A Practitioner's Guide to
UNDERSTANDING INDIGENOUS AND
FOREIGN CULTURES

A Practitioner's Guide to
UNDERSTANDING INDIGENOUS AND FOREIGN CULTURES

An Analysis of Relationships Between Ethnicity, Social Class and Therapeutic Intervention Strategies With Third World Peoples From Other Countries

By

GEORGE HENDERSON, PH.D.

CHARLES C THOMAS • PUBLISHER
Springfield • Illinois • U.S.A.

Published and Distributed Throughout the World by

CHARLES C THOMAS • PUBLISHER
2600 South First Street
Springfield, Illinois 62794-9265

© *1989 by* CHARLES C THOMAS • PUBLISHER

ISBN 0-398-05628-5

Library of Congress Catalog Card Number: 89-20172

With THOMAS BOOKS *careful attention is given to all details of manufacturing
and design. It is the Publisher's desire to present books that are satisfactory as to their
physical qualities and artistic possibilities and appropriate for their particular use.*
THOMAS BOOKS *will be true to those laws of quality that assure a good name
and good will.*

Printed in the United States of America
SC-R-3

Library of Congress Cataloging-in-Publication Data
Henderson, George, 1932-
    A practitioner's guide to understanding indigenous and foreign
cultures / by George Henderson.
        p.   cm.
    "An analysis of relationships between ethnicity, social class, and
therapuetic intervention strategies with Third World peoples from
other countries."
    Includes bibliographical references.
    ISBN 0-398-05628-5
    1. Medical care—Cross-cultural studies.   2. Medical care—
Developing countries.   3. Ethnicity.   I. Title.   II. Title:
Understanding indigenous and foreign cultures.
RA394.H46   1989
362.1—dc20
                                                                89-20172
                                                                CIP

To Jessica, Kimberly, Sterlin and all of my grandchildren yet to be born

Instead, I want to continue the dialogue and action started by the authors of the studies cited.

I am grateful to the many persons whose perceptions and suggestions have greatly strengthened this book. My foremost thanks go to Virginia Milhouse, Maria Cristina Calle of Italy, Amir Barsky of Israel, Katsuya Higuchi and Hiroshi Hasegawa of Japan, Klaus Grawi of Switzerland, De Lourdes Apodaca Rangel of Mexico, and Thompson Olasiji of Nigeria. Several of my students also contributed to this small volume. Special mention is due to William Rose, Sarah Martin, Lori Scarbrough, Martin Sangong, Linda Sterling, Debby Williams-Chambless, Olufemi Somade and Sophie Lam. However, I accept full responsibility for the book's deficiencies. This has been a long and challenging journey of inquiry. It has also been a personally gratifying journey. I wish no less for those who follow.

G. H

CONTENTS

A Practitioner's Guide to
UNDERSTANDING INDIGENOUS AND FOREIGN CULTURES

Chapter 1

PRELUDE TO HELPING

Effective helpers throughout the world utilize themselves as the foremost instrument in the therapeutic process. This is sometimes called the *self-as-instrument philosophy of helping.* Many practitioners who adhere to this philosophy use scientific methods to help clients understand themselves, their significant other persons, and their environment. But methodology is used to improve client insight, not to extinguish it. Also important for this type of helper is the belief that clients "own" their problems, and meaningful behavior change will not occur unless they assume responsibility for their actions. Whatever the modality or its philosophic foundation of helping, successful interventions always take place within the context of cultural beliefs and behaviors.

CULTURAL BELIEFS AND BEHAVIOR

As a whole, members of the various helping professions are not scientists, but many of them use scientific knowledge to affect change. For this reason, a significant number of graduate school courses that are therapy-oriented are designed to teach students to adapt scientific knowledge to individual cases. Ultimately, each practitioner must to some degree make his or her own interpretation of knowledge and the efficacy of various helping techniques. In fact, much of what a helper does can be understood only within the context of his or her values. Unfortunately, ethical therapeutic judgments do not enjoy the relatively high degree of precision that some legal decisions have in deciding what is correct and what is not. Yet, a growing number of educators and practitioners believe that it is important for professional helpers to avoid behavior that restricts individual and group freedom, ignores human dignity and denies due process. Equally important, practitioners must know how to make relevant assumptions, premises or suppositions about clients. The beginning of an effective helping relationship is dependent on the practitioner's knowledge of client behavior.

3

A Paradigm of Client Beliefs and Behavior

Based on my research and review of related literature, I have constructed a paradigm of client beliefs and behavior, which I call the *cultural beliefs and behavior model.* It is drawn from aeronautical engineering principles. That is, I postulate that human beings engaged in interpersonal, intergroup and organization interactions behave as if they were physical objects in controlled flight, and therefore with adequate data we can predict with reasonable accuracy the results of some therapeutic interventions on client behavior. The flight that I refer to is not in outer space but, instead, in the inner space of clients' minds and emotions. Using the engineering concepts "statically stable," "statically unstable," "dynamically stable," and "dynamically unstable," I am able to partially account for and predict human behavior.

Cultural beliefs are static phenomenon; they don't change, but the people exposed to them do. Thus, statically stable beliefs are those which an individual maintains, and statically unstable ones are abandoned. Behavior is a dynamic phenomenon which people may elect to do or not do. Therefore, dynamically stable behavior is that which an individual repeats, while dynamically unstable behavior is extinguished. Simply stated, people exposed to conflicting cultural beliefs and behavior adopt either stable (traditional) beliefs and behavior or unstable (nontraditional) beliefs and behavior. Culturally, the maintenance of a traditional way of life is a static condition, and the change from traditional to nontraditional beliefs and behavior is a dynamic condition. "Static" does not refer to an inferior situation, nor does "dynamic" denote a superior situation. Rather, the terms pertain to cultural equilibrium and disequilibrium.

The major focus of the model is not on the way people behave but, instead, why people in certain circumstances believe they must behave they way they do. Thus, attention is given to purposive action and the anticipated consequences of such action. In a broader sense, the model is concerned with action which involves motives and a choice between alternatives. A statically stable person accepts his or her traditional culture's beliefs, whereas a statically unstable person does not. A dynamically stable person returns to the traditional cultural behaviors, but a dynamically unstable person adopts nontraditional behavior. Traditional beliefs and behavior are strongest when individuals are unaware of alternatives. Based on the preceding assumptions, I further postulate that cross-cultural interaction produces the following four types of people.

1. **Statically stable-dynamically stable.** These people accept a traditional culture's beliefs and behavior; and if for some reason they experiment with nontraditional beliefs and behavior, they will still maintain the traditional way of life. Once equilibrium is established, people within a traditional culture are likely to believe there are no "good" reasons to adopt a nontraditional way of life, and there are ample reasons, in terms of group stability, why they should not. Adherence to group norms is taught and individuality is discouraged in traditional cultures. Statically stable-dynamically stable persons are the least conflicted of the four types. Wilbert Moore and Melvin Tumin (1949) observed that "all socialization processes operate to reduce curiosity and knowledge about the presumed socially dysfunctional alternative of pursuing individual tendencies. These processes act so effectively in most cases that the matter rarely appears as a matter of choice, much less as a conflict" (pp. 791–892).

2. **Statically stable-dynamically unstable.** These people have internalized traditional beliefs and behavior; but if they are exposed to compelling nontraditional beliefs and behavior, they will change to a nontraditional way of life. Dynamic instability is the opposite of the general *law of assimilation* which states that the human organism will respond to new situations in the same manner it responded to familiar situations. Statically stable-dynamically unstable persons typify individuals who are marginal within their ethnic group.

> Being aware of others in the same aggregate and defining oneself as a member may still not guarantee that the individual is involved. Everyone knows people who, although nominally members of a group, nevertheless seem completely uninterested in the group. For them to be real members of a group, they would have to feel kinship or identity with the others—to feel they were significant. Social psychologists would say that these people belong to a *membership group*, since they belong to the group in name only (Kiesler & Kiesler, 1970, p. 27).

3. **Statically unstable-dynamically stable.** These people have not fully accepted traditional beliefs but continue to act as if they have even when exposed to attractive nontraditional beliefs and behavior. This situation typifies many individuals who live in cultural enclaves. Because their survival is dependent upon "fitting in," they maintain traditional behaviors. When a society or subculture demands adherence to behavior that is inconsistent with an individual's feelings about it, stress and trauma develop. Fortunately, every culture has its own unique level of anxiety which its members can withstand without serious psychological

harm of maladjustment (Draguns, 1973; Magnusson & Stattin, 1978; Strauss, 1979).

4. **Statically unstable-dynamically unstable.** These people are sometimes seen as social deviants. Because abnormality refers to descriptive behavior which deviates markedly from what a group considers to be normal, it is essential that helpers understand what the client's culture considers normal. Several studies conclude that social deviance varies across ethnic groups (Torrey, 1972; Sue et al., 1974; Sue & McKinney, 1975; Katz & Sanborn, 1976). In a different environment, statically unstable-dynamically unstable people may be quite normal. For example, immigrants who reject the "old ways" and seek identity with a nontraditional culture illustrate this phenomenon. There is stress in each of the culture types described.

When people throughout the world experience conditions of stress, it is natural for them to use defense mechanisms—repression, suppression, rationalization, projection and so forth—to cope. Coping mechanisms allow people to adjust to problems. In fact, emotional survival is often dependent on being able to regulate personal feelings, beliefs and actions so that anxiety remains at a manageable level. While defense mechanisms do not in themselves solve problems, they can allow an individual time to cope with them until better solutions are found. When defense mechanisms cease to relieve stress, clients frequently turn to behavior that is called "maladjustment" or "maladaptive." But a few words of caution are in order: There is a thin line between normal behavior and neurotic and psychotic behavior. Except for extreme psychoses, what is normal and what is abnormal is difficult to ascertain. It is even more difficult when working with peoples from different cultures (Kleinman, 1979; Draguns, 1980; Guthrie & Tanco, 1980; Tseng & Hsu, 1980). Within all cultures, most people have periods of maladjustive behavior, and most maladjusted people have periods of rational behavior.

Poverty or residence in a socially disruptive area are compounding factors in maladjustive behavior associated with ethnicity and social class. For example, the fact that African American rates of hospitalization for mental disorders are somewhat lower than White rates in the United States (Rushing, 1980) appears to be related to a higher arrest and imprisonment rate for African Americans than for Whites of equivalent behavior. African Americans, in particular, typically receive more severe psychiatric diagnosis (e.g., paranoid schizophrenia) than Whites (Steinberg et al., 1977; Rabkin, 1980; Ruiz, 1982). There is also evidence that social class is linked to the number of incidences of mental illness (Dohrenwend & Dohrenwend, 1969; Eron & Peterson, 1982). The poor are more likely to be more severely diagnosed by practitioners than the affluent. Studies show that neuroses diagnoses are concentrated in middle and upper classes and psychoses in the lower classes (Hollingshead & Redlich, 1958; Torrey, 1972). Anxiety and insecurity are common characteristics of the poor in urban societies, but this does not necessarily lead to mental illness. When these data coalesce, it is clear that there are connections between ethnicity, social class and particular kinds of therapeutic treatment. This raises questions about the efficacy of therapeutic interventions.

The Autoplastic-Alloplastic Dilemma

Cross-cultural helpers have debated what has been called the *autoplastic-alloplastic dilemma* (Vexliard, 1968): How much should the helpee be encouraged to adapt to a given situation and how much should he or she be encouraged to change? Western helping modalities have a strong autoplastic bias; clients are encouraged to abandon traditional beliefs, values and behavior if this will allow them to fit into a dominant society's mainstream. While loss of cultural identity can be personally devastating, the ability to change is a prerequisite for survival in modern societies. At the same time, there is the need of people for continuity of values and life-style. These conflicting expectations often moderate the forces of change. Non-Western helpers tend to be alloplastic; that is, they encourage new behavior if it is compatible with traditional ways of doing things. This approach, like the autoplastic approach, has problems (Taft, 1966). There is the danger that traditional-oriented people will become encapsulated in their culture and therein unable to adequately adjust to technological and social changes. Effective helping involves interventions in which clients are able to abate or adjust to problems and also, if they desire, maintain their cultural identity.

Every culture has a point or threshold around which the majority of its members exist. This is commonly referred to as *culturally typical* or *normative behavior*. Statisticians generally agree that each person's behavior within a given culture falls within three standard deviations of normative behavior. The major point of this calculation is that each person has the potential to engage in behavior that can be described as culturally unusual in terms of their overall behavior. However, the behavior that people usually engage in is culturally determined. Failure to understand a client's cultural imperatives is likely to result in ineffective interventions by the helper. Relatedly, it is important that helpers not project their definitions of what is imperative on clients.

The further a client moves from his or her cultural balance or congruency, the more difficult it is to return to traditional behavior. When people deviate from their normative center, the *law of advantage* takes over: Of two or more inconsistent responses, such as traditional behavior versus nontraditional behavior, one has more advantage and is more reliable in fulfilling an individual's needs. For example, if a particular behavior is likely to fulfill an individual's need for love, she will do it—even at the risk of being ridiculed. People generally change their behavior for three interrelated reasons: (1) to achieve greater fulfillment and avoid pain or destruction, (2) when their emotional needs are not being met, and (3) when different ways of behaving provoke satisfying responses from their significant other persons. Succinctly, people change when different ways of behaving provide a greater emotional or physical payoff than the status quo behavior. Therefore, homeostasis often fluctuates between the desire to retain the status quo and the desire to change if it will be an improvement. This dilemma frequently causes people to seek professional help.

SELECTED HELPING MODALITIES

Professional helpers get their techniques and strategies of intervention from one or more of three psychologies: behaviorism, psychoanalysis, and humanistic psychology (Corsini, 1989). Those who adopt behaviorism believe that behavior change comes about through external manipulation of stimulus and reward. The goal of behavioral helpers is to remove symptoms; they are not concerned with clients' inner experiencing of symptoms nor with establishing a warm relationship with clients. Rather, behavioral helpers try to eliminate symptoms as quickly as possible using learning theory principles: observing, recording, and controlling observable phenomena (Messer, 1986).

Psychoanalytic-oriented helpers interpret for helpees the relationship between past and present experiences. In psychoanalysis, the helper assumes the role of teacher and interprets insights to the helpee. Central to this process is the development of a transference relationship between the helper and the helpee. Psychoanalysis holds the view that humans are basically irrational and, if our impulses are not controlled, we will destroy ourselves and other persons.

Humanistic helpers believe that behavior change evolves from within the individual. This approach focuses on the dignity and value of the individual person in a continuous process of emotional growth. The focus here is on the present, not the past. The term often used by humanistic helpers is "the here and now." The humanistic helper presents himself or herself as honestly and transparently as possible. This also includes the helper avoiding expressions that have evaluative connotations. Nor will the helper interpret meanings for clients, or describe the client.

Certain conditions pertain to all therapeutic situations including release of tension through cartharsis, cognitive learning through trial and error and gestalt interpretations, reconditioning by operant conditioning through implicit and explicit reward and denial of reward, identification with the helper, and reality testing (Marmor, 1971).

Cartharsis refers to tension relief through self-disclosure in a trustful and intimate interaction. A successful helping relationship results in "intersubjective consensus" regarding the meaning of what is told (Johnson, 1975). This is what has sometimes been called the "social construction of reality" (Berger & Luckman, 1967). *Learning* is not based on ascertaining absolute "true" or "false" statements (Reichenbach, 1947). *Operant conditioning* is achieved through various rituals, ceremonial performances, techniques and methods that lead to the acquisition of new insights and behavior. *Reality testing* refers to a helpee trying new behaviors and making the necessary behavioral and attitudinal adjustments (Reusch & Prestwood, 1950). Stated another way, all helping modalities described in this book are methods of learning. They attempt to change people: to help them think differently (cognition), to help them feel differently (affection), and to help them act differently (behavior). Out of the three forces in psychology have come many helping modalities, including the ones that I will briefly discuss. A helper does not have to be a "therapist" to use some of the strategies developed in these modalities. Raymond Corsini and Danny Wedding (1989) provide an inclusive definition of the various modes of helping: "All modes of trying to help people improve themselves via symbolic methods can be called psychotherapy" (p. 2). The review of therapeutic modalities which follows only presents a few of the characteristics. A more comprehensive description is found in the sources cited.

Psychoanalysis

Psychoanalysis is a helping modality based largely on the discoveries of Sigmund Freud (1920). Several persons preceded Freud, including Paul Dubois who treated psychotics in the early nineteenth century by talking with them in a reasonable manner. Pierre Janet is credited with founding a system of dynamic psychiatry to replace those of the nineteenth century (Corsini & Wedding, 1989). But it was Freud who served as the catalyst for the growth of psychotherapy. (Today, there are more than 200 different systems of psychotherapy). Freud refined psychoanalysis to treat persons suffering from hysteria, to interpret dreams, to understand narcissism and aggression, and to develop a structural theory of the mind. Building on insights gained from treating individual patients, he developed the first comprehensive theory of personality. The psychoanalytic theory of personality is based on four principles: determinism, the topographic viewpoint, the dynamic viewpoint, and the genetic viewpoint (Ellis, 1962; Melzoff & Kornreich, 1970; Brenner, 1973; Arlow, 1989).

The first and foremost principle of psychoanalysis is *determinism*. This is the belief that mental events are not random, haphazard, accidental, unrelated occurrences. The *topographic* viewpoint holds that every emotional event is judged according to its accessibility to recall. The process by which certain events are barred from our consciousness is called "repression." The more undesirable an event, the less available it is to our conscious mind. The *dynamic* viewpoint describes the libidinal and aggressive impulses that are part of our biological makeup. These impulses are referred to as either "instincts" or "drives." The *genetic* viewpoint traces conflicts, character disorders, and psychological structure to early childhood, usually the first five years.

Freud postulated that the personality is made up of the id, the ego and the superego. The id consists of the instincts (life, death, sexual libido). The ego in its executive capacity selects which instinctual drives or impulses to gratify—but only after contending with the superego which reflects the traditional values and taboos of an individual's society. The superego tries to repress the ego. Freud also proposed that each person passes through certain stages of psychosexual development which he defined as oral, anal, phallic, and genital. The danger is that a child can become fixated or suffer from arrested development as a result of psychological trauma. In adulthood this condition is manifested by character types which correspond with behavior appropriate to an earlier stage of development.

An individual who seeks help through psychoanalysis must be strongly motivated to overcome his or her problems through long, honest self-scrutiny. The psychoanalytic dialogue is characterized by the frustration of inevitable transference wishes. The analyst is basically passive; he or she listens patiently, uncritically and sympathetically. Important to this mode of helping is nondirective listening. Whatever feelings the analyst has are kept hidden from the client. This, then, is a modality that requires, from a Western perspective, a helpee to acquire a fairly healthy ego.

Person-Centered Therapy

Person-centered therapy, also known as client-centered therapy, was developed by Carl Rogers (1951). Helpers who utilize this modality believe that if their attitude in the helping relationship includes congruence or genuineness, unconditional positive regard, and empathic understanding, then growth and positive change will occur in the helpee (Patterson, 1984; Seeman, 1984; Rogers, 1986; Raskin & Rogers, 1989). This perspective presumes that the helpee is motivated toward self-actualization. Consequently, the helper will assist the helpee to release positive internal qualities and grow into a fully functioning person.

Person-centered helpers try to reduce or relieve destructive inner forces through the use of non-authoritarian, non-judgmental statements and other nurturing behaviors. Basic to this approach is the assumption that all people encounter life conditions which negatively affects their self-image. If we are not forced into socially constricted roles but rather are accepted for what and who we are, positive self-images will thrive. Our natural impulses are constructive and conducive to self-actualization. In short, each of us has within himself or herself the ability to create and direct our own lives. Central to this modality is the ability of the helper to verbally and nonverbally establish rapport or "with-ness." In the words of Rogers (1951):

> The process is not seen as primarily having to do with the client's memory of his past, nor with his exploration of the problems he is facing, nor with the perceptions he has of himself, nor the experiences he has been fearful of admitting into awareness. The process of therapy is, by these hypotheses, seen as being synonymous with the experiential relationship between client and therapist. The therapy consists in

experiencing the self in a wide range of ways in an emotionally meaningful relationship with the therapist. The words—of either client or
counselor—are seen as having minimal importance compared with the
present emotional relationship between the two (p. 172).

The technique of the person-centered helper is simple and understandable.
Application is more difficult, however. Simply put, it takes a long time to
learn to be proficient in dispensing genuineness, empathy and positive
regard.

Reality Therapy

William Glasser (1981) developed reality therapy. The major assumptions of reality therapy are that human beings have five essential needs:
survival, belonging, power, fun and freedom. When people fail to fulfill
these needs, they lose control of their lives. To gain control of our life,
we must first be aware of our needs. Second, we must be able to act on this
awareness and engage in need-satisfying behavior. There are two fundamental ways to control our destiny: first, to identify what in the world
can possibly satisfy our needs and, second, to act upon or control that
which will satisfy our needs. Reality therapy assumes that the answers to
our problems lie within ourselves. The helpee must not only take responsibility for his or her negative behaviors but also learn to modify behaviors to satisfy needs. Personal involvement is the foundation of this
therapy. The past is scanned to select situations and times when the
helpee successfully controlled his or her world. Little attention is given
negative behavior. The following eight steps describe the reality therapy
helping process:

1. **Make friends with the helpee, "What do you want?"** Most people
who seek help are lonely. They desperately want a friend, somebody
who cares about them. While a positive relationship with clients is
important, helpers should not allow clients to control them through
anger, anxiety, depression or threats. A helpee's wants must be realistic—
something he or she can possibly achieve.

2. **Ask the helpee, "What are you doing now to get what you want?"**
Here the helper focuses on helpee behavior that is most amenable to
change.

3. **Ask the helpee, "Is what you choose to do getting you what you want?"**
At this step the helpee evaluates the effectiveness of what her or she has
chosen. Step 3 will not be effective until Step 1 is accomplished. If what a

helpee chooses to do is in violation of a reasonable rule or a law, then the choice is not wise.

4. **If what the helpee is doing is not working, ask him or her, "What else could you do to get what you want?"** This is the planning, advising, helping, and encouraging step. Unlike many therapies that do not have the helper actively participating in giving advice and planning, reality therapists are very much involved in these activities.

5. **Ask the helpee, "When are you going to follow the plan?"**

6. **Accept no excuses.** In essence, the helper says, "I'm not interested in why you can't or haven't done it. I'm only interested in when you can do it and how you can do it."

7. **There is no punishment.** There are only two consequences for inadequate behavior: temporary restriction of freedom or temporary removal of privileges.

8. **Never give up.** The helper perseveres with the helpee as long as he or she is needed.

Significant other persons are often asked to share information about the helpee. It is not always easy for clients to describe accurately what they want. The more aberrant a helpee's view of the world, the more difficult it is to help him or her.

Rational-Emotive Therapy

Rational-emotive therapy (RET) was developed by Albert Ellis (1962). RET defines appropriate feelings and rational beliefs as those promoting survival and happiness (Miller & Berman, 1983; Dryden, 1984; Bernard & DiGiuseppe, 1988; Ellis, 1989). Irrationality leads to needless harm. RET postulates that human values are very important. And the personality consists mainly of beliefs and attitudes. We are healthy when we have rational or empirically based values. Psychological problems are caused by faulty or irrational patterns of thinking. Problems are conceptualized in the A–B–C paradigm. *A* consists of an event in a helpee's life. *B* refers to the helpee's thoughts about the event. *C* represents the helpee's emotions and behavior based on *B*.

One goal of RET is to alter the helpee's thoughts at point B. In order to do this, the helper might ask several questions before the helpee can understand that his or her thoughts are illogical. To the unaware observer, it may appear that the helper is arguing with or belittling the helpee. Another goal is to help individuals stop assigning blame for their difficulties. The need to assign blame is caused by several irrational beliefs, including: we should be loved or respected by almost everyone; things must always be the way we want them to be; every problem has an ideal solution and we are failures if we do not achieve it. The major propositions of RET are:

1. We are born with the potential to be rational or irrational. That is, we have the ability to be self-preserving or self-destructive.

2. Our tendency to self-destruction is frequently exacerbated by our culture and family.

3. We almost always perceive, think, emote and behave simultaneously. Effective change is not likely to occur until we understand how we perceive, think, emote and act.

4. A highly cognitive, homework-assignment, active-directive and discipline-oriented approach is the most effective in extinguishing negative behavior.

5. A warm relationship between helper and helpee is neither a necessary nor a sufficient condition for effective helping to occur. This approach tries to prevent and, where needed, terminate unduly dependent relationships.

6. Rational-emotive therapists are multimodal—they use role playing, humor, operant conditioning, assertion training, desensitization and so forth to help clients achieve cognitive change.

7. Virtually all serious emotional problems are attributed to devout religiosity, dogmatism, magical thinking, intolerance, and whining. Clients are taught to follow the logical-empirical and abandon all forms of magic and absolutism. RET attacks *shoulds, oughts,* and *musts.*

Behavior Therapy

The origins of behavior therapy can be traced to J. B. Watson, the "father of behaviorism," and Ivan Pavlov, founder of classical conditioning. The present form has been greatly influenced by Joseph Wolpe (1958) and B. F. Skinner (1953). Different techniques are used for different problems, and the best way to change people's feelings about themselves is to first change their behavior (Bandura, 1969; Franks et al., 1982; O'Leary & Wilson, 1987; Wilson, 1989). Clients are expected to set specific goals. Compared with psychoanalysts and person-centered therapists, the behavior analyst is more directive, more open and more of a "problem" solver. The helping views of therapists require different questions, e.g., psychoanalysts ask how a client became the way he or she is; person-centered therapists ponder how a person feels about the way he or she is; Adlerian psychotherapists ask what the client is trying to achieve; and behavior analysts wonder what is causing clients to behave the way they are.

Counterconditioning (e.g., desensitization) is used to treat anxiety-related problems such as fear of height or closed space. The anxiety is replaced by a response that contradicts the anxiety. Muscle relaxation and visualizing threatening situations is an example of desensitization. Observational learning or modeling can also be used to treat anxiety-related problems. In this technique, the helper models functional behavior.

Some behavioral therapists use *aversion* therapies to eliminate inappropriate behavior. Here too the strategy is to replace pleasurable reactions to inappropriate behavior with unpleasant experiences such as electric shock or emetic drugs which produce nausea. Other behavior therapy techniques include *operant techniques.* That is, clients are given rewards when they engage in appropriate behavior and punished for inappropriate behavior. A few behavior therapists prefer their clients to have an active imagination and a willingness to be subjected to sometimes harsh physical and emotional consequences. While each client sets his or her goals for treatment, the behavior therapist usually determines the means for achieving changes in behavior.

Gestalt Therapy

Founded by Frederick (Fritz) Perls (1969), Gestalt therapy focuses on *process* (what is happening) rather than *content* (what is being discussed). It is based on existential assumptions, but its main focus is on seeing, hearing, touching, and moving (Feder & Rondall, 1980; Dolliver, 1981; Yontef & Simkin, 1989). Body movements are significant to Gestalt therapists, who deliberately touch their clients in an attempt to make them aware of themselves. Unlike traditional psychology, which in effect fragments the human personality and considers the individual as merely a sum of his or her basic parts, the Gestalt approach focuses on the whole person as greater than his or her parts.

Explicit in this approach is the therapeutic value of enhancing one's awareness of the here and now. Because people exist in relation to each other, human contact is experiencing the boundary between "me" and "not-me." In essence, being fully human requires that we maintain a connection with the not-me while at the same time maintaining a sense of a separate identity from the not-me. Martin Buber (1965) described this as an "I–Thou" dialogue relationship. The dialogic relationship in Gestalt therapy has the following characteristics:

1. **Inclusion.** This is the need to be with people and simultaneously maintain a sense of separate identity.

2. **Presence.** The helper expresses his or her self to the client. The helper expresses preferences and other thoughts.

3. **Commitment to dialogue.** The helper becomes active in the interpersonal process.

4. **No exploitation.** The helper protects the client and himself or herself from exploitation.

5. **Dialogue is lived.** The interaction is done, not merely talked about.

In Gestalt therapy the process of discovery through experimentation is the goal rather than the feeling or idea or content of the interaction. There are no "shoulds." Instead, "what is" becomes the focal point. The entire biopsychosocial field is important. Awareness and dialogue are the primary therapeutic tools. And people are responsible for their own behavior. The goal of Gestalt therapy is *awareness*.

Transactional Analysis

Eric Berne (1958) is the founder of transactional analysis (TA), a therapeutic approach designed to provide clients with an understanding of their personality as it is shaped in social situations or transactions. Believing that the life roles we assume are not limited by chronological age, transactional analysts focus on behavior common to children and adults (Erskine, 1982; Heyer, 1987; Dusay & Dusay, 1989). The three life stages basic to TA are: Child, Parent and Adult.

The *Child* may be defined as the stage of personality development which accentuates the "recording of internal events (feelings) in response to external events (mostly mother and father) between birth and age five" (Harris, 1969, p. 19). According to TA theory, each of us starts out with the Child, and as we grow, we develop the Parent and Adult ego states. To distinguish clearly between Parent and Child, it should be remembered that much of the recording in the Child is preverbal recording—that is, it is recorded before the person has adequate command of language. Hence, the Child is mainly associated with internal feelings or nonverbal events.

The *Parent* is the stage of personality development which accentuates the recording within us of imposed, unquestioned external events perceived by us between birth and age five. The mother and father become internalized in the Parent as recordings of what the child observed them to say and do. In other words, the Parent is a social concept of dominance internalized by the individual at an early age. The fact is that many recordings in the Parent are unquestioned and can either be favorable or unfavorable, depending on the situation.

The *Adult* is the stage of personality development which accentuates the data acquired and computed through exploration and testing. The Adult is frequently thought of as a built-in computer whose functions are to evaluate data gathered from or presented by the Parent, the Child or the environment and to respond appropriately to these data. Transactional analysts believe that the Adult should be in control at all times once a person has completed five years of life. This does not mean that the Parent and the Child are no longer viable; however, it does mean that a person operating in the Parent or the Child ego state (definitions of self) must be aware that he or she is in such an ego state and must accept or reject it.

TA defines Parent, Adult, and Child ego states in a more personal sense than do the id, ego, and superego concepts of Freudian psychoanalysis. Parent, Adult and Child states represent psychological, historical and behavioral realities. In discussing life scripts and script analysis, Berne (1958) credited the research of Freud with helping him arrive at this aspect of TA. The life script or plan fulfills a major human need, namely, that of structuring long periods of time. In the script each person feels "OK" or "not OK." Time structuring allows us to play our roles within a predetermined framework. Helpers using TA try to identify and alter dangerous or tragic scripts. To do so they use diagramed outlines of the client's childhood messages as they are reconstructed from current transactions.

Substance and Style

Person-centered helpers teach clients to be their "feeling selves"; Gestalt helpers teach them to be "fighting selves"; and rational-emotive helpers teach clients to be "thinking selves" (Hill et al., 1979; Meara et al., 1979). Person-centered helpers mainly encourage clients, restate observations, and reflect on clients' observations. Gestalt helpers mainly offer direct guidance, give information, ask open questions, focus on nonverbal behaviors and are confrontive. Rational-emotive helpers are among the most active of the modalities. They use direct guidance, closed questions, restatements and minimal encouragers. Psychoanalytic helpers facilitate "coping"; transactional analysts facilitate "adult" behaviors; and reality therapists teach "functional" behaviors. Psychoanalysts are descriptive rather than prescriptive, while transactional analysts and reality therapists are mainly prescriptive. These helping modalities can be superficially defined in terms of whether practitioners are nonjudgmental about helpees' beliefs and behavior, and whether they are active in the problem definition and resolution. Specifically, the following categories are possible:

Neutral-passive modalities. Helpers are nonjudgmental and not prescriptive. Psychoanalysis and person-centered therapies are in this category.

Neutral-active modalities. Helpers are nonjudgmental but prescriptive. Gestalt therapy is in this category.

Interactional modalities. Helpers are opinionated and active in the problem definition and problem resolution processes. Reality therapy, transactional analysis, behavior therapy and rational-emotive therapy are in this category. In practice, all helpers make judgments each time they respond in therapy irregardless of their modality.

Therapeutic helping occurs in a wide variety of settings. Basic to all helping modalities is the belief that all individuals have the potential to alter their life situations or at least themselves in relation to them. Each helpee is capable of being an active party in the helping process. Because there is no common philosophy that unites all modalities, some of them are better suited for particular cultures than others (Corey, 1977; Brabeck & Wolfel, 1985; Brammer, 1985; Jones, 1985). The study of ethnocultural factors in the helping professions does not mean that one can be an effective helper only after learning the attitudes, values, and family patterns in all ethnic groups. No helper can do this. But each helper can learn about the groups with whom he or she will interact. Relatedly, there is a paucity of quantitative research focusing on cross-national helping (Casas et al., 1986). Our knowledge of the efficacy of various therapeutic interventions in non-Western cultures is based largely on descriptive, qualitative observations. Therefore, it is important for researchers to study therapeutic modalities and helping techniques which may be culturally relevant and will help mobilize resources for nonoppressive interventions.

BEYOND OPPRESSION

In *Pedagogy of the Oppressed,* Paulo Freire (1970) defined oppression as an act of overwhelming control or exploitation performed by one person in order to hinder or prevent the full development of another person. Conversely, liberation is freedom to develop one's full potential. Oppressed people are dehumanized to the point of being viewed by their oppressors as being less than human; they become nonpersons. From this perspective, the oppressors are endowed with characteristics to be emulated by the oppressed. Gradually, the imagined aura of their inferiority subsumes the underclass. And the overriding task of oppressed clients is to liberate themselves—and their oppressors as well.

People who oppress others usually do so by virtue of their power over them. Unfortunately, powerless people can seldom muster enough courage or strength to liberate themselves without additional help. Yet, as Freire points out, freedom for both the oppressed and their oppressors will come by carefully unraveling but not severing this human relations Gordian knot. Within these parameters, the issue of oppression is not only relevant to modern therapies but it is also applicable to traditional therapies. Indeed, it is important to consider the degree of oppression that is explicit or implicit in any helping modality. Freire stated that few traditional or scientific modalities are really liberating processes. A liberating process includes two inseparable stages: reflection and action.

Reflection. This occurs when oppressed individuals try to understand their oppressors, their role in the oppression, and possible avenues of liberation. At this stage the job of helper, according to Freire (1970), is *problem-posing education* which has four prominent features. Because myths bind people to their oppression, the first act of the helper is to encourage clients to rid themselves of myths surrounding their situation. An example of such a myth is a client's belief that she is "stupid" and her stupidity is the result of being born to poor Mexican parents. She is convinced that this is God's will. People in traditional cultures frequently behave as though they are under the influence of magic or myth. That is, they often believe that their suffering or exploitation is the will of a supernatural force. Second, the helper encourages clients to keep the lines of communication open between themselves and their significant others. An open dialogue is indispensable to any act of cognition which tries to make sense of reality. Third, clients are encouraged and assisted to be critical thinkers. Fourth, client creativity is nurtured as the means of achieving intrapersonal and interpersonal transformation.

Action. The process of reflection in a problem-posing therapeutic process is expected to lead to positive (liberating) action. The characteristics of such action include cooperation, unity, and cultural synthesis. Helper-helpee cooperation can lead to a meaningful focus on a client's reality by abolishing hidden agendas during the helping process. Of course, trust is a requisite condition for full cooperation. Unity or fusion in the helping relationship comes from the communion of persons who trust each other. In general terms, positive change is most likely to occur when the parties involved in the helping process exhibit a high degree of unity. Action can create, preserve or destroy social order. In this book we are mainly concerned with action that creates and preserves conditions which help clients to realize their human potential for positive growth. The questions I would ask in this regard are the following:

Does the modality:
- Place the helper in an authority role and the helpee in a submissive role?
- Stress personal growth of the helpee?
- Facilitate reflection on part of the helpee?
- Encourage critical thinking?
- Facilitate creativity on the part of the helpee?
- Focus on problem posing and problem resolution?
- Conceptualize the helping relationship as open communication between helper and helpee?
- Require mutual trust?
- Require helpers to be congruent in their statements and behavior?
- Encourage the transformation of helpees into culturally liberated persons?

Admittedly, this is a subjective evaluation. Even so, this process may help us to determine whether a modality is oppressive or liberating. In reality, all therapeutic modalities are both oppressive and liberating, but some are more oppressive or liberating than others.

Recommendations

It has been proposed by numerous authors that practitioner preparation for using any modality include systematic study of various ethnic group life-styles and alternative strategies for helping them to self-actualize. Practitioner commitment to cultural pluralism and liberation are exemplified by individuals who demonstrate a willingness to first learn about themselves. The role of the helper in the liberation process includes the following dimensions of cross-cultural relations: encourage ethnic consciousness, validate ethnic differences, support minority group advocacy, use collaborative and cooperative strategies, understand conflict resolution and risk taking (Katz, 1985). Clients (and helpers) must be encouraged to affirm their ethnicity, not deny it. Validation of cultural differences requires practitioners to go beyond valuing cultural differences. They must take an active stance in protecting these differences.

Ethnic-group advocacy is most effective when helpers assist clients to establish their own goals. Also, helpers must support positive goals fostered by ethnic clients. In a social context, helpers must collaborate with colleagues who are trying to understand and help ethnic group persons achieve their human potential. But these activities are sometimes laden with conflict, which is inevitable in society. Conflict can be a destructive force in the helping process or it can become a constructive force that encourages open and helpful problem posing and problem solving. Finally, all helpers should understand that social change involves risks. In summary, the following paraphrased principles adopted in 1979 by the American Psychological Association Division of Counseling Psychology are suitable guidelines for practitioners who work with ethnically diverse clients:

1. Helpers must be knowledgeable about ethnic groups, particularly with regard to historical, psychological and social issues.
2. Helpers must be aware that assumptions and precepts of theories relevant to their practice may apply differently to various ethnic groups. Helpers must be aware of those theories that prescribe or limit the potential of clients, as well as those that may have particular usefulness for clients.
3. After formal training, professional helpers must continue throughout their careers to explore and learn of issues related to ethnic groups.
4. Helpers must recognize and be aware of various forms of oppression and how these interact with racism.
5. Helpers must be knowledgeable and aware of verbal and nonverbal process variables (particularly with regard to power in the helping relationship) as these affect clients in counseling/therapy so that the

helper-helpee interactions are not adversely affected. The need for shared responsibility between clients and helpers must be acknowledged and implemented.

6. Helpers must have the capability for utilizing skills that are particularly facilitative to ethnic clients in general and to specific minority clients in particular.

7. Helpers must ascribe no preconceived limitations on the direction or nature of clients' life goals.

8. Helpers must be sensitive to circumstances where it is more desirable for ethnic clients to be seen by a helper of their ethnic group.

9. Helpers must use non-racist language in counseling/therapy, supervision, teaching and publications.

10. Helpers must be aware of and continually review their own values and biases and the effect of these on their clients. Helpers must understand the effect of role socialization upon their own development and functioning and the consequent values and attitudes they hold for themselves and others.

11. Helpers must be aware of how their personal functioning may influence their effectiveness in counseling with clients. They must monitor their functioning through consultation, supervision or therapy so that it does not adversely affect their work with clients.

12. Helpers must support the elimination of racism within institutions and individuals.

Chapter 2

A WORLD VIEW

The developments in both the physical sciences and technology have created a world community characterized by rapid change. Approximately 90 percent of all scientific achievements have been made in the twentieth century. Until the mid-nineteenth century, the speed of transportation never exceeded twenty miles per hour. Today, rockets carry astronauts at more than 20,000 miles per hour, and the speed of some airplanes exceeds the speed of sound. Simply stated, it is relatively easy to travel to two continents within the same week.

The "smallness" of the world is more than a technological illusion. Seventy-five percent of the world's population lives in a narrow strip of land from 35 degrees to 53 degrees north latitudes, or between the southern boundary of the United States to Labrador in North America, from the Mediterranean to the Baltic Sea in Europe, and through the North Temperate Zone in China and the Soviet Union. Ninety percent of the world's industries also lie in that narrow strip of the northern half of the globe. In no comparable period in history have more countries been forced to alter their systems of values, customs, laws, and business practices to coexist. Even so, little progress has been made in training professional helpers to work effectively with cross-national client populations.

In the context of international cultures, cross-national helping involves complex human relations skills. It is extremely difficult to interchange concepts across cultures at appropriate levels of cultural awareness (Asante et al., 1979). Unfortunately, few supervisors of student therapists have adequate knowledge of world cultures (Ridley, 1985). This condition frequently results in graduate programs producing individuals who are not therapists in the traditional sense. Instead, socially and emotionally, they become "the/rapists" when working with culturally different helpees. These helpers intrude in the lives of "foreigners" and do great harm. Successful cross-national helping requires a detailed understanding of the specific cultures of the helpees. Upon close examination of people in their social milieu, we learn that there are many different ways of doing everything required to survive. And the "everything" that people do, which is what culture consists of, are very numerous. Perhaps this is why few helping therapies focus on cross-national behaviors. Ideally, both the helper and the helpee will occupy central positions in the language-culture continuum that is basic to effective helping. Consequently, a helping modality will not be optimally effective until the helper understands and respects the helpee's culture.

BARRIERS TO HELPING

Contrary to popular notion, little empirical evidence supports the assumption that race or ethnic group per se is related to the level of understanding between helpers and helpees. Generalizations about ethnicity and cross-cultural helping should be made with great care. At best, the literature on the subject is inconclusive. Several studies suggest that cultural barriers, such as language and folkways, make the development of successful cross-national helping very difficult (Poortinga, 1977; Sue, 1983; Atkinson, 1985). Yet other studies conclude resolutely that well-trained empathic helpers can establish with minimum difficulty effective relationships with people from other racial or ethnic backgrounds (Ibrahim, 1985; Pedersen , 1985; Suinn, 1985; Pedersen & Lefley, 1986; Ivey et al., 1987). It is emphatically this latter perspective that I advocate. Although the chapters which follow address specific helping modality issues, it seems appropriate here to provide an overview of areas in which it is important for helpers to be both knowledgeable and understanding. Bilingualism and biculturalism present a special kind of challenge. Language, culture, and ethnicity play the most important role in the formation of the self-concept and in the development of cognitive coping skills. Most bilingual-bicultural subcultures have not assimilated into surrounding dominant culture melting pots because they prefer not to assimilate. Mainly Third World organizations have mounted national civil rights campaigns to gain racial desegregation during the twentieth century.

Helpers must be aware that individuals living in traditional families have to function according to the norms of their kinship network and also according to the norms of other societal institutions (Anda, 1984). This conflict was vividly captured by D'Arcy McNickle (1968) when he summarized the dilemmas of traditional American Indians:

The problem of being an Indian, and being obliged to function at two levels of consciousness, for many individuals reduces itself to this: They are aware that their communities, their people, their kinsmen are Indians, but they do not want the low-status equivalent. They look for some way in which they can share in the status ascribed to middle-class Americans without ceasing to be Indians (p. 119).

The lack of cultural sensitivity is seen when practitioners mispronounce clients' names. Mispronouncing a person's name, whether through carelessness or laziness, can easily be interpreted as a lack of interest. In the case of Spanish, pronunciation is much more consistent than English because each vowel is pronounced the same way in all words. When in doubt about pronunciation, the helper should ask the helpee.

Ethnic group language shapes one's philosophy of life. Consider the following example: To English-speaking people, the clock runs; to the Spanish, *el reloj anda* (the clock walks); and for most Third-World peoples, it just ticks. The former group is preoccupied with hurrying to be on time, whereas the latter two groups adopt a slower pace of life. Structuring relationships around clock-measured business appointments vary according to the culture, not because of the definition of time, but instead the perception of time versus relationship.

Helpers who do not know the various social class dimensions of ethnic groups are also unlikely to know that despite common language, color, and historical backgrounds, all members of a particular ethnic group are not alike. It is presumptuous and counterproductive to talk about *the* African or *the* Indian or *the* Hispanic or *the* White people as if members of these and other groups have only one set of behavior characteristics. This book focuses on ethnic characteristics, but the reader is reminded that social class differences often are more determinant of an individual's behavior than ethnic background.

Also, some thought should be given to non-Western helpers who ostensibly have everything in their favor when working with individuals from their own ethnic group. Several factors frequently mitigate against them being effective helpers. First and most important, non-Western professional helpers are frequently Western in terms of their education and professional associations. They are, in short, carbon copies of their Western colleagues. Of course, some non-Western helpers are able to maintain their ethnic identity with a minimum loss in credibility. In terms of their verbal and nonverbal communication, however, some non-Western helpers appear condescending to non-Western helpees. In other instances, these helpers feel quite marginal—not really like their Western counterparts, yet no longer comfortable with members of their own ethnic group. These individuals appear cold and detached to both worlds. A related issue seldom explored in depth is the lack of empathy and sensitivity some helpers have for helpees other than those of their own ethnic group. Germans, for example, might display hostility towards Turks, and Chinese frequently reject Africans. No doubt you can think of other illustrations. It is also worth noting at this juncture that practitioners are affected by institutionalized racism, and awareness of this fact will allow them to better deal with it (Katz, 1985).

CULTURAL PERSPECTIVES

To the extent that helping beliefs and practices can be measured, we are able to postulate universal cultural characteristics. Furthermore, to the extent that helping beliefs and practices characterize subgroups of humanity, there are identifiable transcultural modalities. For the sake of analysis, I shall presume that when a given ethnic group has to solve its social and psychological problems in a given environment, most of its members will develop patterns of behavior that can be conceptualized in the same way (Dohrenwend & Dohrenwend, 1974). The world is a place of great cultural diversity. Although all segments of the world share common elements in life patterns and basic beliefs, there are significant differences in subcultural attitudes, interests, goals, and dialects. No two cultures are precisely alike. Optimum utilization of human resources is a cultural value shared by most social services professionals; however, not all people actively promote this value. Failure to understand this can result in practitioners defining clients who have values different from their own as "bad," "uncooperative," or "difficult."

The Efficacy of Therapies

The crux of Western and non-Western helping interventions is that they are culturally determined (Thomas, 1985). The essence of helping techniques in both Western and non-Western societies can be understood only as social phenomena. On close scrutiny, traditional and modern helping beliefs and practices are more interrelated than many researchers admit. Traditional cultures usually bend to make room for modern knowledge, but such unilateral change can have negative consequences.

There is a growing belief that modern societies must reciprocate and accommodate traditional systems. There are culturally functional and dysfunctional good and bad practices in both systems.

Non-Western social services systems tend to be more holistic or comprehensive than Western systems. The Western mind-body dichotomy gives way to defining helpees as a biological, psychological, and spiritual whole existing in a specific environment (Henderson & Primeaux, 1981). The traditional non-Western helper tries to maintain a balance between humans, their society, and their physical environment. By removing the neat line between physical and mental symptoms, indigenous helpers sometimes achieve remarkable results. Relatives and friends are an integral part of the therapy plan. When effective, non-Western therapeutic techniques do indeed relieve physical and emotional pain.

Because non-Western therapies are internally oriented and subjectively based, they have for the most part not led to the development of "rational" modalities (Tseng & McDermott, 1981). Similar to Western systems, indigenous therapies tend to be based on trial and error and passed on by oral tradition. It is not surprising then that the same problem might be treated by greatly different techniques depending on the helper involved. The efficacy of non-Western therapies is not easily evaluated, because little empirical research data are available. Even so, when using the criterion of client satisfaction in terms of the religious, social, and psychological functions they fulfill, non-Western therapies compare favorably with Western therapies.

Although most contemporary therapies are based on Western beliefs and practices, the vast majority of the world populations are non-Western. In some instances, the differences between the cultural context of Western and non-Western life-styles are dramatic. The *cultural context* of a client's behavior refers to the implicit and explicit tendencies of subgroups to respond to stimuli according to their learned styles of coping. Each subgroup has its own unique ways of seeing, interpreting and coping with its environment and the people in it. Practitioners concerned with the "why" and "what" of a specific ethnic group's social problems can get most of their answers by becoming familiar with the group's history, religion, kinship patterns and social class systems.

David Ho (1979) pointed out some of the basic contradictions between Western and Eastern psychological and therapeutic orientations. Traditional Western values are likely to focus on freedom of choice, the uniqueness of the individual, independence, interdependence, nonconformity, competition, expression of feelings and fulfillment of individual needs. Conversely, traditional Eastern values are likely to focus on group decision making and conformity, compliance, cooperation, harmony, control of feelings and achievement of group needs. Chapter 4 discusses these differences in greater detail. The issue is not which approaches are culturally relevant. All of them are relevant in particular instances. Rather, the issue is which psychotherapies and helping techniques are most relevant for a given population. Charles Patterson (1985) maintains that the methods of Western therapeutic approaches are appropriate in other cultures and do not have to be adapted to conform to the characteristics of other cultures. Chung Saeki and Henry Borow (1985) take the opposite approach. The psychotherapies of the West and non-West, Saeki and Borow argue, require a cross-cultural therapy that will adapt principles and techniques appropriate to particular cultures. It is realistic to assume that effective cross-cultural helpers are eclectic. They adhere to a particular theory and use particular modes of helping based on the needs of their clients. True, they are better versed in one or two art forms of helping than others, but they are skilled enough through intensive training to utilize a variety of specific methods associated with other modalities (Corsini & Wedding, 1989).

Cross-cultural therapy is a twentieth century phenomenon (Morrow, 1975). I use the term "cross-cultural" to include "cross-ethnic." Currently, most of the cross-cultural research and therapy are being conducted by White, middle-class, English-speaking, male practitioners whose clients are African American or Hispanic citizens in the United States or Great Britain. Much of this research attempts to expand and clarify Kurt Lewin's classic formula (1935): $B = f(P,E)$, or behavior is a function of person-environment interaction. And language is important in this process.

People who speak different languages live in different worlds. Too often, practitioners are not aware of this fact. African Americans who speak Black English clearly illustrate this condition (Dillard, 1972). Dorothy Seymour (1972) was one of the first researchers to argue that Black English, which has a West African language foundation, is not "bad" English but a dialect with a structure and form of its own. Other linguists have made it clear that language systems that are different are not necessarily deficient. From the West African point of view, "standard" English is difficult to comprehend because it: (1) lacks certain language sounds; (2) has language sounds for which others may serve as substitutes; (3) doubles and drawls some of its vowel sounds in sequences that are difficult for non-Americans to imitate; (4) lacks a method for forming an important tense; (5) requires several ways to indicate tense, gender and plurality; and (6) does not mark negatives sufficiently for words to make optimally strong negative statements (Seymour, 1972, p. 80).

Consider also, for example, the possible therapeutic problems that can result from accepting a traditional Chinese client's description of his wife. Unlike the English language, the Chinese language does not have past-tense verb forms. Thus, the Chinese client who says, "My wife is very beautiful," when she is dead, is not necessarily grieving. Relatedly, Luis Marcos et al. (1973) addressed the problem of Hispanic patients for whom English was a relatively unfamiliar second language:

> When the patient attempts to speak a language other than his mother-tongue he creates problems for both himself and the psychiatrist. Communicating his thoughts in a relatively unfamiliar language imposes an additional burden on the patient's already failing efforts to organize a fluid and chaotic subjective experience. Under these circumstances disturbances in fluency, organization, and integration occurred in English while they were absent in Spanish. These disturbances were not simply related to linguistic competence. It is possible that demanding the patient express himself in English acted as a distraction to cause further deterioration in his cognitive functioning. At points of affective arousal, patients frequently attempted to evade the linguistic constraints imposed on them by shortening their responses and lapsing into their native tongue (p. 657).

The patients in Marcos' study had difficulty in understanding questions asked in English. Also, they had difficulty finding suitable English words to satisfy their communicative intent. In addition, they had difficulty using past-tense communication when interviewed in English. The latter behavior mislead clinicians attempting to assess just how active a patient's symptoms were. Speaking across the language barrier frequently arouses complex socially learned perceptions which distort the helpee's behavior.

As noted earlier, the social class of an individual is another important cultural factor in shaping views. A cursory look at world cultures reveals that variables such as education, income, residence and religion vary greatly in most communities (Bagley, 1973; Stadler, 1985; Wehrly, 1988). Higher occupational status has been associated with depression. In modern Western communities the types of social and psychological disorders and the kind of treatment received tend to be a function of social class (Jones, 1974). This is less often the case in non-Western cultures where there is less stratification in terms of income and social status. Compared with Western countries, Third-World counties in particular have fewer affluent citizens. Indeed, most Third-World countries have a large lower class, almost no middle class, and a small upper class.

In the causes of psychological disorders there are dramatic ethnic differences. Culture defines the situations that arouse certain local and national responses, and it also determines the degree to which responses are regarded as normal and abnormal (Dunham, 1976; King, 1978; Morley & Wallis, 1978; Wehrly & Deen, 1983). Although all types of psychological disorders occur in non-Western cultures, they frequently differ from their Western counterparts in form and treatment. In addition to individual experiences that develop fears and anxieties, cultural beliefs cause members of societies to avoid certain behaviors. For example, in some societies individuals publicly exchange verbal abuse, whereas in other societies such abuse is taboo. By now it should be clear that people who come from varying cultural backgrounds have varying beliefs and practices.

THE PEOPLE INVOLVED

The terms *therapist, practitioner* and *helper* are used interchangeably, as are the terms *clients, patients* and *helpees*. While the type and degree of training will differ, all helpers use specific techniques in order to help people to accomplish something beneficial. That "something beneficial" is usually culturally determined. John Mann (1965) described several kinds of professional helpers:

> There are many ways to induce a constructive behavior change in individuals. The *practitioner*, or change agent, the man who tries to bring about such a change, is not a researcher; he devotes himself to working directly with people on problems of immediate, practical importance. Among the practitioners who devote themselves to treating the mentally ill are the *clinical psychologist* and the *psychotherapist*, who usually have Ph.D. degrees and who use certain techniques of psychological therapy on their patients; the *psychiatrist*, a medical doctor whose specialty is mental illness; and the *psychoanalyst*, usually a psychiatrist who has taken further training in a particular kind of psychological therapy at a psychoanalytic institute. Other practitioners are more interested in attempting to bring about a more overt kind of behavior change related one's social environment, the *social worker*, for example,

or the *human-relations trainer,* who works with psychologically normal persons to help them improve their skills in relating to others (p. 9).

Much of the cross-cultural literature focuses on racial and ethnic groups, particularly Third-World groups. It is important to note that the terms "racial groups" and "ethnic groups" are not synonymous. Race refers to a system by which humans are classified into subgroups according to specific physical characteristics. These characteristics include skin pigmentation, stature, facial features, texture of body hair and head form. The three commonly recognized racial types—Caucasoid, Mongoloid and Negroid—greatly overlap each other. There are no pure races. Ashley Montagu (1974) correctly observed that the concept of race is humankind's most dangerous myth. There are more similarities than differences between racial groups. For these reasons, I have elected to focus on ethnicity.

Ethnic groups are groups of individuals who share a unique cultural and social heritage passed on from one generation to another. Racial groups and ethnic groups should not be confused with "culture." Stated another way, culture is the profile of learned behavior and the results of behavior whose components and elements are shared and transmitted by the members of a particular society. Races do have different cultures, and ethnic groups within races differ in cultural content. Furthermore, people of the same racial origin and of the same ethnic group may differ in their cultural matrices. For example, all Hispanics, Africans, Indians, or Britons are not alike in the cultures in which they live. Understanding the culture of another person, or of groups other than one's own, demands knowledge of varied elements within a culture. It is precisely this kind of understanding that we seek as we explore cross-cultural helping beliefs and practices.

Most higher education programs that train social services practitioners pay little attention to cultural influences of people who are not local ethnic minorities. This pedagogical approach ignores the variety of cultural groups found throughout the world. Andrew Greeley (1969) predicted that future historians will ponder why North Americans in particular stood in the midst of tremendous ethnic diversity and did not bother to study it. He wrote:

> They will find it especially astonishing in light of the fact that ethnic differences, even in the second half of the twentieth century, proved far more important than differences in philosophy or economic system.

Men who would not die for a premise or a dogma would more or less cheerfully die for a difference rooted in ethnic origins (p. 5).

There is ample empirical evidence that ethnic values and identification are retained for several generations after people migrate from their native land (Greeley, 1969; Staples, 1980), and are central in family life and development throughout the life cycle (Gelfand & Kutzik, 1979). Indeed, second-, third- and even fourth-generation immigrants tend to maintain traditional culture values, life-styles and behavior.

Ethnicity subsumes group commonality which is crystalized over generations by the community and reinforced by the family. It incorporates conscious and unconscious processes that characterize group identity and historical continuity (Giordano & Giordano, 1977; Green, 1982). Psychological studies document that ethnicity shapes an individual's thinking, feeling, and behavior in both overt and covert ways (Giordano, 1973; Endo & Munoz, 1981; Smith, 1985). A cursory survey of related literature reveals that ethnicity plays an important role in determining an individual's diet, work habits, religious beliefs, philosophy of life, and methods of coping with illness and death (Blalock, 1982; Feagin, 1984).

Ethnic groups differ in their inclination to seek help outside the family. They also differ in the kind of help they will accept. For example, Italians generally rely on family members and turn to outsiders as a last resort (Fondetti, 1976; Gottesfeld, 1981). African Americans tend to mistrust social services agencies staffed by non-Blacks (Ponterotto et al., 1988). Some groups, including Puerto Ricans and Chinese, are culturally conditioned to somatize when they are under stress and prefer medical rather than mental health treatment (Smith, 1985). Furthermore, members of some groups are taught to define their problems in terms of their own inadequacy, action or sin, while other groups tend to see their problems as a result of somebody else's inadequacy, action, or sin. It is helpful for practitioners to determine which of these perspectives is operative for each client.

This brings us to the final term, *Third World*. I use it to refer to countries sometimes called "newly developing." The First World is composed of economically developed capitalistic countries, the Second World consists of economically developed socialist countries, and the Third World is made up of developing countries in Africa, Asia, and Latin America.

FAMILIAL CHARACTERISTICS

The sections focusing on cultural differences are at best introductions to the topic, but even so these data vividly illustrate the importance of understanding familial characteristics. Practitioners must understand that most behaviors exhibited by foreigners are neither capricious nor malicious; rather, they are socially prescribed ways of dealing with life situations. Furthermore, family practices play important roles in human relationships. The modern Western family has relinquished some of its traditional functions and gained importance in others. Unlike most Third-World families, the Western family has lost most of its economic functions and is now mainly a unit of economic consumption. The protective functions have declined, giving way to institutions outside the home. The socialization function is being shared largely with the school.

However, the Western family is still the primary agent in passing on social skills. The shift of world populations from rural to urban setting alters family relationships and activities. In most developing Third-World countries the move towards urbanization has not resulted in the decline of the extended family. Nor has it drastically changed the values upon which cultural exchanges occur. Most Third-World families still consist of the immediate family units. Extended families are philosophical and psychological systems much less based on individual existence than nuclear families (Mindel, 1980; Allen & Stokes, 1981; Smith, 1985; Ho, 1987). Although they do not share the same residence, most extended family members share similar beliefs and values.

Not all spouses consist of living persons. The "ghost marriages" in traditional Chinese families is such an example (Tseng & McDermott, 1981). In Taiwan, a shaman may decide that an illness in a family is caused by a ghost who needs a living husband. Until the unmarried ghost is wed, the illness will continue. Therefore, a family member or an outsider enticed with money must go through a wedding ceremony. Once married, the ghost spouse becomes a member of the living mate's clan. Traditional Chinese belief frowns upon a woman dying before getting married. Until a woman is married, she has little chance to be worshipped after death. An ancestral tablet on the family alter accrues to her only through her husband. Thus, a ghost marriage provides a woman, living or dead, with status and security.

Family units differ greatly in the following ways: first, the demands for responsibility made on children, that is, the number and kinds of duties expected of them; second, the emotionally positive behaviors of parents to children such as praise, absence of physical punishment, and general warmth; third, the degree of control demanded over aggression toward peers; and, fourth, the degree of child obedience and aggression toward parents and other adults (Staples & Mirande, 1980).

Asians

As I have noted earlier, people within and across cultures are different and these differences require different styles of helping. Client behavior and its underlying motivations or causes can best be objectively understood from their cultural orientations. A major task for helpers is to learn basic concepts of human motivation, which requires learning the culture of an ethnic group, a geographical region, a national minority, or a nation. In international relations this means learning about the influences of national cultures. For example, most non-Asians do not understand Asian family values and therefore do not understand Asian people or their patterns of interaction (Henderson, 1979; Ho, 1987). Many of the following generalizations about traditional Chinese and Japanese families are applicable to other Asian families too (see Chapter 4).

Filial piety. There is unquestioning respect for and deference to authority. Above all else, there is the expectation that each individual will comply with familial and social authority.

Shame and guilt. Since they are taught to respect authority and maintain filial piety toward their parents and ancestors, a violation of these norms results in feelings of shame and guilt.

Self-control. Individual achievement is pursued in order to enhance the family name. But verbal, assertive, and individualistic people are considered crude and poorly socialized. Strong negative feelings are seldom verbalized.

Social milieu. Most Asians are other-directed and are greatly concerned with how their significant others view and react to them. Social solidarity is highly valued.

Inconspicuousness. Taught to avoid calling attention to themselves, Chinese and Japanese are likely to be silent in public settings.

Fatalism. Resignation and pragmatism is the manner in which they deal with changes in nature and social settings.

A "good son" in the traditional Chinese family accomplishes several things. He fulfills obligations and pays honor to his parents and ancestors, and this in turn brings him health, success, and happiness. Through his behavior these blessings also flow to his descendants, even unborn grandchildren and great-grandchildren. Ancestors who are honored are at peace; they send beneficial influences. Neglected and dishonored ancestors send harmful influences. A good son is a "good person."

The norm of *enryo* is characteristic of Japanese behavior. This concept originally referred to proper role behavior among "superiors" and "inferiors," mainly deference and obsequiousness in order to avoid confusion, embarrassment and anxiety. As an illustration, if a practitioner would ask a traditional Asian, "Do you understand what I said?" the client who does not understand will answer, "Yes," meaning "I have respect for you and don't want to embarrass you." It would be impolite for the client to say, "No, it is not clear," implying that the helper is either confused or unable to correctly communicate, or both. The blank stare, noncommittal answer and passive group behavior reflect *enryo*.

Ha zu ka shi ("Others will laugh at you") is part of the *enryo* syndrome. Publicly making a fool of oneself publicly shames one's family. Reticence in order to avoid embarrassment is seen in job situations. *Hi-age*, or refusing to praise self or family, particularly in public, does not prevent the Japanese from being highly competitive. Like the Chinese, the Japanese are taught to do the best they can, no matter what they are doing, but to be humble and self-depreciating if they succeed. This outward modesty in a quest for personal excellence often seems strange to non-Asians.

Latinos

Cultural similarities and differences become even more evident when we compare Asian cultures to Latino cultures. It is important to remember that what is normal and functional behavior in one Latin country may be abnormal and dysfunctional in another. Even so, the following characteristics are generalizable to most traditional Latin American and Latin European cultures (Henderson, 1979; Mindel, 1980; Hardy-Fantana & MacMahon-Herra, 1981; Ho, 1987). Variations and regionalisms of the Spanish language are almost as numerous as the countries in which they are found. Hispanics are composed of the people from all the countries of South and Central America, Mexico, some of the Caribbean countries, and Spain. Common Hispanic family values include the following.

La Raza (*The Race*). All Latinos are united by cultural and spiritual bonds believed to have emanated from God. Because God controls all events, Latinos tend to be more present oriented than future oriented. The influence of the Roman Catholic Church on *La Raza* is pervasive— most Latinos are born, get married, work, die and are buried under the auspices of religious ceremonies. But not all Latinos are Roman Catholics.

Family loyalty. The familial role is the most important, and the family is the second most cherished institution in Latino society. A Latino owes his or her primary loyalty to the family. The worst sin is to violate one's obligations to God, and next comes the family.

Respect. The oldest man in the household is the family leader. Respect is accorded on the basis of age and gender. The old are accorded more respect than the young, and men are accorded more respect than women. Latino families are based on family solidarity and male superiority.

Machismo. Latino culture prescribes that the men are stronger, more reliable, and more intelligent than women. *Machismo* dictates that the man will show a high degree of individuality outside the family. Weakness in male behavior is looked down on. (This does not result in "weak" females. Within their prescribed roles, Latino females are very strong.)

Compadrazgo. The Latino family is extended by the institution of *compadrazgo*, a special bond between a child's parents and godparents. Often, the bond between *compadres* is as strong as between brothers and sisters.

Intervention programs that work well for Mexican Americans might not work well for other Latino persons because of subcultural differences. For example, knowing that a client speaks Spanish may be inadequate cultural knowledge. There are qualitative differences in the language of Latinos who are monolingual Spanish or bilingual Spanish-English. Furthermore, Spanish has many dialects.

Africans

Finally, I call your attention to African family characteristics. It is difficult to categorize Africans because of the many clans and ethnic group divisions found in Africa, the second largest continent in the world (Disara, 1988). Out of this diversity, we find the following common characteristics which are also seen in traditional African American families (Henderson, 1979; Sudarkasa, 1980; Allen, 1981; McGoldrick et al., 1982)

Extended family. The African family is sometimes extended bilaterally but often it is maternally oriented. The African extended family is a closely knit group, frequently consisting of grandparents, aunts, uncles,

nieces, nephews and cousins. In many Central and West African countries the concepts of "superior" and "inferior" with regard to gender is
meaningless (Weekes-Vagliani, 1976). However, in all African countries
there are prescribed sex roles.

Kinship bonds. Kinship is the most important aspect of the African
society. And bearing children is an obligation of parents. The more
children parents have, the more glory they receive. Because children are
proof of an individual's manhood or womanhood, caring for them is
proof of an individual's humanity. When children marry or otherwise
reach adulthood, they leave home but often settle close to their parents
or other relatives. Family unity, loyalty, and cooperation are part of the
African life-style. (These values are also strongly held by the other
Third-World ethnic groups discussed in this book.)

Authority and discipline. Childhood in African countries revolve around
learning community customs, traditions and values. Traditional life-
style is highly prized and it is taught through both formal and informal
education. Through these processes African children learn acceptable
behaviors. Discipline tends to be harsh, strict and preoccupied with
teaching children respect for their elders, respect for authority, responsibility for themselves and an understanding of what it means to be a
family member.

Religious orientation. On the whole, Africans are highly religious.
Many of them are Protestant. The church offers spiritual hope to many
persons who live in oppressive environments.

Achievement and work orientations. Contrary to popular notion, most
African parents pass on to their children high achievement aspirations.
However, most African homes lack middle-class role models for children
to emulate. The desire to survive has forced many families to internalize
a strong work orientation that makes palatable the unskilled and semi-
skilled jobs available in the economically depressed job market within
which most African people work.

Stable Families

Basic to our discussion of the Third-World family are the concepts
self-actualization and *social equilibrium.* The need to develop oneself to
maximum potential as an integrated, fully functioning, unique person
often clashes with the need to be like one's relatives. The actualization
need is most likely to be realized in societies or families that do not

devote disproportionate amounts of time and energy to biological subsistence. As demands for maintaining bodily existence decrease, the opportunity for self-actualization increases. Within any society individual variations of two kinds exist. First, some persons may elect to waste their opportunities to self-actualize. Second, the drive to self-actualization may under unusual circumstances be realized by impoverished people. Great literature, renowned art, and profound philosophical insights have come from individuals continuously living close to the survival level.

The equilibrium process is a chain of events occurring at an optimal rate so that the social system can maintain its functional integrity. The notion of a family being "healthy" because it is in equilibrium during cultural changes (e.g., new factories, infusion of foreign workers, racial disturbances) is not new to the behavioral sciences. James Miller (1955) presented several provocative ideas about the subject in the *American Psychologist.* The personal equilibrium of families in an international context can be judged from two perspectives: first, the extent to which they routinely carry out their traditional functions and, second, the extent to which they adjust to or absorb nontraditional ways of interacting. Families unable to maintain their equilibrium frequently produce misfits, troublemakers, and unstable citizens.

Never before have as many people throughout the world been so free from restrictions to self-actualization. But lack of practical restrictions is not enough to alter centuries of cultural inhibitions. The progression of theories and models promulgating individual freedom have not automatically provided individuals with the skills or courage needed to use this freedom responsibly. It is not easy to move from being colonized or dominated to being free. Generally, it is easier for people in industrialized areas to use this freedom than people in rural areas. The family tends, on the one hand, to reject new values and, on the other hand, to foster new ones (Sertorio et al., 1976). It is common practice for each family to filter cultural changes through its traditional lenses. By the nature of their own restricted folkways and mores, traditional families are slow to try new patterns of social interaction and healing.

USEFUL MODALITIES

All of the therapy modalities discussed in Chapter 1 have been used extensively in the Anglo countries of the United States, Great Britain and Canada. They have had considerably less use in India, Australia and New Zealand. Also, the modalities are widely applicable for the Germanic countries of West Germany, Austria, and Switzerland; and the Scandinavian countries. The Western influence, spearheaded by conferences, student exchanges, and book translations, is analogous to a helping modality common market. Contributing to this worldwide extension of Western therapies are multinational corporations that have created world communities whose residents suffer similar maladies and seek similar therapeutic services.

Neither Western religions nor Western helping modalities have been widely exported to the Arab countries. The Arabian Middle East includes the area bounded by the North African states of Morocco, Tunisia, and Algeria on the west to the Arabian Gulf states on the east. Egypt has the largest number (approximately 70%) of mental health practitioners in the Arab countries (King, 1983; Seligman, 1985). On the whole, there are relatively few mental health practitioners in the Arabian Middle East. The vast majority of them were trained in the West, and those who have attempted to fuse their training with indigenous practices have been generally unsuccessful (Moracco, 1985). The family, especially the father and not professional helpers, is responsible for problem resolution. Women in the Middle East generally hold lower status than men. But in most Arab countries women have equal rights in many areas, including education and suffrage. Even so, masculinity is perceived as responsible, rational and controllable, whereas femininity is considered sexually irresponsible, irrational and uncontrollable (Gulick, 1976; Moracco, 1983). Consequently, problems centering on sexual relationships are seldom discussed outside the family.

Despite changes toward Western dress and cultural activities, basic traditions have not changed in Arab countries. Most Arabs are Moslems and this fact alone restricts the use of Western helping practices. The Islamic religion is the foundation upon which Moslem life and culture are based. The history of Moslems necessarily begins with the Prophet Mohammed, a son of a poor merchant. Born in A.D. 570, Mohammed traveled throughout the Middle East with trading caravans. At age 40 he had the first of a series of revelations from God through the angel Gabriel. While in trance-like states, Mohammed received the contents of what is now Islam's Holy Book, the Qur'an (Koran). God (Allah) controls everything for Moslems, and individuality is not a primary goal of most Arabs. Expressing one's feelings and thoughts are not part of traditional

Arab socialization. The laws of Islam prescribe appropriate behavior. Thus, role-appropriate behavior does not include the kind of introspection required in most Western therapies. The utilitarian Western modalities would be reality therapy and other behavioral therapies. But care must be taken to focus on behavior change consonant with Islamic laws.

The Latin European countries are considerably more diverse in lifestyles and beliefs than the Arab countries. Many of the Western religions and helping modalities discussed in this book are found in some form in France, for example. Faith healing as well as psychodynamic and humanistic modalities fit well into Italian socialization patterns. Transactional analysis is of more limited value because of the negative connotations given to much of the Parent ego state. Anything that suggests being disrespectful of parents will be resisted by traditional Italians (Gottesfeld, 1981). Behavior modification therapies conceivably would also be resisted if the helper insists that nothing we do, feel or think is a reaction to external events. Italians are likely to believe the opposite. The Portuguese are the least likely Latin Europeans to accept Western modalities. Sharing intimate family and personal problems to an outsider is not typical behavior. Nor are the Portuguese likely to actively seek ways to disrupt the status quo. The Portuguese saying *"Se deus quizer"* ("If God so wills") is not just a slogan, it is a philosophy of life. Behavior and multimodal therapies have been suggested for Latinos by researchers (Padilla & DeSnyder, 1983; Ponterotto, 1987).

Behavior modification has been studied in several parts of the world, particularly Australia, Europe, Japan, Mexico, New Zealand, South America and Southeast Asia (Sheehan & White, 1976; Ardilla, 1978; Kazdin, 1978; Higginbotham, 1979). The data substantiate that intervention programs cannot be isolated from the cultural milieu in which they are implemented. Any helping modality used with Hispanics must allow for *afecto* (warmth and demonstrativeness), *dignidad* (dignity), *fatalismo* (fatalism), *machismo* (male superiority), and *respeto* (respect for authority, family and tradition). Unlike psychoanalysis and person-centered therapies, behavior therapies are straightforward, immediate and goal-oriented—procedures preferred by Hispanics. Furthermore, it is important to know that Hispanics are less willing to self-disclose than Anglos and Africans (Acosta & Sheehan, 1976).

Western helping modalities which are based on personal growth through self-exploration must be significantly adapted for Hispanic populations. Among the cultural values of Hispanics is the belief that one does not reveal personal or family information to persons outside the home if it has no relevance for them. Personal and family problems are private matters and as such they must be kept within the kinship group. There are times when an Hispanic will not even share personal matters with other family members in order to spare them anxiety (Murillo-Rohde, 1979). The reluctance of traditional Hispanics to disclose self and family problems make them very cautious candidates for a "talking therapy." The privacy of confession is more comfortable for Catholic Hispanics.

Similar to Africans, Italians and Latin Americans subordinate individual goals to group goals (Papajohn & Spiegel, 1975). The temporal focus is based on the present; the past receives little attention; the future is seen as unpredictable. Yet, there is a qualitative difference between Italians and Latin Americans. Both have a code or hierarchy that respects the family, age and men. While there is abundant literature about Latin Americans (Mindel, 1980; Werner, 1983; Sanchez & Atkinson, 1983; Padilla & DeSnyder, 1985; del Portillo, 1987; Taussig, 1987; Ponce & Atkinson, 1989), the Italian experience has not been similarly researched. This is yet another reason to believe that modalities which require self and family public disclosure will be met with resistance by Italians (Gottesfeld, 1981). They value individuals who will not publicly tell their secrets.

The colonization of African countries by Western nations have rendered most African countries receptive to Western religions and helping modalities. However, religious leaders and helpers who require public sharing of family and personal problems are likely to meet resistance. Also, situations that place African men in subordinate relationships with women will create blockages. Thus, humanistic modalities are the least likely to receive large-scale reception in African countries. Here too the most promising modalities would be the ones that are the least socially disruptive. Behavior modification techniques that focus on satisfying basic survival and security needs are amenable to cultural adaptation in most African countries. As a whole, Africans are structure oriented. They are accustomed to authorities teaching or telling them what to do (Esen, 1972; Idowu, 1985). The traditional African religions and healing system are authoritative; healers structure and direct the helping process. Democratic, nondirective helpers are often seen by African and African American clients as incompetent and weak (Harris & Balgopal, 1980; McFadden, 1981; Allen & Stokes, 1981; Anosike, 1982; Ridley, 1984; Jones, 1985).

Psychotherapy techniques are not unique to Western countries. African and Latin American indigenous helpers used similar techniques long before Freud and his colleagues. At least one writer has described indigenous helping techniques as being "psychiatry without psychiatrists" (Collomb, 1972). Indigenous psychotherapy has been the subject of several researches (Sanua, 1966; Torrey, 1972; Pedersen et al., 1976; Prince, 1980). When we consider the many techniques of helping used in Africa and Latin America, it is evident that psychotherapy has existed in some form for centuries (Wachtel, 1977). Even so, descriptions of individual psychotherapy within African cultures suggest processes very unlike Western modalities (Olatawura, 1975). Western psychotherapy is unsuitable in Africa without considerable modification. The form that a Western helping modality takes must be compatible with the traditional cultural ethos (Torrey, 1972; Draguns, 1973). Unlike traditional healing systems, Western modalities give little attention to the cultural link between individuals and their emotional states (Idowu, 1985). Africa healers utilize clients' beliefs to alter their emotional and body states. Illnesses are viewed by most Africans as symbolic expressions of internal conflicts or disturbed interpersonal relationships, or both. The role of the African healer is authoritative and his or her position is supported by the family and community.

Traditional African healing is a community process. Furthermore, healing is directed toward complete personal integration of the client into the community. For this reason, Western "psychoanalysis and other insight or behavior-oriented approaches may be inappropriate. Rather, group counseling and other techniques that emphasize the client's significant groups and cultural identity seem more appropriate" (Idowu, 1985, p. 83). Few Western helpers fully comprehend the importance of community to Africans. The Swahili proverb *Mgeni siku mbili; siku ya tatu mpe jembe* ("You should treat a guest as a guest for two days, but on the third day, give him a hoe so he can work like one of the family") illustrates the East African concept of sharing work and problems. Of course, this also includes sharing pleasant things. The most successful African helpers integrate indigenous methods into their Western-based modalities (Lambo, 1978).

The question is not whether a particular modality can be effective in a particular country but in what forms? Hard data on this subject are not available, but it is likely that practitioners who are culturally literate can adapt their modality to fit a large number of clients (Copeland, 1983; Beutler, 1983; Ponterotto, 1987). Even so, as I have suggested, some modalities and cultures are more adjustable than others. Studies of health beliefs and practices in Melanesia, the Republic of Panama, Peru, Chile, and Guatemala conclude that when a treatment is quickly effective, dramatic and evident, it will be chosen over others (Simmons, 1955; Gonzales, 1966; Egeland, 1967). Alternative modes of curing are arranged in a hierarchy of effectiveness, with different alternatives being used as the illness or problem progresses without cure or resolution (Schwartz, 1969). A *hierarchy of resort in curative practices* is found in all cultures. This results in simultaneous or serial use of Western and traditional modalities. As an example, psychoanalysis is favored by Jewish people who are taught to look for and discuss the deeper implications of social interactions (Meadow & Vetter, 1959), while it is not favored by Japanese who learn to be private, shame-oriented people taught to hide family-related problems (Doi, 1964). Yet, depending on the severity of their problem, Jewish clients will abandon psychoanalysis for other therapies, and Japanese clients will try psychoanalysis.

Any modality which ignores the etiological categories of severe emotional upset, ritual uncleanness, evil spirits, and bad air are likely to be assigned low priority in many Third-World countries. Observing similar behavior among Bahamians, Cubans, Haitians, Puerto Ricans and Southern American Blacks, Clarissa Scott (1974) offered the following advice to Western practitioners:

> 1. Gain knowledge of the health beliefs and practices of local ethnic groups.
> 2. Respect the fact that these beliefs and therapies, although perhaps running counter to the scientific medical system, have survived in these populations for generations and may indeed be measurably effective. To try to change a deeply rooted health belief either by ridicule or by treating it as unscientific may not only fail but may also alienate the patient.
> 3. Use a treatment plan which shows understanding and respect for the patient's beliefs and which builds on these in a positive way (p. 230).

Romantic conceptualizations assign different values to rural (folk) and urban (scientific) communities. Some writers create idyllic images of rural life. "Rural" conjures up the smell of freshly mown fields, herds of cattle or sheep, fields of crops, a country store and people in native dress. From this perspective, the indigenous curer is the prototype of the sturdy, independent religious person in a natural, unspoiled environment; while the modern health care practitioner works in the unnatural, spoiled religiously hostile environment. Somewhere between these two extremes is a more accurate picture of rural and urban life. In terms of religions and life-styles, there is much similarity between urban-oriented and rural-oriented people throughout the world.

Before the introduction of rapid transportation, mass communication and other intrusions of urban culture into rural communities, rural dwellers were isolated very much like the mythical people in Washington Irving's *Sleepy Hollow.* There was an overriding sense of independence, on the one hand, and ethnic solidarity, on the other. The range of acceptable behaviors were greatly restricted. This set of circumstances resulted in community efforts to retain folk beliefs and practices. Contact with the outside world was intermittent and slow in coming, but once contact was established through explorers, exploiters and churches, folk beliefs and practices were altered forever. This mix of old and new beliefs and values is the stuff out of which relevant helping modalities must be shaped.

Chapter 3

RELIGIOUS FOUNDATIONS

Traditional folk health care practices exist side by side with formal health care practices. In fact, they overlap at many points. Though these beliefs and practices are not well described historically, we can, according to George Foster (1953), deduce them by subtracting formal medicine of the sixteenth century from folk medicine of today and making allowances for New World influences. Sixteenth century Spanish folk medicine was the accretion of centuries of influence by numerous invaders. For example, the significance of fire and water to Spanish health systems, particularly in Northwest Spain, reflects the pre-Christian beliefs of the Celts and other early European invaders. Pre-Arab Mediterranean influences are reflected in votive offerings which have been traced back to Greek and Roman temples. Also, the indigenous Spanish practice of using religious prayers and invocations in curing rituals represent the Christian influence. And the belief in the evil eye may be due to Arab contact or earlier Mediterranean invaders.

THIRD-WORLD HEALTH CARE SYSTEMS

Third-World peoples are likely to explain their emotional and physical illnesses in terms of imbalance between the individual and his or her physical, social and spiritual worlds. In short, health and illness come from the supernatural (Snow, 1974; Endo & Munoz, 1981). Although all medical systems focus on preventive and curative medicine, good health in most Third-World cultures centers on personal rather than scientific behavior. From this perspective, it makes sense to burn incense or to avoid certain individuals or cold air or evil eyes.

All religious systems have elaborate rules that determine appropriate and inappropriate health care behavior. This includes rules for giving care and receiving it. Religious experiences may consist of blessings from spiritual leaders and apparition of animate as well as inanimate objects. The key concept in all religious systems is *faith*. In traditional

45

Third-World societies some of the most significant religious rituals are those that mediate between events "here" in this world and those "out there" in the nether world. To mediate these worlds, folk practitioners may effect cures and work protective and evil magic. These helpers are known by many names such as *dang-ki* (Taiwan), *mudang* (Korea), *yuta* (Okinawa), *fu-i* (Manchuria), *hougan* (Haiti), *haka* (Hawaii), *babalawo* (Yoruba), *miko* or *rebai* (Japan) and *hodja* (Turkey). It is interesting to note that modern health care practitioners are also concerned with "here and now" (present) and "there and then" (past) conditions that affect a client's health.

> *First case* (Western "middle-class" psychotherapy): The psychiatrist looked thoughtfully at his patient. "You looked angry when you were just talking about your father. You often look angry when you talk about him. I wonder if something happened to you once that made you very angry at him." At this point the patient broke down sobbing, blurting out a forgotten history of neglect and deceit by a thoughtless father toward a little girl. Afterwards the patient felt better.

> *Second case* (Psychotherapy with an "indigenous" healer): The witch doctor stared solemnly at the small shells. They had landed in a pattern resembling the shape of a large animal. He picked one shell and examined it minutely. "You have broken the taboo of your family. It has offended the sacred bear that protects your ancestors. That is why you are sick." The patient and her family breathed a sigh of relief. It was as they had suspected. Now that they knew for certain what was wrong they could proceed with the necessary sacrifices. After these had been made, the patient began to get better (Torrey, 1972, p. 70).

It is important to remember that the folk health care systems I describe are not restricted to Third-World cultures. For instance, portions of these systems are found among North American groups as diverse as the Hutterites, Amish, Appalachian Whites, Midwestern farmers and Pennsylvania Dutch. Also, similar beliefs are found in the rural South and Southwest, throughout the Ozarks, and as far north as the Upper Peninsula of Michigan. Therefore, they are characteristic of a great many people.

Loudell Snow (1974) summarized three major themes in Third-World health care systems: the world is a hostile and dangerous place; the individual is vulnerable to attack from external sources; and because the individual is helpless and has inadequate internal resources to combat external attacks, he or she must depend on outside help. Survival in a hostile world requires one to be wary of nature, faithful to a punitive God and suspicious of other people. This latter belief often leads to distrust of relatives, friends and strangers. Consequently, success in interpersonal relationships is often seen as the ability to manipulate others. The use of magic is a natural outgrowth of such beliefs. Feelings of loneliness, normlessness, emptiness and helplessness are prominent in folktales and religious music.

Humoral pathology is an important aspect of Latin American and Spanish health care. This simplified form of Greek humoral pathology was elaborated in the Arab world, brought to Spain as scientific medicine during the period of Moslem domination, and transmitted to the Americas at the time of the Spanish Conquest. According to humoral medical beliefs, the basic functions of the body are regulated by four bodily fluids or humors—blood, phlegm, black bile and yellow bile—each of which is characterized by a combination of heat or cold with wetness or dryness (Clements, 1932). Blood is hot and wet; phlegm is cold and wet; black bile is cold and dry; and yellow bile is hot and dry. Most foods, herbs, beverages and medicines are classified as "hot" (*caliente*), "cold" (*frío*) or "cool" (*fresco*). The wet-dry conditions are less important; the secret to good health is believed to lie in maintaining a balance between hot and cold humors. The hot-cold syndrome is operative in most of Latin America, including Chile, Columbia, Guatemala, Mexico and Peru. It is also prevalent in Haiti, Jamaica, and Puerto Rico.

African indigenous health care practices make little distinction between physical, emotional, and spiritual needs. According to traditional African beliefs, both living and dead things influence an individual's health. In addition, health is directly related to nature. To be in harmony with nature is to be in good health, whereas illness reflects disharmony with nature. The secret to good health is maintaining a balance between the forces of good and evil. Faith healers, root doctors, and spiritualists carry out the ancient rituals of casting out evil spirits or demons. American Indians, Latin Americans and Africans believe in *bad magic* —spells, evil eye, and other harmful magic. To counter bad medicine, *good medicine* —taboos and magic—are used. A taboo is an injunction to do or not to do something. Indian medicine men (shamans) were the original folk healers in North America.

So that you will not attribute taboos only to primitive people, I call your attention to modern social taboos such as women wearing high-heel shoes that deform their feet or men wearing too much clothing in order to conform to beauty taboos. Or I can point to religious persons who would not leave home without a miniature cross. Nor should we overlook people who believe that broken glass or walking under a ladder will bring bad luck. Generally, nonprimitive people call their taboos "etiquette," "customs" and "conventions."

Blacks from Africa and the West Indies brought their own magical rites to the Americas. Black magic, *obeah*, was once a widely practiced form of healing in the West Indies, the Guianas in Latin America and the southeastern part of North America. Obeah is not the same as voodoo which is a form of African religion or serpent-god worship requiring an animal sacrifice. Obeah has little to do with religion. Rather, it is a form of witchcraft or black magic. There have been instances when obeah doctors have been able through autosuggestion and fear to perform remarkable feats. For example, they have been able to put pins, needles and other objects in the flesh of their subjects without drawing blood or causing pain (Metraux, 1959). Conversely, they have been able to cause a person to exhibit painful medical symptoms without being sick. In extreme ire, an obeah doctor can frighten to death an otherwise healthy follower (Engel, 1971).

Spiritualism

Spiritualism is an integral part of most folk health care systems, especially among Hispanics, Africans, African Americans, and American Indians. For our discussion, spiritualism is defined as the belief that the visible world also includes an invisible world inhabited by good and evil spirits who influence human behavior. Spirits make their presence known through *mediums:* Voodoo men and women, coranderos, espiritas, and shamans or medicine men and medicine women.

> In addition to conferring protection and enabling the medium to function, spirits can both cause and prevent illness. One's spiritual protection acts as a shield, turning away evil spirits and hexes while at the same time bringing one good luck. If one loses spiritual protection . . . one can become ill. The illness may be manifested by such signs as pain, lethargy, nervousness and bad luck (Fisch, 1968, p. 378).

Mediums treat both emotionally related and physical illnesses. Unlike Western-based practitioners, mediums treat the whole person. For example, in Puerto Rican culture psychological symptoms are frequently expressed as a somatic illness. Western practitioners tend to minimize the importance of psychosomatic illnesses or ignore them. Mediums have a distinct advantage when compared with Western-oriented practitioners.

This advantage is due to the fact that most mediums share the ethnic background, language, social class and community of their followers. They are not visitors to the community. Here, too, the essence of their success resides in the faith that their followers have in them.

There is virtually no incompatibility between religion and spiritualism. Religion, similar to spiritualism, is based on the belief in spirits. Furthermore, similar to a medium, a religious leader's authority is of a spiritual nature. However, one person's religion may be another person's magic, witchcraft or superstition (Kay, 1978). Thus, it is easy to understand, for instance, why the Roman Catholic Church and Hispanic spiritualism have appealed to overlapping populations. All religious systems have elaborate rules that determine appropriate and inappropriate health care behavior. This includes rules for giving care and receiving it. The key concept in religious systems is "faith." It is important to note that the distinction between the indigenous helper, whose powers derive from the supernatural, and the professional helper, who learns a codified body of interventions and helping techniques through formal training, is not always easy to make. Both frequently engage in similar behaviors.

It is wise to remember that in all ethnic communities, both Western and non-Western, health care practices are used. To be aware of which ones are accepted is to be able to be an effective helper. How people attempt to heal their minds and bodies is influenced by the place and cultural norms in which they live. Wen-Shing Tseng and John McDermott (1981) suggest that practitioners ask themselves the following questions:

> If I am incorporating the patient's cultural customs in therapy, am I doing this because they have real therapeutic value or because I find them fascinating? When I ask a patient for cultural information, do I make it sufficiently clear that my purpose is to use this knowledge to help him, not to educate me? Do I sufficiently demonstrate that my interest is in the patient's problems, not in the patient as a kind of "cultural specimen" to be studied? Am I allowing my interest in this culture to make my Japanese or Icelandic or German patient more essentially Japanese or Icelandic or German than he really is? Do my sympathies toward a minority group cause me to see a minority patient as a social victim and neglect the psychological aspects of the patient's condition? (pp. 268–269).

Although there are significant differences in the many types of folk and modern helping modalities, they share certain elements of healing or therapy. Both of them foster hope, require faith in the helper, tend to be lead by empathic personalities who are authoritative, and work best

when there is active participation by the helpees. Also, they make allowances for religious beliefs.

RELIGION AND HUMAN RELATIONS

The collective attempt of the human race to understand its own history is a classical study in frustration. This frustration notwithstanding,
human beings have tried continually to understand their present by
extracting significance from their past and even by imposing upon their
present a social order which is shaped by their expectations of the future.
Despite the time gaps inherent in the juxtaposition of such words as *past,
present* and *future,* the life of an individual—as well as the human
race—testifies to a mind-boggling oneness between time, however distant,
and human experiences, however disparate. This condition prompted
artist-philosopher Samuel Beckett (1965) to observe in *Proust* that
"yesterday is not a milestone that has been passed but a daystone on the
beaten track of the years, and irremediably a part of us, within us, heavy
and dangerous" (p. 3).

It is certainly understandable that attempts to define and relate practi-
cally to one's existence is difficult. More likely than not, confrontations
with the universe arouse complex emotions within us. That is, most
people are puzzled by the cyclic patterns of the seasons, the unerring
polarities of days and nights, the conflict between their own reason and
emotion, the glorious process of birth and the inevitable call of death.
Most people are mentally shaken when they consider the idea of infinite
time and compare it to their limited consciousness of a single moment.
Yes, they are terrified when they realize their smallness in comparison to
the magnitude of the universe. But if, on the one hand, people are forced
to submit to the unknown "powers that exist," they may become, on the
other hand, significant by the growing realization that they are unique
pieces of the universal picture of life. In short, human life seems to have
a complexity beyond the powers of comprehension.

Historically, religion is one of the institutions every society has perpetuated in an attempt to work out the meaning of existence. For that
reason, religion is both a catalyst to understanding basic elements of a
people's makeup and a philosophic border within which they try to give
at least a semblance of order to these elements. Because the varieties of
religious beliefs and practices are almost unlimited, students of human
relations are faced with the tremendous problem, as Archie Bahm (1964)

points out, of selecting "representative perspectives that will do justice to the numerous complexities and at the same time provide insights into the authentic vision of each major religious movement" (p. 32). Given the magnitude of the task, I have elected to focus on selected religious contributions of Western and non-Western cultures.

The Western Genesis

Religion contributes to the healing process because it offers what is perhaps our most comprehensive evidence of the basic nature of human beings, evidence which can significantly affect the theory and practice of effective human relations. This is borne out in a brief glance at the religious orientation of primitive peoples, specifically in the societies of ancient Egypt and Mesopotamia where Western religions originated. (The word *primitive* is used here in the sense of *ancient*, not with the negative or culturally prejudiced connotations it has acquired over the years.) The religious beliefs and practices of primitive societies were animistic and reflected preoccupation with *mana*, a term adopted by anthropologist to designate the force or forces which primitive people believed to pervade the world (Bahm, 1964). Therefore, mana is indicative of a mentality which gave rise to early religious beliefs and practices that have influenced some of the religious attitudes of modern people. Mana encapsulates the primitive belief in a powerful, invisible, all-pervading force at work in the universe. Primitive deity took many forms and had many names. It was manifested in humans, animals, plants and minerals. Some North American Indians called it the "Great Spirit"; Central African tribes called it *Leza* or "Cherisher," maker of the world.

The primitive deity influence on modern consciousness is obvious. Today, many people still believe in invisible powers that affect their lives. In fact, our entire scientific, industrial and commercial way of life depends on our belief in electrons, that is, in invisible powers. Mana also encompasses the ancient belief in one total, universal Energy, for primitive people felt little necessity to give consistent answers regarding the number of manas. Even this attitude is deeply embedded in the modern temperament: "We still do not know whether existing power is all one or whether it is distributed among dispersed parts" (Bahm, 1964, p. 40).

Since mana's affects on us may be good or evil, we, like primitive people, cannot help experimenting with ways of controlling it. Manas which manifest themselves in the wind, sun, thunder and time seem beyond our power to influence. Other manas such as those in rocks, animals and persons are frequently within our power. It should be clear by now that knowledge of primitive religious beliefs can provide a basis for grasping the nature of healing in general, especially as it has evolved into modern ritualistic practices. Christian Holy Communion services, for example, involving "eating the Body and drinking the Blood of Christ," signify the Christian's need for partaking of the substance of divinity, for attaining more mana; recognition of its possession provides the believer with a feeling of confidence and attainment, even immortality. But the chief contribution of the religious nature of primitive people as they related to their gods lies in their attempt to act out their belief in mana and to explain their participation in the process of life.

A sense of paradoxical unanimity and complexity is primitive religion's most lasting contribution to human relations. Despite the later polytheistic entities which primitive people accepted as the embodiments and causes of mana, they were well aware of the commonality of the human predicament. In modern times this awareness is still a prime motivation for therapeutic programs.

Western Religions

We can now focus on the genesis of Western religions, specifically Egypt and Mesopotamia where animism influenced a complex polytheism which, in turn, gave way dramatically to a belief in one supreme God, Yahweh (Smith, 1932). From Yahweh, Moses eventually received the Ten Commandments, a contract or covenant under which Yahweh was to protect the Hebrews. In return, the Hebrews were to serve Yahweh forever by living out the terms of the contract. Thus, two contributions to human relations are apparent: monotheism, a theological reference point which not only articulates our relationship to the question of ultimacy but also suggests the ideal relationship between humans (our relationships to people in the Western world depends to a large extent on our view of God and on the relationship between God and humans); and the existence of a contract which spells out our responsibilities to God and humans.

Academic human relations training began in the field of business management, and the idea of the contract still prevails in the helping professions. Perhaps even more crucial to the nature of Judaism's contribution to human services is the fact that the modern contracts which govern areas of personal and professional behavior often attempt to embody the spirit of the Ten Commandments, at least in the idea of equality of regard between people. The spirit of neighborly equality and love permeates the last five of the Ten Commandments: "Six days shalt thou labor and do all the work. . . . Honour thy father and thy mother. . . . Thou shalt not kill. . . . Thou shalt not commit adultery. . . . Thou shalt not steal." Obviously, the social impact of these five commandments is immeasurable; they deal with crucial aspects of communal living, including attitudes toward work, family, marriage and crime.

Furthermore, Judaism's contribution to human relations includes its aggressive and theistic tone as well as its body of literature. The documented religious history of the Jews as recorded in the Old Testament of the Bible provides us with a picturesque look at many facets of human relations — alternative ways in which religion can be used to affect both personal and community behavior. Although organized religion is no longer the center of culture (as it generally was in the early days of Judaism), churches still exercise great influence over their members. For good or ill, organized religion's influence on the life-style of nations is not to be dismissed.

The impact of primitive Greek religions on Western society is seen in the United States philosophic, rational and scientific characteristics. Edith Hamilton (1942) maintains that the Greeks' religious beliefs and practices make us aware that Westerners are their descendants, intellectually, artistically, politically. "Nothing we learn about them," she writes, "is alien to ourselves" (p. 7). With the advent of Homer's Greece about 1000 B.C., humankind became the center of the universe, the most important thing in it. It may have been in Greece that humans first realized what mankind was. Reflecting this ideological revolution, the Greeks created gods in their own image:

> Until then, gods had no semblance of reality. They were unlike all living things. In Egypt, a towering colossus, immobile, beyond the power of the imagination to endow with movement, as fixed in the stone as the tremendous temple columns, a representation of the human shape deliberately made unhuman. Or a rigid figure, a woman with a cat's head suggesting inflexible, inhuman cruelty. Or a monstrous mysterious sphinx, aloof from all that lives. In Mesopotamia, bas-reliefs of bestial shapes unlike any beast ever known, men with birds' heads and lions with bulls' heads and both with eagles' wings, creations of artists who were intent upon producing something never seen except in their own minds, the very consummation of unreality. . . . These and

their like were what the pre-Greek world worshipped. One need only place beside them in imagination any Greek statue of a god, so normal and natural with all its beauty, to perceive what a new idea had come into the world. With its coming the universe became rational (Hamilton, 1942, p. 9).

The effect of this egocentrism and rationality on human relations is prodigious. All of the Western world's modern institutions—universities, churches, governments, banks, social services agencies and so forth—accept rationality as one of the cohesive elements of their programs. But there was more than idle rationality in the Greek religious approach. They used rationality to confront and come to terms with the intangibilities and mysteries of human existence. When Paul says in the Bible that the invisible must be understood by the visible, he was borrowing the idea from the Greeks. In the Greeks' relationship to their gods we see the first attempt to free people from the paralyzing fear of the omnipotent, omnipresent Unknown. Magic, a powerful force in the world before this period, was significantly downgraded. It is true that often the Greek gods were only slight improvements upon their worshipers and that there were beast gods, but the rationality of Greek mythology is astonishing.

Although Greek mythology is not, of course, a religion in the true sense of the word, religious elements are present. The degree to which the Greek myths enlighten us about what human beings needed in their gods and what they got from their gods reflects the degree to which the Greeks were religious. From Homer through the tragedians (and even later), most Greek literature revealed a deep realization of the dependency relationship between humans and the gods. Zeus, in fact, is similar in many ways to the Christian God: "Our Zeus, the giver of every good gift, the common father, and saviour and guardian of mankind" (Hamilton, 1942, p. 14). This brief review of Greek mythology and religious beliefs and practices clearly reveals their several distinct contributions to the helping professions: the accent on human life, the concern with the psychological well-being of people as reflected in the nature and quality of their activities, and the quest for excellence in human affairs.

Finally, it is important that we examine the contributions of Christianity as one of the major influences on the helping professions. The most obvious contributions evolve around the teachings of Christ. The essence of Christ's wisdom is contained in the Sermon on the Mount, the Lord's Prayer and the parables. Although two thousand years of conflicting interpretations leave most investigators unsure of their views, some of the historical interpretations have become quite influential and are generally recognized as part of the Christian doctrine. The foremost Christian contribution to human relations is the concept of love. The Greeks emphasized self-love and the Old Testament portrayed Yahweh as a God of fear and justice, but Jesus said "God is love." This simple idea was new. Thus, Jesus commanded: "Thou shalt love the Lord thy God with all thy heart, and with all thy soul, and with all thy strength, and with all thy mind." Faith in the power of love has deeply affected the Western world, but the effect has not been totally positive. Wars, racism, poverty and sexism are a few negative conditions that have been supported under the guise of love.

To deny that human relations are not sometimes motivated by values less humane than love is to deny the obvious. And yet the love which Christ described as being God and consequently recommended for human beings has become a challenge and guide for millions of persons. It has become the yardstick by which many people measure the humaneness of their relationships. Christ's love ethic has ample room for justice and forgiveness; he urged that we forgive "seventy times seven." The clash between ancient and modern Christian temperaments is clearly portrayed in the conflict of love versus justice. The distorted view that a society cannot have both seems to be especially pronounced in our technological twentieth century. Jesus, the psychiatrist, was concerned with the healing of souls, and he taught psychological principles, many of which are embodied in twentieth century approaches to psychological health. "The Kingdom of Heaven," he said, "is within you, and whosoever shall know himself shall find it." He also urged his followers to "take no care for tomorrow." Application of the present rather than anxious concern for the future is highly recommended by various helping professions in modern society.

As debate over the merits of religion continues, it is indisputable that the Christian church still wields much influence over millions of minds. For this reason, the life of Christ continues to be a source of considerable interest. Admittedly, there are some points of controversy within the Bible. There are discrepancies, for example, between what Christ taught and what Paul recommended. And, of course, Protestant and Catholic organizations have at times used Christian dogma to achieve horrifying ends. But such details are not the major foci for our discussion of Christianity's contributions to human relations and the other helping professions such as social work, education and psychology (Strong, 1980).

One fact is inescapable: Christianity has directly affected the entire modern ethos.

FAITH HEALING

The major goal of professional helpers is to assist clients to become healthier, more mature in terms of being able to effectively cope with their adversities. This is true of traditional helpers, too. The term "traditional" is not used as a synonym of *past* or *nonurban.* Nor is it equivalent to being *old-fashioned.* Rather, traditional refers to a particular cultural system with specific rules and values. Therefore, traditional helpers are as legitimate in the eyes of indigenous people as professional helpers. In many instances, they are more utilized, if not more legitimate, than professional helpers. Within Western and non-Western societies, faith healers comprise the largest number of traditional helpers. In the Western world most faith healing occurs within Christian churches.

Faith or miracle healing has existed in every society from the earliest times in history to the present day (Hamilton, 1942). During the past century, modern medicine has accepted the premise that many diseases are psychogenic in origin and may be helped by faith healing. Diseases in this category include gastric ulcers, high blood pressure, coronary thrombosis, diabetes, vasomotor rhinitis, rheumatoid arthritis and asthma. One verse in every seven of the Gospels and one in fourteen of the Acts provide Biblical references to therapeutic activities that suggest faith healing. Of the scores of miracle events ascribed to Christ, approximately three dozen fit the description of faith healing: lepers, the blind, and the crippled were cured. Christ's techniques—praying and commanding the sick to be well, laying on hands, and instructing the afflicted person to pursue a specific course of action—have been adopted by modern evangelists. Basically, this healing system states that distressed persons will be healed if they have strong faith and engage in fervent prayer. An individual who is not healed is unworthy and he or she lacks spiritual grace.

Four principles of Protestantism lend themselves to faith healing: a resolution to live by faith; freedom to initiate a new life; openness to truth which is revealed in both scientific and nonscientific experiences; and the call to a vocation in the world such as caring for the poor, sick and orphans. Evangelical Conservative Christians relate their healing activities to belief in authentic and authoritative Holy Scriptures; in the life, teachings and sacrificial death and resurrection of Jesus Christ; and in an eternal life (Vayhinger, 1973). Evangelists reject the notion that healing occurs by God in only some situations. They believe that it is God who heals in *all* situations although through different persons, modalities and techniques. Many people throughout the world are ministered to by deliverance evangelists—itinerant male and female preachers who claim the Holy Ghost has given them the gift of divine healing. On a broader scale, Pentecostalism is composed of many fundamentalist or evangelical denominations, sects and cults concerned primarily with holiness (a state of moral and spiritual purity), literal interpretation of the Bible, and a renewal of the Pentecostal experience. Most Pentecostals believe in divine healing, prophecy, speaking tongues (ecstatic speech induced by religious emotion) and working miracles.

There are distinct differences among faith healers, however. Some faith healers believe that all disease is the work of the devil and that the only cure is to place our trust in the Lord. Others believe that both disease and medicine (including herbs) are the work of the devil. Yet, other faith healers believe in divine healing but not to the exclusion of scientific medical cures. Several non-Pentecostal groups believe in elements of faith healing. Mormons utilize "holy handkerchiefs" which are part of a healing tradition dating back to Joseph Smith in the nineteenth century. Baptists, Congregationalists, Methodists, Lutherans and Unitarians are part of a long list of other religious groups that have a history of faith healing. Now we will look at a few churches whose interventions sometimes run counter to scientific Western health care practices.

Church of Christ Scientist

Christian Science presents a metaphysical approach to religion, sickness and healing (DeWitt, 1971). The ultimate human reality, Christian Science asserts, is mental or spiritual, not material or physical. Therefore, because sickness, whether of mind or body, is of a mental origin, it can be cured through proper mental processes. Consequently, there is no mind-body dilemma for the Christian Scientist. The body is its own laboratory. Christian Science treatment consists of prayer and counsel with the sick person; however, there are no clergy in Christian Science. Healing is facilitated by certified practitioners who employ three dimensions of therapeutic treatment. The first dimension focuses on "affirmation and denial" or "argument," that is, the practitioner tries to destroy the sick person's belief in suffering. The second dimension of treatment consists of "absolute consciousness of good"—convincing the individual that he or she is well and knows it. The third dimension, "impersonal treatment," is carried out alone by the practitioner who focuses on his or her own thoughts to free the inflicted person of belief in sickness.

Christian Science therapy is not like other forms of spiritual healing. There are no prayers that involve emotional, ritualistic appeals to God. Rather, healing is private, abstract and highly intellectual. Nor do Christian Science practitioners lay on hands as do some practitioners in other religious sects. Drugless healing as found in osteopathic and chiropractic medicine are accepted by Christian Scientists; so too are natural methods of healing—dietary regulation and manipulation of the body.

Native American Church

The Native American Church has more American Indian members than any other church in America (Bergman, 1971). It is a Christian church whose rituals and beliefs represent almost every North American Indian tribe. The most controversial healing practice is the use of the peyote cactus; thus, the designation of its members as "Peyotists." Members of the Native American Church believe in both the Great Spirit of Indian religions and the Christian Trinity—the Father, the Son and the Holy Ghost. Peyotists believe that through prayer and communion with God our sins are forgiven and we can be cured of illness; the earth is our mother and she must not be abused or treated disrespectfully; all people are brothers and sisters; and the universe is an harmonious creation and each of us must fit into it with love, peace, charity and humility.

Peyotists also believe in abstinence from alcohol. The peyote service is a total audience participation activity. All members participate equally in the praying, drumming, singing and speaking. In this Indian tradition, tobacco is part of the service. By consuming peyote the members believe that they are able to establish a closer contact with God. The entire peyote ritual is performed under the guidance of a road chief. The attraction of the Native American Church is clear when we recount the insensitive deeds of early missionaries.

> Missionaries looked at the feats of medicine men and proclaimed them to be works of the devil. They overlooked the fact that the medicine men were able to do marvelous things. Above all, they overlooked the fact that what the Indian medicine men did *worked*. Most missionary

activity centered on teaching and preaching. The thrust was to get the Indians to memorize the Large Catechism, the Small Catechism, the Apostles Creed, the Nicene Creed, the Ten Commandments, and other magic rites and formulas dear to Christianity. Salvation became a matter of regurgitation of creeds. In a very real sense, then, Christianity replaced living religions with magic (Deloria, 1969, pp. 108–109).

The religion of Native Americans are religions of the land. To understand this, we must understand the nature of sacred mountains, sacred hills, sacred rivers, sacred burial places and other sacred geographical features. The Native American Church incorporates these concepts into its doctrines. Finally, it is important to note that Peyotists also believe that scientific medicine can be used to supplement peyote services.

Eastern Orthodox Church

Christian churches are divided into three major sects: Roman Catholic, Eastern Orthodox, and Protestant. The Eastern Orthodox (Greek) Church claims to be the "direct heir and conservator" of the original Christian (primitive) church (Constantelos, 1967). Historically, the Eastern Orthodox Church has been divided into independent ethnic churches—Albanian, Bulgarian, Georgian, Greek, Romanian, Russian, Serbian and Syrian. The Eastern Orthodox Church does not believe that God created humans in His image; however, we have the potential to become like God in terms of His goodness. Nor does the Orthodox doctrine subscribe to the original sin of Adam; rather, each of us is guilty if in our freedom we elect to imitate Adam. In the Eastern Orthodox Church salvation is a community, not an individual, activity. Thus, we are not saved *from* the world but *with* the world. In essence, salvation is achieved through reconciliation with God, ourselves, our neighbors and nature.

The Eastern Church believes that humans need the Spirit of God for healing to occur. Caring for the sick has a special place in the church. For example, if a man is sick, the priest visits him to pray over him. If the man is gravely ill, the priest will administer the sacrament of Holy Unction. Since this latter activity consists of seven lessons about the miracles of Jesus, it is preferable, but not mandatory, that seven priests be present, each to read a lesson and to anoint different parts of body with oil. Furthermore, members of the family and the congregation are present during the Holy Unction. Eastern Christians, like other Christians, are encouraged to pray for and visit sick persons. Persons "possessed" with spirits are exorcised by priests who have special healing powers. In addition to religious healing services, Orothodoxy encourages the sick to seek out scientific medical cures.

Church of Jesus Christ of Latter-Day Saints

Latter-Day Saints are better known as Mormons. Based on the Bible and Joseph Smith's *The Book of Mormon*, the religious doctrines of Mormons are similar to those of many conservative Protestant churches (Smith, 1971). However, unlike conservative Protestants, Mormons believe that two personages of God—the Father and the Son—have bodies of flesh and bones, whereas the Holy Ghost does not. Salvation for humans will come through the atonement of Christ and by obedience to the laws of the gospel. Explicit in the Mormon's faith is belief in baptism by immersion in water. Healing takes on an aspect of faith healing discussed earlier: laying on of hands. Mormons also believe in speaking in tongues, visions and prophecy. Mormons will seek scientific relief for illness and poverty. They have established worldwide missions to spread their gospel at home and abroad.

HEALTH CARE RAPPROCHEMENT

It is erroneous to cling to the stereotype of the traditional curer who, according to George Foster and Barbara Anderson (1978): "Is known to us all: a wise and skilled person who knows not only the patient but also the patient's family, who is aware of the social and personal tensions of the patient's life, who sees relief from interpersonal stress as essential to relief from physical symptoms. The stereotypic curer is, in short, a social pathologist, able and willing to spend unlimited time with a single patient, little concerned with payment" (p. 249). A few of these types still exist in both indigenous and scientific health care systems, but most care givers are very much concerned with remuneration for their services. For example, Irwin Press (1971) noted that urban *curanderos* in Bogota used techniques identified with both traditional folk and modern medical sources. Many of the curers that Press observed scheduled as many as seventy patients a day, and each visit lasted less than 15 minutes. With few exceptions, the Bogota curers charged fees—some of them quite high.

The behavior of Third-World clients is also changing. Many of them have adopted Western religions and utilize the services of curers in two or more health care systems. Sometimes, this is done simultaneously. The reason of this behavior is simple. Clients want a wide and hopefully sound variety of opinions and advice to select from. It is not uncommon for persons in all ethnic groups—Western and non-Western—to try one curer after another to secure effective treatment. Nor is this sampling process limited to indigenous curers. Western religious leaders and health personnel also are consulted about problems in which they are believed to have expertise. The process of shopping around for indigenous curers and modern health care personnel is occurring throughout the world. For example, this behavior has been documented in several Third-World communities, including Taipei, Kota, Hong Kong, Bangkok and Borneo.

Robert Edgerton and associates (1970) studied *curanderismo* in East Los Angeles and concluded that in spite of a long tradition, "its importance has diminished greatly. Both ethnographic observations and formal interviews indicate that for Mexican-Americans in East Los Angeles, the preferred treatment resource for mental illness is the general physician, not the curandero" (p. 133). From these data we can surmise that when effective medical treatment is available in Western systems, is delivered by empathic persons at a price Third-World people can afford and at convenient times and places, it will be the first choice for many and perhaps most persons.

Based on recorded observations of several countries in Southeast Asia (Higginbotham, 1979) and the Ivory Coast of West Africa (Claver, 1976), it is evident that the role of traditional practitioners is being eroded as populations shift from rural to urban settings. This is not to suggest that traditional religions and healing techniques have no value in urban settings. Yoga, Zen and transcendental meditation, for example, have been incorporated into several modern therapies. And sometimes encounter group leaders appear to be exorcising evil thoughts from the minds of participants. Aware of these trends, a growing number of traditional curers are engaging in a process that David Landy (1974) called *role adaptation* —the process of updating traditional therapies by incorporating elements of scientific medicine. Role adaptation involves a wide range of behavior. Some curers convert almost completely to a Western system of helping; others select only those elements that will preserve their status while at the same time minimally altering their behavior. In any case, the pattern of the interrelationship between traditional health care and modern health care appears to be universal and irreversible. Thus, all health care systems must meet the needs of non-Western and Western people.

Integration or Pluralism

Whether or not to integrate into Western society is a question that most Third-World people ponder. The dilemma is somewhat similar to that of the early European immigrants to the United States. When they initially came to this country during the nineteenth century, the Poles, Greeks, Germans, Italians, and other groups clustered together in their own ethnic enclaves. Gradually, either they or their children moved out of their ethnic neighborhoods into the larger community. With this change came a merging of languages, customs, habits, dietary patterns, and medical practices. While the European ethnic groups were assimilating into a nebulous American melting pot, most Third-World people present at that time were not assimilated (Fresh, 1982; Smith, 1985). Some Third-World activists argue that pluralism, not assimilation, was the most viable goal for Third-World people. Switzerland, Canada, and Belgium are examples of pluralism that may be the most acceptable to Third-World and non-Third-World people:

> The standard example of cultural pluralism is Switzerland, a country that maintains a high degree of national unity although it has no national language and is religiously divided. In Switzerland, Protestants and Catholics have been able to live agreeably under the same government, while speaking either German, French, or Italian. Since the Swiss citizen does not feel that either his religious loyalty or his ethnic identification is threatened by other Swiss, he is free to give complete allegiance to the Swiss nation as a common government that allows for the tolerance of distinctly different cultural groups. Canada, with a division between the French and the English, and Belgium, with a division between the French and the Flemish-speaking populace, are other examples of cultural pluralism. The different groups that make up a pluralistic society in these nations frequently engage in a struggle for influence, but the essential ideal is that national patriotism does not require cultural uniformity and that differences of nationality, language, or even race do not preclude loyalty to a common government (Horton, 1965, pp. 310–311).

Perhaps within a similar framework it would be possible for Third-World people to adopt Western religions and health care practices without losing other aspects of their ethnicity. If this is not possible, what will happen to individuals who against strong community injunctions maintain their traditional beliefs and practices? Intracommunity health care conflicts have left many Third-World people, especially curers, feeling marginal. According to Robert Park (1928), the marginal person is one whom fate has condemned to live in two societies and in two not merely different but antagonistic cultures. Although Park used the term "fate" in his definition, I consider marginality not to be the result of accidental phenomena but predictable occurrences within a social framework. One may or may not feel "condemned." Or, as Milton Goldberg (1941) observed, if:

(1) The so-called "marginal" individual is conditioned to his existence on the borders of two cultures from birth, if (2) he shares this existence and conditioning process with a large number of individuals in his primary groups, if (3) his years of early growth, maturation and even adulthood find him participating in institutional activities manned largely by other "marginal" individuals like himself, and finally, if (4) his marginal position results in no major blockages or frustrations of his learned expectations and desires, then he is not a true "marginal" individual in the defined sense, but a participant member of a *marginal culture*, every bit as real and complete to him as the non-marginal culture to the nonmarginal man (p. 53).

Health care marginality therefore is characterized by the following conditions. First, there must be a situation that places two health care systems in lasting contact. Second, one system must be dominant in terms of legal and political power. This is the nonmarginal of the two systems. Its members are not particularly influenced by or attracted to the marginal system. Third, the boundaries between the two systems are sufficiently defined for the members of the marginal system to internalize the patterns of the dominant system and the minority groups are not satisfied with their socially prescribed inferior status.

We cannot fully appreciate the present without understanding the past. A culture's religious and health practices are derived from basic needs and fears. Although religions and health care practices of indigenous curers may be defined as "primitive" or "marginal" by outsiders, they are functional for the persons within their culture. It is important to start where the helpee is in terms of religious and health care beliefs and practices. Western religions and the scientific method are not always the best intervention. Whichever method is used, the helpee's beliefs should be respected. In fact, in all situations respect, trust, and positive regard are needed for effective helping to occur.

Frequently, cultural values are based on needs that may have little basis in environmental realities. Social scientists have not been able to clearly separate interrelated variables such as politics, religion and education. Most attitudes are learned and they are reinforced in a variety of behaviors. As we have seen, religious beliefs and traditions are integral aspects of folk medicines. The semantics of a culture are captured in their definitions of life, illness, and death. Each individual's concept of the spiritual universe shapes his or her behavior. Consequently, religion is an important factor in shaping an individual's readiness to utilize a particular helping modality.

Chapter 4

FAR EAST CULTURES

The dynamics of becoming an effective helper in transcultural situations are threefold. First, the facts that constitute the problem must be understood by a person with credibility to the helpee. These facts consist of both Western and non-Western definitions of socially and psychologically appropriate interactions. Second, the facts must be carefully thought through. Specifically, they must be probed into, reorganized, and recast into appropriate cultural contexts. One society's taboo may be another society's norm. Finally, decisions must be made by all parties that will result in culturally appropriate action. This almost always involves changes in attitudes and beliefs.

CROSS–CULTURAL PROBLEM SOLVING

To achieve optimum results in a helping relationship both the helper and the helpee must be actively involved in the process of conceptualizing health-related problems. As in Chapter 3, the term "health" is used here in the broadest sense to refer to any physical or emotional state of functioning. The ultimate goal of the helper is to assist the helpee in achieving a satisfactory state of health. It is possible for helpers to unilaterally define a helpee's problems and prescribe solutions, but this would weaken or destroy the client's sense of responsibility. When focusing on non-Western clients, it is helpful to keep the following principles in mind.

A transcultural problem cannot be solved if the necessary information is missing. A helper may want to understand non-Western clients but not be able to do so because he or she has inadequate information. A major deficit in most practitioner's training is the paucity of systematic transcultural coursework and clinical experience. It is understandable therefore that many Western practitioners feel grossly inadequate when working with non-Western clients.

Information alone is seldom enough. Memorizing words, sentences or phrases from books and journals will not in itself produce transculturally literate professional helpers. A few minutes of positive interaction with people from another culture might do more to enhance a practitioner's cultural sensitivity than hours of reading about it. A firsthand examination of the conditions impacting on various ethnic groups is vital to understanding their problems.

Cultural sensitivity is the capacity to identify and empathize with the values, beliefs and feelings of others. Ideally, all helpers will be culturally sensitive. Understanding and accepting another person's cultural reality is the beginning of a positive helping relationship. Helpful, as opposed to harmful, relationships do not require either party to abandon their own values and beliefs. Value differences should not lead to individual ego or ethnic group destruction.

Most practitioners need to learn how to explore new and contradictory ideas and facts. The greater the cultural distance between the helper and the helpee, the more likely the ideas and facts that characterize the helpee will be misunderstood by the helper. Knowledge of basic anthropological, sociological, psychological and economic data will provide a solid foundation for transcultural problem solving. If practitioners remain wrapped up in their own cultural definitions of acceptable behavior, they will not be able to perceive clearly the feelings and needs of clients from other cultures.

Both Western and non-Western practices are social systems, and both have interdependent parts or variables that Thomas Weaver (1970) described as "the whole complex of a people's beliefs, attitudes, practices and roles associated with concepts of health and disease, and with patterns of diagnosis and treatment" (p. 141). Differences in foci in Western and non-Western health practices are discussed in Chapter 3. Some of the differences are more significant than others. For example, non-Western societies have multiperson helping relationships consisting of parents and nonparents, relatives and nonrelatives as helpers.

EASTERN RELIGIONS AND PHILOSOPHIES

Asian, or Eastern, cultures provide a clear view of philosophies and helping modalities that are relatively independent of Western psychologies (Saeki & Borow, 1985; Ho, 1985; Leong, 1986; Paranjpe et al., 1988). India, China, and Japan have been the repositories of intellectual ideas that have greatly influenced other Third-World countries with similar cultural, socioeconomic and political conditions. I speak of Eastern religions, philosophies, and psychologies in global terms. In reality, the Far Eastern countries have been the birthplace of a large number of religious and philosophical schools of thought. What binds them together is the common concern with the quest of reaching the outer limits of human potential. Hinduism, Yoga, Taoism, Confucianism, Zen, and Sufism are the most practiced forms of Eastern thought.

Indian *Hinduism* is one of the world's oldest religions. It maintains that only the permanent is real. And because all things change, only the Ultimate Reality, the unchanging, is real.

Indian *Yoga* consists of systematic sets of exercises designed to aid an individual in identifying with, or "yoking" himself or herself to, the divine. The four major systems of Yoga are: Bhakti (love), Hatha (bodily control), Raja (control of thought), and Jnana (philosophic insight). Shakti, or Kundalini, Yoga focuses on direct work with spiritual energy.

Chinese *Taoism* stresses intuition, simplicity and the attainment of profound insight through the ability to perceive "Tao," the primal cause in daily activities and surroundings. Taoists believe that humans can find harmony by being good to all things, being humble and quiet, avoiding honors and distinctions, and enjoying the forces of nature.

Chinese *Confucianism* is a system of ethics, education, statescraft, and religion designed to produce a superior person who has self-respect, sincerity, benevolence, and earnestness.

Japanese *Zen Buddhism* seeks a direct experience of enlightenment. It differs from Taoism mainly in the intensity of its approach and the development of a series of training procedures designed to facilitate the enlightenment.

Persian *Sufism* is a form of mysticism in which followers view God as an idealized beloved, similar to Bhakti Yoga. The recurrent theme in Eastern beliefs is human perfectibility. This central theme is found in Eastern religions, philosophies and psychologies. Now let us review the four most prominent Eastern religions and philosophies.

Hinduism

The people of India have had a continuous civilization since about 2500 B.C., when the inhabitants of the Indus River developed an urban culture based on commerce, trade and, to a lesser degree, agriculture. This civilization declined about 1500 B.C., and Aryan tribes originating in Central Asia absorbed part of its culture as they spread out over the South Asian subcontinent. Asian sages developed a particular way of thinking which was expressed in the Upanishads, in the Bhagavad-Gita, in Yoga, later in other Hindu systems, and finally in the ideas of Buddhism. Buddhism spread to China and ultimately to Japan where it took on new forms. From there these concepts spread to Burma, Ceylon, Thailand, and to other parts of southern and southeastern Asia.

Hinduism embraces a myriad of human needs and aspirations. Furthermore, it is tolerant of every person and every religion. For this reason it is often described as attempting to be all things to all people. It has had special attraction for scholars, mystics, detached persons and selfless seers (Welty, 1970). Hinduism is based on ancient writings known as scriptures, which are divided into two parts—the Vedas (the primary and revealed source) and secondary scriptures (authoritative elaborations upon the Vedas). Most of the content in the Vedas was handed down by word of mouth and finally put into written form from 2000 to 500 B.C. There are four Vedas: the *Rigveda*, the *Samaveda*, the *Yajurveda* and the *Astharaveda*. Each Veda is divided into three parts: the *Mantras* (basic hymns and verses and the core of the Vedas), the *Brahamas* (ritualistic interpretations of the Mantras), and the *Upanishads* (profound mystical and philosophic truths revealed in the Mantras). In some writings the Mantras are referred to as the Vedas because they are the foundation upon which the latter evolved. The Brahamas consist mainly of the work of priests and deal with ritual worship. The Upanishads, which literally means "sitting near," focuses on knowledge acquired sitting around a teacher.

Hinduism teaches that the countless gods revered and worshipped merely symbolize and represent One Ultimate Reality that transcends measurable form, name and personality. All things in the universe, not only the gods, are manifestations of an Ultimate Reality. Consequently, animate and inanimate objects are interrelated. Equally important, in every human there is an essential self, *atman*, which is divine and transcends mind, body and the senses. The atman is a non-material realization of the real self as opposed to the material form of self which consists of thought, sensations and desires. When the Hindu discusses the "individual," it is not to analyze but to denigrate (Marsella et al., 1985). Thus, atman is subjectively the Ultimate Reality. The Upanishads declares: "The essential self or the vital essence in man is the same as that in a gnat, the same as that in an elephant, the same as that in these three worlds, indeed the same as that in the whole universe." Everything is one.

Hindus believe there is a supreme and absolute power called *Brahman*. And there are three gods who are reflections of Brahman: *Brahma* (the Creator), *Vishu* (the Preserver or Renewer), and *Siva* (the Destroyer). The goal of Hindus is to be united with Brahman, where they will achieve perfection. But before this can happen, the human soul must undergo a transmigration. That is, the human soul must be reborn many times until it becomes pure enough to unite with Brahman. This transmigration is a process of the soul passing from one body to another—human or animal. An individual's character in the present life determines what the next life will be. For example, if a woman lives like an animal, she will return to earth in the body of an animal. If she lives a relatively wholesome, good life, she will return as a human being.

Because the essential self has no beginning, it can have no end. From this perspective, a baby is old beyond the conception of time. Life is a journey over a bridge, across which we must travel to reach our destination but upon which we do not build permanently. Human existence is a lower stage of experience necessary before passing to the higher stage of identification with a Supreme Reality or Ultimate Reality. The final passage is brought about through adhering to the virtues of truth, nonviolence, sacrifice, purity and detachment from all ties to material things.

Central to Hindu religious thought is the belief in *karma* which determines one's rewards and punishments. Karma is fate in the sense that it is inherited from a previous life, but it differs from fate because each person makes his or her own karma and determines the character of his or her next birth. Charles Eliot (1925) summarized this idea as follows:

> These views of rebirth and karma have a moral value, for they teach that what a man gets depends on what he is or makes himself to be, and they avoid the difficulty of supposing that a benevolent creator can have given his creatures only one life with such strange and unmerited disproportion to their lots. Ordinary folk in the East hope that a life of virtue will secure them another life as happy beings on earth or perhaps in some heaven which, though not eternal, will still be long. But for many the higher ideal is renunciation of the world and a life of contemplative asceticism which will accumulate no karma so that after death the soul will pass not to another birth but to some higher and more mysterious state which is beyond birth and death (p. xxvii).

Buddhism

Adherents of Eastern religions have always sought maximum human development. Ideas, beliefs, and values pertaining to human nature are *means* to an end, not ends in themselves. This general approach is seen in the life and teachings of Gautama Buddha, who founded Buddhism in the sixth century before Christ. He did not debate the relevancy of gods, nor did he stress the need for gods to intervene in human relationships. Instead, he argued that the human condition is surrounded by fear, disease, and death; the wise person realizes this situation and looks for a way to resolve it. All things, including human beings, will inevitably disintegrate. Consequently, Buddhists are instructed to not make plans in this world without reckoning with death. But death is not something to fight against, for it will always win; it is instead something we must accept. Buddha's message focuses on the experiences or path that leads to liberation from the human condition. Actually, Buddhism grew out of Hinduism. Most Buddhists live in Asia. The following Four Truths are the Foundation of Buddhism:

1. The Noble Truth of Suffering states that suffering is omnipresent and an important part of life.
2. The Noble Truth of the Cause of Suffering cites the cause to be desire—desire for possessions and selfish enjoyment of any kind.
3. The Noble Truth of the Cessation of Suffering states that suffering ceases when desire ceases.
4. The Noble Truth of the Eightfold Path which leads to the Cessation of Suffering prescribes the means to achieve cessation of desire. This path is also called the Middle Way because it avoids the two extremes of self-indulgence and self-mortification. It includes right views, right desires, right speech, right conduct, right occupation, right extinction of all cravings and the final release from suffering is the reward for people who are able to stay on the path.

Knowledge of one's self and love are two of the most important Buddhist virtues. "Buddha" means enlightened. Ignorance of the self results in self-centeredness, desire, and sorrow. The best way to self-knowledge is proper conduct: self-control, humility, generosity, and mercy. Love, according to Buddha, is universal goodwill. Indeed, love of one's enemies is the apex of a Buddhist's life. Only love can conquer hatred. One can achieve nirvana only if he or she has achieved perfect self-control, knowledge, unselfishness, and enlightenment. This means that we must reject all anger, passion and sin. These and other principles are found in the sacred book of Buddhism, the *Tripitaka* (the three baskets); *Lotus of the Good Law;* and *Paradise Scriptures.*

Buddhism differs from Hinduism mainly in the denial of a changeless inner entity. For the Buddhists there is no personal Atman waiting to reveal itself when the mental states are removed. Rather, the mental states are the reality and, therefore, there is no persisting soul through all the changes. Chinese Buddhism grew within the influence of the ancient philosophical-poetic system of Taoism, the philosophy of Lao-tse, which defined a "The Way" or norm underlying major events of life. Chinese Buddhism is also a fusion of the practical system of laws of living defined by Confucius, who lived at the same time as Lao-tse and was only a few years younger than Gautama, the Buddha. Chinese Buddhism incorporates the rules, obligations and practical principles of the Chinese family and social order.

Sixth-century Japanese Buddhism took several forums—psychological, mystical, esoteric in particular. Until the thirteenth century, various Indian and Chinese philosophies were imported into Japan mainly by Buddhist priests. Prince Taishi Shotoku (574–622 B.C.) built the oldest Buddhist temple in Japan and encouraged his people to adhere to the following tenets: "Give up anger. Don't be angry at the mistakes of others. Everyone has a mind and opinion. If the other person's opinion is right, yours is wrong. If yours is right, the other's is wrong. You are not always wise; nor is the other person always stupid. Both of you are *bombu* (mediocre persons). When in doubt about who is right, ask the opinions of other people." Buddhism was supported by the emperors in China and Japan as a way to counter Christianity and its emphasis on life beyond death.

Buddhism in Thailand illustrates a form of Asian outer- and inner-directedness. Thais try to keep relationships peaceful and avoid conflict, to prevent anger or passion from being displayed overtly. This is seen in the Thai expression *"mai pen rai"* ("It doesn't matter" or "Never mind"). Each person is responsible only to himself and therefore his actions are no one else's concern (Fieg, 1979; Weisz et al., 1988). Consequently, Thais resist continuous regimentation. Yet, they are extremely group-centered. Smooth interpersonal relations rather than individuality, which characterizes Western cultures, is the Thai norm. This results in the development of people who have strong personalities and convictions controlled by family norms and cultural traditions.

Taoism

Edwin Harvey (1933) stated that the Chinese mind is syncretistic; it absorbs only what it can use. Indeed, the Chinese have shown the remarkable ability to absorb many things. They have absorbed the ancient philosophies of fetishism, the doctrine of spirits embodied within us, attached to objects or conveying influence through certain material objects and animals. They have absorbed filial piety or ancestor worship. They have absorbed Confucianism, a system of social ethics taught by Confucius and given imperial recognition in the second century A.D. And, finally, they have absorbed Taoism, Buddhism, Islam, and Christianity. John Fraser (1980) noted that Taoism is the prominent religion in the Peoples Republic of China because the ruling party considers it the most malleable. It can incorporate Christ as easy as the Green Dragon. Whatever works is good and is part of the Taoist correct order of things.

Asian folk medicine and philosophies have a strong Chinese Taoist religion base which seeks balance in all things (Henderson & Primeaux, 1981). From a Taoist perspective, humans are microcosms within a universal macrocosm. The human energy of the microcosm interrelates with the universe. Both energy (*chi*) and sexual energy (*jing*) are vital life energies kept in balance by *yin* and *yang*. Yin is feminine, negative, dark and cold; whereas *yang* is masculine, positive, light and warm. An imbalance in energy is caused by an improper diet or a strong emotional feeling. Balance or good health may be achieved through the use of appropriate herbs. And both the universe and humans are susceptible to the laws of earth, fire, water, metal and wood.

Early Chinese migration throughout Asia spread Taoist philosophy and medicine. This is seen in the similar philosophies concerning nutrition and herbology in China, Japan, the Philippines, Thailand, Malaysia, Korea, Vietnam and other Asian countries. The art and science of Chinese medicine goes back at least 5000 years to Emperor Huang Ti (2697–1597 B.C.). Unlike Western medicine which emphasizes disease and cure, Asian medicine focuses on prevention.

The philosophy of Taoism is named after the Chinese word *Tao* which means "The Way." It is the first word in *Tao Te Ching* ("The Classic of The Way and Its Power"), the Taoist book. Although there were three principal teachers of Taoism—Lao-tse, Tang-chu and Chuang-tse—Lao-tse, the "Old Master," was the founder. He was also the author of *Tao Te Ching*. According to Taoism, the best way to live is the natural way. Our fears, sufferings and problems are largely due to living an unnatural life. Thus, the way to freedom is to liberate ourselves from all artificial restraints. This is called "The Way of the Uninhibited"—spontaneity and simplicity. It is difficult to describe accurately what Tao is because, as the ancient saying goes, "Those who know of the Tao do not speak of it; those who speak of it do not know it."

In essence the Tao is like the stream of time, drifting without a set goal and without purpose (*wu-wei*). Indeed, certain of Tao's characteristics are analogous with moving water. As water overcomes obstacles by flowing around them, so too does the Tao overcome obstacles by yielding. As oceans and rivers are great because they occupy the low places of the earth, so also is the Tao great because it is lowly. Because it is the ultimate reality, the Tao is present in all things. Although the Tao is continuously changing the physical forms inhabiting the universe, such change is always in accordance with the individual nature of each form. Taoism supports the right of each person to spontaneously express his or her nature. The fact that societies exist with rules and regulations is contrary to human nature. To get back to a natural state requires that people do things without the intention of acting, give without the intention of pleasing, and not pass judgment on themselves.

The state of harmony with the Tao is called *te* or *virtue of te*. This harmonious existence is characterized as trusting in wu-wei and yin-yang as a unified system (Watts, 1975). Everything is part of a natural, universal flow and we can be in harmony with it. The emphasis is away from rational thinking toward our own intuitive logic. From this perspective, *wu-wei* is not inertia. Rather, it allows individuals to honor conflict and allow themselves to be in conflict. The basic process is *acceptance:* "To try to control the mind forcefully is like trying to flatten out waves with a board, and can only result in more and more disturbance" (Watts, 1975, p. 118).

David Knoblauch (1985) provides an extensive discussion of ways to apply Taoist thought to counseling and psychotherapy. Throughout the years several prominent Western therapists have espoused Taoist concepts (Jung, 1961; Maslow, 1971; Kopp, 1972; Watts, 1975; Brandon, 1976; Bolen, 1979). Person-centered therapy, existential psychotherapy and Gestalt therapy draw upon Taoist concepts.

Confucianism

Confucianism is named after its founder Kung Fu-tse (Confucius) who was born in 551 B.C. The content of Confucianism is drawn from many sources, including ancestor worship, sacrifices to the dead, and the belief in spirits. It also draws from other Eastern philosophies, including Buddhism and Taoism. However, most of the doctrines are taken from the speeches and writings of Confucius and his disciples, Mencius and Hsun-tse. Several hundred years before Jesus stated the Golden Rule, Confucius said, "What you do not like done to yourself, do not unto others." The Confucian Canon consists of nine works which are divided into two groups called the *Four Books* and the *Five Classics.* The *Four Books* are: *The Analects* (Sayings of Confucius), *The Book of Mencius,* the *Great Learning* (a short treatise on Confucian ethics), and the *Doctrine of the Mean* (a treatise on universal harmony and ethics). The *Five Classics* are: the *Book of History,* the *Book of Changes* (fortune-telling based on sixty-four hexagrams), the *Book of Poetry* or *Book of Odes* (folk poetry of the Chou period), *Ch'un Ch'iu* (*Spring and Autumn Annuals*), a history of Confucius' native state of Lu and the *Li Chi* (*Book of Rites*).

Unlike Taoism, Confucianism considers it natural for people to live in societies. In fact, it is only in society that people can reach their fullest development and self-actualize. The universal need for communal life is called *jen* by Confucians. The Chinese character *jen* combines the symbol for *man* and the symbol for *two* to describe the relationship between persons. In English jen is equivalent to "human-heartedness," "human relationships," "empathy" and "benevolence." It is the desire to understand and help others. But, first, it is the desire to understand oneself. Confucianists are taught, "The man of jen is one who, desiring to develop himself, develops others, and in desiring to sustain himself, sustains others. To be able from one's own self to draw a parallel for the treatment of others; that may be called the way to practice jen." The central focus of jen is the proper position of the individual in terms of one's wishes, anxieties and predilections oriented to contributing to group life (Yum, 1988). Therefore, jen is a basis for understanding Asian behavior with reference to social interactions. It is a state of dynamic equilibrium. The Chinese epitomize the supremacy of kinship. Throughout their history the Chinese have developed few renown world travelers and conquerors. Partially for this reason, the Chinese have developed few secondary groups outside their kinship boundary. (This is also true of most other Asian ethnic groups.)

The "right action" is defined in terms of duties and obligations implicit in five basic social relationships: ruler and subject, father and son, elder brother and younger brother, husband and wife, friend and friend. Except for friends, the relationships involve the authority of one person over another. Confucians believe that the inferior owes loving obedience and loyalty to his or her superior, and the superior owes loving responsibility to the inferior. The person of the lowest status must advise the other as to the right course of action. The "just action," or *ji*, should be carried out once it is decided upon. But Confucian justice is not blind obedience to intellectual or legal principles. Rather, it is akin to compassionate wisdom in which the facts are weighed with a feeling of human concern.

The family is emphasized in Confucianism. It is in childhood and through familial interactions that morality is developed and nourished. Indeed, it is in the family that we learn responsibility and attitudes toward obedience and authority—the same things valued in the state. Although the family is central to Confucian thought, it is not considered an end in itself. The self not only lies in the center of relationships but also as a dynamic process of spiritual development (Wei-ming, 1985).

Perhaps the most important characteristic of human beings in Eastern religions is that they can cease to exist as unique individual personalities. They can instead become universal beings and transcend their existence by surrendering their existence to what is called God, Atman or simply "the void." The goals outlined by Buddha, Confucius, and Lao-tse do not by themselves change anybody in any way. Rather, they offer directions toward which efforts might be directed to achieve greater emotional balance and improved physical health.

EASTERN PSYCHOLOGIES

The preceding Eastern systems are religious, in that they are directed toward immediate freedom from suffering and ultimately salvation from suffering. They are psychological systems because in the process of defining religious and ethical practices they become, as Gardner Murphy and Lois Murphy (1968) stated, more definitive as to what the human mind is and how it works, and how it can be freed of delusion and self-imposed misery. Interestingly, the Japanese were the first to recognize the relationship between mind and body in what we now call psychosomatic illness. Compared with Western psychology, Eastern psychology seems pessimistic in the quest of a sound mind and a good life.

In the Upanishads, we find a denigration of the body and the world. The Bhagavad-Gita and Yoga encourage a retreat into inner discipline. Even the middle course espoused in Buddha's noble *eightfold way* leads to a loss of individuality, a state of *nirvana.* Despite the upbeat mood of most Chinese literature, there is little place for human fulfillment in this world. Through self-control, discipline and extremely limited immediate gratifications we can, according to the Eastern psychological approach, get rid of some of the misery, suffering and frustration which characterizes human life. The goal then is freedom from individual suffering and frustration. The liberation process begins when the battle of self versus non-self is given up and cosmic order reigns within one's self as it does without. This view is not limited to Asians. In previous chapters, I have illustrated other cultures where the self gives way to collective strivings.

Basic to Eastern psychology is the method of self-control through which we keep our eyes open and let the nature of reality come as it will. As in the Upanishads and in Yoga, this is a long, tedious process. It is illustrated in Lao-tse chiding Confucius for looking everywhere—in the sequence of numbers, in the doctrine of yin and yang—for "The Way" but not finding it. This kind of enlightenment, Confucius is told, comes from living the good life. (Centuries later, Western existentialists wrote about self-realization as a process of being.) Each person is a living laboratory whose truth can be learned through arduous self-examination. This is an opposite view to Western psychology which advocates knowledge through direct observation and precepts passed on by "experts." Clearly, the methods we use to define reality will determine our philosophy of life whether it looks inward or outward.

Both Eastern and Western therapies are based on the premise that in order to achieve significant personal growth a great amount of dedicated work is necessary. But work alone without the guidance of an experienced teacher will not be productive. A teacher/helper who is knowledgeable, impartial and benevolent is necessary. Of equal importance is the need for the helpee to be guided by a helper who can detect areas and issues the helpee would avoid or cannot see clearly. The nature of this helping process, whatever its specific content, is painful and difficult for the helpee to deal with. Thus, the helpee grows emotionally by fighting his or her natural tendency to avoid pain. The helper facilitates growth by creating the right kind of verbal obstacles and showing the helpee how they can be overcome. But none of these interventions will work until the individual recognizes his or her own helplessness and asks for guidance. Finally, in both Eastern and Western therapies the helping process is gradual, though the rate of development at different times may vary greatly.

Arthur Kleinman (1977, 1979), Edward Maupin (1962) and Alan Watts (1961) discussed several psychotherapies in relations to Eastern thought. Zen Buddhism provides a cogent point of reference for Western psychotherapy. Both Zen and psychotherapy share the common characteristic of a helper assisting a helpee in losing himself, redefining his boundaries, and coming to grips with hidden and rejected aspects of his reality. Indeed, both the Zen master and the therapist use their knowledge and skills not to reinforce accustomed patterns of behavior in the helpee but to guide him to new experiences and relationships. Regardless of the particular exercises to which the Zen follower is subjected by the master with whom he or she studies, three stages of development evolve. In the first stage, the individual engages in some form of relaxation and self-immersion. When relaxed, thoughts and feelings emerge which disturb the individual's inner tranquility. If the individual is able to accept these disturbances calmly, his attempts to concentrate become effortless and he gains a feeling of quiet power.

It is during the second stage that the individual is most free and most vulnerable to various illusions including a desire to withdraw from social contact with significant other persons, feelings of ecstasy and attacks by "demons." Now the individual recognizes his inability to permanently solve his illusions. At this point, the third stage, if he gives up the hope of being free of problems, he may attain the experience of enlightenment called *satori* which enables him to integrate and temporarily resolve all his problems within one unified and universal conception of himself and his world. Zen does not offer permanent enlightenment. Although the exercises must be repeated, with repetition the general level of one's existence is slowly raised. Gradually, a diligent student of Zen requires less effort to get to a specific level of enlightenment. Upon close analysis, it is evident that the main aspects of Zen training are similar to the Western therapies that promote spontaneity and free association of inner experiences. Becoming aware of oneself as a subject and object of reality allows the helpee to control himself. This is the essence of Eastern and Western therapeutic exercises. Recently, Western therapists concerned with reducing stress within individuals have adopted exercises similar to the following fundamental Buddha exercise called "the setting up of mindfulness":

> Let a brother, going into the forest, or to the roots of a tree, or to an empty chamber, sit down cross-legged, holding the body erect, and set his mindfulness alert.
>
> Mindful let him inhale, mindful let him exhale. Whether he inhales a long breath, let him be conscious thereof; or whether he exhales a long breath, let him be conscious thereof. . . . Let him practice with the thought: "Conscious of my whole body will I inhale." Let him practice with the thought: "Conscious of my whole body will I exhale." Let him practice with the thought: "I will inhale tranquilizing my bodily organism"; let him practice with the thought: "I will exhale tranquilizing my bodily organism."
>
> . . . And moreover a brother, when he is walking, is aware of it thus: "I walk"; or when he is standing, or sitting, or lying down, he is aware of it . . . whether he departs or returns, whether he looks at or looks away from, whether he has drawn in or stretched out his limbs, whether he has donned underrobe, overrobe, or bowl, whether he is eating, drinking, chewing, reposing, or whether he is obeying the calls of nature—sitting, sleeping, watching, talking, or keeping silence, he knows what he is doing (Davids & Davids, 1939, pp. 328–329).

The particular content of the helper's message is not as important as the assumption that the experience of liberation from one's social condition could be achieved following a known path. Whether one believes in an Eastern religion or Western therapeutic process, seeking change has its own intrinsic value. It either leads one to greater objectivity and personal understanding or it does not. Eastern systems comprise many practical procedures that are designed to elevate people to higher levels of existence. This is particularly compatible to Western therapy modalities which emphasize reflecting on past events.

The Yoga exercise, a meditation on the past, resembles certain psychoanalytic techniques. Students of Yoga try before going to sleep at night to review in reverse the events that occurred during the day. They continue this process by reviewing the dreams of the previous night until they cover the twenty-four-hour period and return in their memory to the time when they last performed the exercise. They attempt to objectively and vividly look at their behavior and motives as if they were an impartial observer. Such detached introspection is commonplace in most Western therapies.

By focusing on the similarities between Eastern and Western thoughts, we risk blurring the lines of demarcation. East and West *are* different in many important ways, especially in family life-styles. Inability to understand these differences will result in helpers using inappropriate interventions.

EASTERN CULTURES AND CHARACTER

Religious and philosophical differences provide clear points of cultural demarcation between the East and the West. Generally, Western cultures focus on three concepts of ultimate reality—God, human beings, the universe—and the quest for many Westerners is to manipulate the environment, repent their sins, and achieve universal salvation by adhering to the principle attributed to a personified god. As we have seen earlier, Eastern religions and philosophies perceive the universe as a mere illusion and there is no personified god. The Ultimate Reality is mystical. The impact of Eastern thought on cultures and character are seen in Chapter 2 and the following examples.

Koreans have developed a national personality which combines endurance and flexibility (Yum, 1976; Kim et al., 1981; Yu & Philips, 1983; Rhee, 1984; Kim, 1987; Howe, 1988). Buddhism, Confucianism and Taoism are evident in the Korean tendency to exhibit moderation. Centuries of being dominated by China and Japan caused the Korean people to learn to survive through accommodation while simultaneously resisting cultural extinction through assimilation. As with other Asians, there is a strong sense of family identity and unity in Korea based on the Confucian principles of filial piety and kinship interdependency. But this is not to imply that Koreans are docile as a people. Unlike the traditional Japanese, the traditional Koreans have developed a strong predilection for individuality within the context of the family.

The Vietnamese family is the life force for each person who in turn gains his or her self-identity mainly from it. A traditional Vietnamese's personal goals are a reflection of those of his or her family (Marr, 1981; Atkinson et al., 1984). The influence of Taoism is seen in the Vietnamese quest for harmony and order. Consequently, the Vietnamese are eclectic and indirect when dealing with problems. Survival also is related to *tanh can cu*—thriftness, endurance, patience, tenacity and industriousness. Yet, the Vietnamese are an extremely sensitive people who value dealing with others from the heart as well as the mind. In their nonaggressive, indirect manner, the Vietnamese have been able to achieve family goals.

The name Thailand ("Free Land") captures the essence of Thai culture and character. While they respect hierarchal order, Thais value their individual freedom as much as their national freedom (Weisz, 1988). In interpersonal relations they are polite and exercise restraint and moderation, but, unlike most Asians, they exhibit individualism. As a whole, they value their serenity and peace — avoiding confrontation as much as possible.

The Filipinos comprise large extended family relationships based on a system of reciprocity called *utang na loob* (Lott, 1976). This is a highly personalized network of friendship bonds that cement kinship and friendship. Indeed, Filipino life evolves around social acceptance which results from respecting persons of higher authority, fulfilling one's social responsibilities, and not bringing shame on the family. This behavior is supported by cultural norms which place a high value on *pakakisma* — maintaining harmonious relationships among significant others. Often, Filipinos walk a thin line of nonconflict, indirection and nonconfrontation in order to foster positive interpersonal relationships. Now, let's look at some common characteristics for these groups (see also Chapter 2).

Family. Korean, Vietnamese, Thai, and Filipino cultures, similar to other Asian cultures, are mainly family oriented. One derives his or her identity, status and sense of self-worth from the family. It is therefore the basic unit for social, emotional and economic support. Furthermore, the family demands loyalty from each of its members. It is usually extended to include several generations. Most Asian families are patriarchal, but females play important and respected secondary status roles. Even when working outside the home, women are expected to maintain their traditional nurturing roles of wives, mothers and sisters.

Filial piety. Filial piety is the basic foundation upon which the Thai, Filipino, Korean, Vietnamese family is built. First, each person is indebted to his or her parents for bringing them into the world via the family. Family lineage and respect is maintained through the Confucian concepts of filial peity and ancestor worship. Simply stated, filial piety is respect for parents, grandparents and other significant elders. From this ideology comes the expectation that parents and other significant elders will be treated with respect and cared for by the younger generation. Obviously, this expectation manifests itself in strong interdependence. The Asian penchant for collective identity fosters interdependence. Indeed, interdependence is a way of life among relatives, friends, neighbors, employers and employees. And it has a positive connotation.

The norm of reciprocity spills over into most activities. But it is the norm of harmony that prevents interdependence from getting out of control.

Harmony. If filial piety is the foundation upon which the Vietnamese, Korean, Thai, and Filipino family is built, the concept of harmony is the load-bearing principle that prevents the interactions from falling apart. Maintaining peaceful and agreeable interrelationships, which includes accommodation and compromise, are the behavioral means by which harmony is achieved. As an example, an individual may turn away from an angry person as a sign of harmony rather than responding in an angry manner. To the uninformed, this may be misinterpreted as defiance or anger or even disrespect. This kind of self-restraint or behavior moderation is more noticeable in some Asian cultures such as the Japanese and Chinese. In most Asian cultures, however, it is shameful to be aggressive or confrontive. The Asian way of dealing with confrontation and aggression often shows up in psychosomatic illnesses. Turning into oneself as a method of handling conflict leads to high incidences of suffering without complaining. To *gaman*, as the Japanese call this behavior, is to exhibit dignity. To complain is to show what the Vietnamese call *ki ga chiisai*, that your spirit is small. Thus, Asians learn to suffer quietly.

Saving face. Asians are taught to save face, or *chaemyun* in Korean. This means to maintain one's respect and status. Usually one loses face when a socially appropriate role behavior is not carried out. This is not merely a personal embarrassment — it is a family shame (*haji* in Japanese, *chang pi* in Korean, *hiya* in Filipino). As an example, the individual who does not pay back a favor or who is accused of a crime and the accusation appears in the news media experiences a loss of face. It is also important to note that this shame afflicts all members of a family — the living, the dead, and the unborn.

Acceptance of fate. Buddhism, Hinduism, Confucianism, and Taoism all to some extent foster the notion of fatalism. This is not a negative life adjustment. On the contrary, it is a pragmatic way to cope with life situations. Instead of challenging a situation or event, traditional Asians accept things as a given condition of their fate, or *palja* as the Koreans call it. This then is adopting the Filipino attitude of *bahalana* ("come what may"). It would be a great disservice if practitioners misread this behavior as being negative.

An Illustration

The traditional Japanese family living in Okinawa has been molded by *family, field* and *form.* The family is extended vertically to include all generations deceased, and horizontally to include all living relatives through fourth cousins. Family honor, prestige and respect are inculcated during early child training when the Japanese learn their religious, moral and ethical obligations. Child rearing is an act of deliberate love and permissiveness. Once the intense love is firmly rooted, anything that threatens the Japanese family, however remote, is a threat to each individual's personal existence. This is drastically different from most Western nuclear families. Furthermore, the traditional Japanese family in Okinawa is highly religious—mainly Buddhist and Shinto.

Using Margaret Mead's (1970) terminology, Japanese society has strong *postfigurative* traditions. Particularly noteworthy is the powerful influence of ancestral veneration. Within the home, the family shrine is the focal point for formal recognition of prior generations and their contributions to the family lineage. Important anniversaries are observed in the home with feast days, and offerings and prayers are presented by the shrine's custodian. This privilege usually falls to the female head of the household, but sometimes it is delegated to an elderly family member. Thus, unlike Americans who mourn their dead, the Japanese honor their "ghosts" with happy events.

Although child training is extremely permissive (Japanese children are "punished with love"), this training is conducted within the parameters of respect for and honor of the family. Or stated another way, Japanese mothers tend to "suffer" their children rather than inhibit their behavior by using chastisement or physical punishment (DeVos, 1985). The Japanese derive ultimate satisfaction from belonging to the family. A sense of group identity gives one the psychic energy to go beyond personal defects or limitations. Older siblings are trained to take care of younger ones, and these obligations become lifetime moral, ethical and practical responsibilities. *Otoosan* (honorable father) is the family protector, responsible for the welfare of the family members. *Okaasan* (honorable mother) is the head of the physical household, ensuring the security and upkeep of the home and providing for the physical needs and comfort of the family members. Elders (grandparents, uncles and aunts) are cared for with the same permissive treatment as children in family units whose *Otoosan* may be a grandson, nephew or cousin.

The basic sense of family is so strongly a part of the traditional Japanese character that it is transferred to industry, government, bureaucracy and national politics. Paternalistic industries are commonplace, and bureaucracies are extremely sensitive to citizen welfare and the integrity of the family structure. In many ways, the entire Japanese society becomes a "national family." Nonfamily Japanese males in the community are the equivalent of uncles, and nonfamily Japanese females are treated like aunts. For example, a well-known businessman might be greeted by neighborhood children with *"Konichi wa, Ojisan"* (Good afternoon, dear [or honored] uncle).

To some extent, Japanese adult roles match those found in many small, conservative American communities. But this kind of cross-national transposition is not reliable. There is a tendency for tourists who never go for outside Tokyo to view Japan as a completely westernized country and culture. The Japanese interest in Western technology, literature, clothing, art, and government are in fact built on traditional Japanese social organization, not Western culture. The core structure of Japanese life is *iemoto,* a master-disciple relationship. Each master has several disciples (clients) with whom he maintains mutual dependence (Hsu, 1985). Other terms important to understanding Japanese behavior are *amae* (acknowledgment of dependency), *on* (ascribed obligation), *giri* (contractual obligation) and *chu* (loyalty to one's superior). Unlike Americans who tend to view their role expectations as *obligations,* Japanese tend to view them as *an expression of gratitude.* For the Japanese, duties fall into a hierarchy with two distinct categories. The highest level of adult obligations are *duties which can never be fully repaid:*

1. Duty to the law.
2. Duty to one's parents, ancestors and descendants.
3. Duty to one's work.

The second level consists of *duties which are to be fully repaid:*

4. Duty to one's name.
5. Duty to the world (non-related others).

From this ranking, it is understandable that the Japanese spend a considerable amount of energy preserving the family and home and striving for the best education possible in order to succeed as workers. Japanese parents and students are taught to place a high value on education. This commitment is seen in the willingness of families to undergo considerable, often drastic, financial hardship so that their children can receive the best education. Traditionally, Japanese students are dedicated scholars. Japanese students from kindergarten through higher education are commonly seen with a bag of books. In Japan, probably more than in any other post-industrial nation, the interdependence of the industrial technocracy and institutional education is recognized and supported.

The field is the area (or environment) in which adult livelihood and social interaction take place. Basically, the field is represented by the neighborhood, place of employment, and places where friends and colleagues conduct their avocations. The Japanese concepts of work and leisure differ from American concepts. The work ethic is very much a part of the Japanese character; to an uninformed outsider, the Japanese seem to live to work, while U.S. citizens seem to work to live. Of course, these are generalizations, but is it fair to say that it is difficult to get Japanese to take leisure time. Typically, the Japanese do not take long vacations. Instead, they like to take a few vacation days here and there — usually in May, August and early January — at the same time as their friends. In 1987 Japanese factory workers averaged 2,180 hours on the job compared with 1,934 for Americans; and Japanese workers averaged 10 days of paid vacation compared with 20 days for American workers.

Form transcends both the family and the field. *How* one does something is just as important as *what* one does. Perhaps form is important because most Japanese live in extremely high-density areas. They compress their living patterns into crowded groups, and this partially explains their efforts to conserve space. Japanese forms optimize individual movements and minimize inconveniences or interference in the movements of other persons. United States citizens might initially find little elbow room in Okinawa or Japan, but it is there — although somewhat difficult to find.

The custom of leaving outdoor footwear at the household portico illustrates the symbolic Japanese demarcation of public and private space. American space requirements are sometimes interpreted by the Japanese as rudeness in seeking more space than is individually required. Large offices with big desks and many furnishings are not characteristic of the Japanese. Furthermore, loud talk offends Japanese sensibilities, conditioned to controlled speech necessitated by close living patterns. Tone, volume, hand movements, and posture are closely monitored by the Japanese. Drastic changes are not usually necessary, but some change is required if Americans are to be accepted by their Japanese hosts. As Chuang Tsu (1974) observed, this requires a "three in the morning" change:

> When you wrack your brain trying to unify things without knowing that they are already one, it is called, "three in the morning." What did I mean by "three in the morning"? A man who keeps monkeys said to them, "You get three acorns in the morning and four in the evening." This made them all very angry. So he said, "How about four in the morning and three in the evening?"—and the monkeys were happy. The number of acorns was the same, but the different arrangements resulted in anger or pleasure. This is what I am talking about. Therefore, the sage harmonizes right and wrong and rests in the balance of nature. This is called taking both sides at once (p. 30).

THERAPEUTIC IMPLICATIONS

Traditional Asian families vary by locality (urban versus rural) and social class. It is rare in urban areas for parents, siblings, uncles, aunts and cousins to live together. Even when they do not live in the same household, members of a traditional Asian family often maintain strong emotional bonds. Relatives visit each other frequently and a sense of family pride is maintained, including responsibility for mutual aid in times of crisis.

Roles, Status, and Communication

A traditional Asian wife devotes herself to the care of her husband, children, and home. If her husband is unhappy or her children misbehave, she tends to blame herself. Betty Chang (1981) pointed out that Asian females historically have occupied an inferior position to males. Females are thought of as liabilities because they generally are raised to marry into someone else's family and consequently transfer their loyalty to the new family. Married women become integrated into their husband's family, and they rarely visit their own family except for special occasions. Therefore, male children receive preferential treatment.

Roles and obligations are well-defined in the traditional Asian family. Father is the head of the family, and authority is passed to the eldest son when the father is absent. The saying that there are four things Japanese fear the most—earthquakes, thunder, fire, and fathers—is more than humorous chatter (Barnlund, 1975). When major issues are discussed, the male head of the household is responsible for making decisions which affect the whole family. There are also well-defined roles for the aged; the younger persons are expected to defer to their elders. It is the duty of a child, usually a son, to care for parents in their old age. The teachings of Confucius clearly outline the duty of a son to his parents.

Interpersonal interactions in the Asian family tend to be less verbal than in the Western family. This does not mean that family members are deficient in communication skills. On the contrary, they have well-understood means of communicating. While generally not overtly affectionate, during times of illness family members are quite demonstrative. Asian children are taught self-control and to be ashamed of emotional outbursts. Asian girls are taught to be submissive and repress their feelings. The Japanese language in particular involves the use of tonal control and indirect terms so that people can conceal their feelings. The paucity of outward signs of feelings is modeled by parents. Sadness and disappointment as well as happiness are seldom accompanied by much expression in Asian homes.

> The relationships between Chinese parents and children shows entirely different characteristics. Chinese parents are amused by infantile behavior and youthful exuberance, but the measure of a child's worth is determined primarily by the degree to which they act like adults. Chinese parents are rather proud of a child who acts "older than his age" whereas some American parents might take a similar child to a psychiatrist. Or what Chinese consider rowdiness in a child's behavior, American parents might approve as a sign of initiative (Hsu, 1953, pp. 80–81).

The individual who expresses conflict is looked upon with commendation. If anger is expressed, males are more likely to express it than females because the culture prescribes that such behavior is more acceptable in males. The communal behavior controls the expression of anger. This is also true for expressing pain. Asian patients seldom respond to pain by crying for help or thrashing out. Instead, they will deny its intensity. The word "stoic" correctly describes this behavior. To Asians, emotional expression is a sign of immaturity. In traditional Chinese culture, for example, it is acceptable to have a somatic illness but it is unacceptable to be psychologically ill. Therefore, a Chinese who experiences emotional distress is not likely to want to talk about it or ask for understanding and empathy; instead, he or she might complain of a physical disorder and thereby receive attention. Somatic complaints are commonplace in Asian cultures (Tseng & McDermott, 1981; Chin, 1982;

Nevis, 1983; Brammer, 1985). One of my Chinese students described her difficulty in expressing anger:

> As my mind wanders close to the edge of my subconsciousness, memories start to flood my head. I suddenly remember something that I know very well. I remember how resistant I was last summer, when trouble drove me into the couseling office of the handle-bar mustache counselor, Y. M. There, I was confronted for the first time of my life. Whenever Y. asked me, "Are you angry?" I said "No!" Then he asked me, "How are you feeling?" I smiled and said, "I don't feel anything...I don't have feelings! And I don't like to feel!" As I felt the pressure from Y. to verbally *and* behaviorally express my feeling of anger, I repeatedly stated that I would stop coming for counseling. I was offended by Y. when his stern face stared at me, saying, "We have only just begun to deal with your serious problem with 'feeling,' specifically 'anger,' and you are thinking of quitting already?" I did not like to hear such a provocative statement. Yet it ringed so true to my ears that I hated it...and hated Y. for pinpointing the weak side of me — my emotional side. Helplessly, I ended up listening to the naked truth about myself. To my own surprise, I stayed on with counseling and attended ten counseling sessions.

It is extremely difficult for the traditional Asian to go outside his or her home to seek help with a personal problem. They believe that understanding one's motivation may be important, but the primary cause of a personal problem is insufficient willpower. Therefore, the solution can be found in trying harder through introspection, not going for professional help. On a more personal level, family problems are to be resolved within the family. Admission and display of personal inadequacy is a sign of familial failure and shame. Consequently, if a problem persists and continues to cause pain and unhappiness, the Asian is likely to adopt a fatalistic attitude and stoically accept it.

Therapy Modalities

Therapy modalities that require self-disclosure are alienating to most Asians. Even more disconcerting are activities that require individuals to confront each other. Traditional Asians consider this kind of behavior to be rude and impolite. Besides, it is in poor taste to publicly embarrass people. As noted earlier, Asian cultures value the individual who sacrifices himself or herself to avoid conflict even when it would be justified.

Thus, Asians are likely to disengage themselves from conflict, even if their position has more validity.

Helping strategies that have little formal group structure and direction can unnerve traditional Asian clients. They prefer the goals of the sessions to be clearly delineated and followed. When group members deviate from the original goals, an Asian client will probably try to get the group back on track. Impromptu behavior is seen as a sign of immaturity and lack of personal discipline. Traditional Asians are likely to feel more comfortable in well-structured, unambiguous situations (Sue & Morshima, 1982; Sue & Sue, 1985; Fernandez, 1988). Furthermore, failure to understand Eastern religions, philosophies and psychologies will greatly minimize the effectiveness of practitioners who indiscriminantly apply Western helping modalities to Asian clients.

In the early 1920s a Japanese psychiatrist named Shomo Morita, who was influenced by Zen Buddhism, established what is now called *Morita therapy* (personal experience therapy). Building on the accepted clinical practice of prescribing rest as treatment in neurasthenia, which was believed to result from exhaustion of the central nervous system, Morita added guidance, physical rehabilitation, and work therapy to the treatment regimen (Kondo, 1953). For the first four to ten days the patient is told to lie in bed all day. Only when he eats and goes to the bathroom does the patient interrupt his rest. All other activities, including conversation, reading and smoking, are prohibited. After this isolation period, the patient is gradually allowed to leave his room to do light physical work such as gardening or household chores. Slowly, he is allowed to engage in occupational, recreational, and social activities. During this phase, the patient keeps a diary which the therapist reads and comments on. Almost always, the patient initially fills the diary with complaints. Typical therapist comments may include the following: "Do you think you are the only person with these kinds of problems?" "It is natural to suffer." "Learn to accept your symptoms." In this way the therapist gives the patient the insight needed to live with himself, his symptoms, and his total environment.

Morita therapy operationalizes the Zen concept *arugamama*, literally, "as it is," or loosely defined "accept things as they are." This is not an attempt to change the patient's objective reality; instead, he is guided toward changing inner attitudes of his reality. In this aspect Morita therapy is similar to some Western behavior therapies. But there are some major differences. Morita therapy is group-centered, behavioristic, and ritualistic in contrast to most Western therapies that are individual-centered and require more talk than action (Reynolds & Kiefer, 1977). Morita therapy's focus on the here and now places little value on verbally recounting one's problems or the search for their origins. Compared to Western therapies that foster the notion of rationalistic idealism, Paul Pedersen (1979) observed that Morita therapy emphasizes the acceptance of phenomenological reality as it is.

Another Japanese therapy, *Naikan therapy* (introspective therapy), utilizes the central role of guilt in Japanese life (Murase, 1976). While the goal of Morita therapy is to help the patient to live with himself, Naikan therapy seeks to achieve interpersonal and social harmony through introspection. The term *naikan* means "inside looking." This modality was developed by Inobu Yoshimoto and it is based on Jodo-Shin, the most widely accepted Buddhist sect. Succinctly, the patient sits alone from early morning until almost bedtime for a week. During this time, he meditates alone using the therapist's structured directions in self-observation and self-reflection. The patient shares with the therapist his memories of kindness received from a particular significant other person, usually a family member. He is also asked to reflect on what he did in return for the kindness. This remembrance may be extended to other significant persons. After a week of therapy, the patient is told to continue this reflective process without the intervention of the therapist.

The Naikan therapist is an uninvolved teacher, who in the context of Jodo-Shin Buddhism, considers wrongdoing a part of human nature. To harm someone close, especially parents, is a severe violation of the Japanese social code of ethics. The Naikan method does not remove guilt. On the contrary, it reinforces guilt as a useful, socially accepted quality in family and business life. We cannot escape guilt; we must learn to live with it. In Japanese culture to say "I was wrong," "I am sorry" is an admirable trait. Recollecting the experiences that caused the guilt can lead to accepting one's faults and virtues. This then is the process of becoming worthy of love. Asians are much more likely to forgive transgressions of significant others who return to the group than are Europeans (Okonogi, 1978; Henkin, 1985). In Buddhist scriptures there are strong feelings of love and hostility between mother and child, with the theme of forgiveness when the child returns to the mother. Harry Kitano (1981) presents a compelling analysis of the relevancy of Japanese therapeutic modalities for Japanese Americans:

If one were to ask the question, "Are Japanese therapeutic models appropriate for Japanese Americans?" the overall answer would have to be a general "no," but with reservations. The Japanese therapies take place in a local context, within a local situation, and within the context of a specific culture so that, unless conditions for the Japanese in the United States are similar, the models may be less appropriate. However, if someone were to ask, "Are therapeutic systems developed for Europeans appropriate for Japanese Americans?" The overall answer would also have to be a general "no" (p. 240).

West Meets East

Humanistic psychology has clear Eastern perspectives. Martin Buber (1957) and Carl Rogers (1951) were greatly influenced by the teachings of Tao. Indeed, person-centered and Gestalt therapists are much like the man who internalizes the Taoist virtue of *wu-wei* (non-action):

> To interfere with the life of things means to harm both them and one's self. He who imposes himself has the small, manifest might; he who does not impose himself has the great secret might. . . . The perfect man does not impose himself on them, but he helps all beings to their freedom (Buber, 1957, pp. 54–55).

This is the kind of helper that person-centered and Gestalt therapists try to become. This behavior is also consistent with the Zen principle of each person finding *the* answers within himself or herself. Although different methods are used by Tao, Zen, person-centered and Gestalt helpers, their goals are similar.

Japan and Korea exemplify many traditional Asian folkways and mores. Yet, the Japanese and Koreans are open to new ideas and technology. Other Asian countries have followed. Even so, traditional beliefs resist disrespectful behavior and egocentric thoughts. Therefore, psychoanalysis is theoretically the least likely of the modalities discussed in Chapter 1 to be accepted. The philosophy of psychoanalysis centers on the human tendency to seek pleasure and avoid pain. Eastern philosophies do not encourage one to seek out pain, but if it comes we should learn to accept it. Nor are traditional Asians taught to aggressively pursue pleasure. As with the Japanese, other Asians are motivated to change, but not if the change will lead to disrespectful and publicly embarrassing behaviors. The general Asian population can fairly easily accept the time commitment of psychoanalysis, but they will resist the process of critical self-examination. Nor can most Asians financially afford lengthy treatment. But a major drawback of psychoanalysis is that it attributes evil thoughts and behaviors to one's relatives, particularly parents.

As noted earlier, person-centered and Gestalt therapies are consistent with the Asian emphasis on self-improvement. Because each individual is encouraged to set his or her own pace and determine the appropriate time to share secrets, these modalities have become quite popular among some Asians. However, frequently a considerable amount of guilt is produced as helpees try to make sense of their obsequious behaviors. In many ways, traditional Asians are like David Riesman's (1950) "other-directed" men and women—unable to distinguish thoughts from feelings and unable to express feelings even when recognizing them. This type of Asian is indeed attuned to the attitudes and opinions of others and has an insatiable psychological need for approval.

Asian behavior similar to the Japanese *enryo* syndrome is to deflect from oneself praise or positive reinforcement (Kitano, 1976). If praise is directed at a traditional Asian or a member of his family, he may respond by saying, "No, I am not outstanding," or "No, my children are not outstanding," or "Where?" meaning "Not true, where did you see this happen?" To praise oneself or members of one's family is considered poor manners, and the accepted behavior of the person offering the praise is to ignore the denial. Non-Asians often mistake this behavior as a lack of positive self-esteem. The communal behaviors related to restraint and modesty are more pronounced in females than in males because of the former's lower status in Asian countries.

Asians and many other Third-World people respond best when therapy is directive, nurturant and practical (Banks, 1975; Atkinson et al., 1978). Consequently, Adlerian, person-centered and Gestalt therapies gain credibility in these cultures by being nurturing, but they lose credibility by being non-directive. Gestalt therapy is too confrontive for most Asians. Behavior modification modalities are practical and directive, but they too are confrontive and seldom nurturing (Marmor, 1971). The goals of Hinduism, Tao, Confucianism, person-centered therapy, Adlerian psychotherapy and Gestalt therapy are somewhat compatible. Each of them places much value on achieving the ideal self. For Hindus and Taoists the ideal self is not encapsulated in the body or the mind; instead, it is found in a consciousness that transcends worldly parameters. The Hindu and Tao *Ultimate Reality* and Confucian *right action* are as noble goals as person-centered *self-actualization,* Adlerian *right choice* and Gestalt *awareness.*

Transactional analysis is of questionable value to traditional Asians. They can identify with the Adult *thought concept* and the Parent *taught concept* as outlined by Thomas Harris (1969), but they are likely to reject the Child *felt concept.* The creativity, emotion, and rebelliousness of the Child is not characteristic of Asian children. By cultural socialization and societal reinforcement many Asians internalize the "I'm not OK, you're OK" life position.

Behavior modification is a familiar modality to Asians. Many aspects of the business world evolve around reinforcement, punishment, extinctions and stimulus control. Behavior therapy, reality therapy and rational-emotive therapy provide direct reactive approaches that are less culturally confrontive. Behavior therapies are similar to Morita therapy (Gibson, 1974). But if a traditional Asian's behaviors are changed to challenge traditional socialization (e.g., female submissiveness, lack of intragroup competitive effort, deference to parents), then additional problems will occur. Frequently, this change results in creating marginal people — individuals rejected by their relatives and not accepted outside their culture. Some writers argue that behavior therapies are more appropriate for Asian peoples than traditional psychodynamic therapies (Hayes, 1980; Smith et al., 1978). I question this view. On the one hand, any therapy that ignores a client's conceptualization of reality as it pertains to past events is not totally adequate. On the other hand, Western helping modalities which encourage personal growth through self-exploration might cause increased problems as clients become aware of the oppressive nature of some of their ethnic group traditions (Halleck, 1971). A combination of behavioral, psychodynamic, and humanistic helping techniques might be more appropriate for Eastern cultures (Wachtel, 1977). This is often called *multimodal therapy* (Lazarus, 1981). Asian family problems in particular are not easily resolved with Western modalities.

People often go to a therapist to try to "work things out." What can *therapy* mean here? Usually it means focusing on the interpersonal situation, on the inevitable distortions each partner is pushing on the other, on the feelings of hurt and inadequacy, on the needs each partner has; on secrets, on faulty ways of communicating needs and feelings, on the necessity to work harder as "partners" in the relationship; on the different families each partner has come from, and on how different cultural/familial perspectives have added to the quagmire (Glen and Kunnes, 1973, p. 120).

This is mainstream Western-oriented therapy. The problems clients bring to the helping process are almost always reduced to individuals. This kind of helping encourages individualist thinking and distorts the significance of group conditioning and environment.

> Yet with all this emphasis on the relationship, [Western] "therapy" almost always ignores the overriding realities the partners live with: the unequal power distribution, the culture-bound expectations for marriage, the different role choices available to the couple, the politics of their class position (Glen & Kunnes, p. 120).

It would be accurate to say that few Eastern cultures allow individuals to "be themselves" or to express their "real selves" in public. Regardless of the culture, the self can be viewed as a composite of many selves; the personality can be viewed as a learned repertoire of roles. From this perspective, Asians seldom have the opportunity to learn a wide range of roles. Even so, they do subjectively experience differences in the "realness" of their behavior when compared with non-Asians. Erving Goffman (1959) wrote that all social interaction is composed of performances, with each person composing and playing the part of his or her chosen character. Traditional Asians seldom compose their parts; they are assigned to them at birth. Goffman differentiated between behavior in "front stage" and "backstage" behavior. Western people tend to use one language of behavior for informal or backstage interaction and another language of behavior when a performance is being presented. When they are backstage, Western-oriented people can relax; they can speak their mind and step out of character. Backstage they can be authentic as opposed to polite. Western helpers frequently do not realize that traditional Asians are taught to almost always maintain a proper cultural front. It is extremely difficult to alter such behavior. Yet, it is backstage behavior that is encouraged in most Western therapies.

A "changed" Asian is likely to discover that his or her new beliefs and behaviors are culturally alienating. A typical response to this alienation is for changed persons to clarify for those around them the exact nature and extent of the difference between their new reality and the old one. The general result of such a confession of change by an Asian is that his family will label him as "strange" or "different." There is a predictable sequence of events which normally occur when Asians abandon traditional values and behaviors. First, family members will direct an increasing amount of communication toward them, trying to change them back to the old ways and beliefs. If this fails, one after another will abandon them as hopeless and an embarrassment to the family. In the end the changed persons will be ignored or excluded from family decision making.

It is important for practitioners to realize that there is no justification for facilitating a change in a helpee if it will create conditions more deplorable than the present one. This does not preclude the possibility of successfully exporting Western therapies (Draguns, 1981). But unless such therapies are adapted to fit non-Western cultures, the range of usefulness of Western helping modalities will remain greatly circumscribed.

Chapter 5

WORK-RELATED ISSUES

Significant changes have occurred in the concept of *work* since prehistoric days when people had to work only enough to meet very basic needs for food, clothing and shelter. As time passed and human needs became symbolic, work and work-related activities began to take on meanings that went beyond basic survival. The earliest recorded ideas about work referred to it as a curse, a punishment, an activity not included as part of the "good life," and at best a necessary evil needed to sustain life (Lofquist & Dawis, 1969). People of high status did not work. Only slaves, indentured servants and peasants worked. The masters or ruling classes were preoccupied with intellectual contemplation that could not be sustained through physical labor. Many of the religions, philosophies and helping modalities discussed in the early chapters were founded by men who did little physical labor.

WORK ETHIC

As Christianity spread, the Western meaning of work began to change. Martin Luther subscribed to the principle that work is a form of redemption. The Western religious decree was that all people who are able to work should work, including affluent intellectuals and ascetics. Thus, whether an individual's economic position was high or low, he or she was expected to work in order to serve God. According to Luther, the best way to serve God was by performing work more perfectly. The philosophies of John Calvin and Luther were very similar in regard to work, which they both thought curbed the evil in people. Max Weber (1930) hypothesized that the belief that work is the highest means of asceticism and the strongest proof of religious faith had the greatest influence in shaping capitalism. Work became the religious spirit of capitalism.

In the twentieth century, the meaning of work changed to a way to get consumer goods and maintain dignity and self-esteem rather than as verification of religious salvation. In discussing the importance of work, C. Esco Obermann (1965) concluded that the most observable contributions by individuals to their society are made through their work or occupations. In Western urban cultures, work or occupation more nearly defines a person's importance. Consequently, job success is likely to satisfy the need for recognition and status. Several writers have concluded that the Protestant ethic provided the impetus for a scientific, rational approach to Western psychology, and this in turn resulted in a proactive rather than passive approach to job-related success (Draguns, 1973; Rotenberg, 1974). Another result of the Protestant ethic is the separation of people into healthy/sick and good/bad categories. Currently, occupation is one of the most important aspects of a Western individual's life; it defines his or her place in the community. Generally, in Western communities social status is related to one's occupation.

> In our society, there is no single situation which is potentially so capable of giving some satisfaction at all levels of basic needs as the occupation. With respect to the physiological needs, it is clear that in our culture the usual means for allaying hunger and thirst, and, to some extent, sexual needs and others is through the job, which provides the money that can be exchanged for food and drink. The same is true for safety needs. The need to be a member of a group and receive love is also one which can be satisfied in part by the occupation. To work with a congenial group, to be an extrinsic part of the function of the group, to be needed and welcomed by the group are important aspects of the satisfactory job.
>
> Perhaps satisfaction of the need for esteem from self and others is most easily seen as a big part of the occupation. In the first place, entering upon an occupation is generally seen in our culture as a symbol of adulthood, and an indication that a young man or woman has reached a stage of some independence and freedom. Having a job carries a measure of esteem. What importance it has is seen most clearly in the devastating effects upon the individual of being out of work (Roe, 1956, pp. 31–32).

What about non-Western people? Few educators today would question that the period since World War II in most Western nations and Japan has been one of ever-increasing correlation between formal education and economic status. Current United States history books still devote at least one chapter extolling those native-born and immigrant citizens who became wealthy, influential, and beloved though born in humble surroundings in which there was little opportunity for more than the most rudimentary learning. This is a fantasy for most peoples of the world for whom economic mobility is as far removed from reality as the world of log cabins and prairie schooners.

Non-Western Work Ethic

One of the most vivid distinctions between Western peoples and non-Western peoples is in the meaning of work (deKeyser et al., 1988; MOW, 1988). As noted earlier, Westerners work to earn a living; it is what people are expected to do and they need not enjoy it. Leisure or recreation, however, is pursued to get relief from the monotony of work. Thus, Westerners tend to dichotomize work and leisure. And they generally carry out leisure activities with the same seriousness of purpose as attached to work. This is not the case for non-Westerners who generally do not discriminate between work and leisure-time activities. Third-World peoples in particular work at a more leisurely pace than Westerners. An even clearer distinction is seen in the concepts of work as related to temporal orientation.

Western concepts of work reflect an orientation toward the future. That is, by doing something today we can bring about a desired future result. From this perspective, the drudgery of work can culminate in progress. Some non-Western cultures place more importance on the present (e.g., Latin American and African cultures) than the future, while other non-Western cultures (e.g., Asian cultures) focus on the past. These views foster fatalistic outlooks of working—one is neither lazy nor worthless if he does not succeed on the job; rather, he merely has bad luck or is not destined to succeed. Thus, in this situation, much of the helpee's initial conversation pertaining to a failed job situation is likely to evolve around agonizing over bad luck of ill fate.

Motivation for work varies among cultures. Success in work is an integral aspect of the Western worker's self-image (Brockner, 1988; Strasser, 1988). Indeed, the Western worker's invisible concept of self-image becomes visible and measurable in his or her external performances and achievements, many of which are work-related. Western workers fit Erich Fromm's conception of the "marketer" (1967), individuals who derive their self-esteem from their value or salability as a commodity or an investment ("I am what I do"). *Doing* describes the Western worker, while *being* describes the non-Western worker. Being-oriented cultures are built on reciprocal interpersonal relationships within the family and community. The major focus within these cultures is on preserving or improving one's position within the social structure.

The obligations that accrue to persons in being-oriented cultures transcend personal goals. For example, in Latin America a patron may be the godfather of persons who work on his estate, and he has obligations to them which go beyond superior-subordinate obligations. Traditional Asian employers are also expected to assume similar paternalistic responsibilities for their employees—even during adverse financial times. Third-World workers tend to spend little time trying to determine the source of their job motivation. They know that it is in the family or work group. Therefore, they carry out the obligations, duties, and privileges inherent in their social positions. Helpers who ask these workers, "What do you want to do to make things better on the job?" are likely to receive blank stares. To ask group-oriented workers to make "I" statements is to challenge the essence or their group identity. I am not suggesting that the question is inappropriate. I am suggesting, however, that the question will often cause an individual to examine his or her cultural conditioning.

Competition is the primary method used by Western employers to achieve production goals (Hofstede, 1984). Employees in Western cultures who have been socialized to be individualistic respond well to this emphasis, but the same approach applied to workers in cultures that do not value individualism will be ineffective. People who value saving face more than winning a competition will not accept the challenge to be competitive with the same enthusiasm as competition-oriented people. Their communal ethos does not include the norm to excel over one's group members. It is understandable then that, unlike Western workers who tend to fear failure in the competitive work place, non-Western workers tend to fear success in it (Applebaum, 1984). Also, in societies where each person has a fixed position in a vertical, hierarchal tier, status-restricted persons often adopt an attitude of contentment and even dignity within their narrow sphere. Contrary to a popular Western notion, as a whole non-Western workers are not unhappy with their restricted social situations. After all, happiness is a relative condition. And compared to their co-workers, they are equally well off.

Poverty is a predominant condition of workers in developing countries (Gonzales et al., 1984; Nash, 1984). In a strict sense, poverty is the same no matter where it is found, and rural and urban poor people have many traits in common—ill health, low levels of education, and substandard housing. Yet, poverty is more pernicious in rural areas. Tradition-oriented cultures perpetuate old, familiar ways of life; there is a strong resistance to change. Along with this commitment to the status quo comes passive resignation to unequal opportunities. Poverty is not likely to be defined as bad but, instead, the way things have been and probably will continue to be. When this happens, poverty becomes a vicious circle from which the tradition-oriented person in a developing country can seldom escape (Norwine and Gonzales, 1988). In short, most workers with these beliefs and values seem to expect to live today in the same manner as their ancestors lived yesterday. But this is not an irreversible situation.

Traditional people exposed to nontraditional life-styles often develop aspirations for consumer goods and urban living. Politically, rural communities seldom are able to maintain their autonomy once a country begins large-scale urbanization (Mohan, 1984). When the process beings, a growing number of rural dwellers derive their political, educational, and economic role models from nontraditional persons. Perhaps it is counterproductive to focus very long on the differences between traditional and nontraditional workers. Concerned, caring persons in all countries seek the creation of a home where their family can walk in dignity, eat a wholesome diet, sleep in a decent house, live in an emotionally supportive community, and finally die a timely death unhurried by lack of adequate medical services. Unfortunately, for low-income traditional and nontraditional workers, this usually is a dream unrealized.

The peoples of the developing nations, with a few exceptions, will do well if they manage to get and hold a menial job. Attempting to find work which will allow them to rise above their parents economically and give their children certain fundamental benefits is an arduous struggle for most workers in non-Western nations. Deficient in basic technological survival skills, these workers are obviously vulnerable to others who would seek to manipulate them. Within Western and non-Western nations the workers who are in greatest jeopardy are found mainly in inner cities and rural areas. Because these persons are at manifest disadvantage in the skills of reading and writing, relatively untutored in basic science, and less interested in civic matters than most others, they become institutionalized failures.

With the preceding thoughts in mind, we can now turn to management theories to gain additional perspectives of non-Western workers.

Professional helpers who have been educated in Western higher education institutions are likely to have an extremely limited view of non-
Western workers. To provide more balance, it is helpful to examine
popular Western management theories to see how well they describe
non-Western workers.

RELEVANT MANAGEMENT THEORIES

Theories of human behavior reflect the work environment in which
people exist. For about seventy years, the United States has been the
world's largest producer and exporter of management theories. Prior to
this time, the centers of management theory were in the Old World. The
earliest theories are found in parts of the Old Testament of the Bible and
in Plato's *The Law* and *The Republic.* Some leadership concepts can be
traced to sixteenth-century European writers such as Niccolo Machiavelli
(Italy) and Thomas More (Great Britain). Early twentieth-century theorists include Henry Fayol (France) and Max Weber (Germany).

The orientations and values which managers hold about job outcomes
are to a great extent culturally determined. That is, they learn attitudes
and behaviors toward other people when they are socialized in their
native culture. If we are to clearly understand international cultures, we
must understand cultural variations in leadership style. A large number
of interpersonal problems involve some aspect of job-related maladjust-
ments. Geert Hofstede (1980) was one of the first persons to develop a
conceptual framework to determine whether North American management theories apply abroad. He noted the international relevancy of
North American theories of management in the areas of motivation,
leadership and organization. His observations have been corroborated
and refuted by other researchers (Sekaran, 1981).

Motivation

Motivation theories in the field of management are almost the exclu-
sive domain of North American writers, particularly David McClelland
(1961), Abraham Maslow (1954), Frederick Herzberg (1959), and Victor
Vroom (1964). McClelland's *achievement theory* states that people perform tasks because they have a need to achieve. Maslow's theory of the
hierarchy of needs postulates the human drive to fulfill basic physiologic
needs, first, then the other needs in the following order: security, social,

esteem, and self-actualization. Herzberg's *two-factor theory of motivation* consists of hygienic factors (the equivalent of Maslow's lower needs— physiological, security and social) and motivators (Maslow's higher needs— esteem and self-actualization). The hygienic factors may motivate only negatively, while only the motivators may motivate positively. Vroom's *expectancy theory* states that economic rewards are meaningful outcomes for people who have a desire (valence) for economic benefits, see a positive relationship between job performance and economic rewards, and expect to complete assigned tasks.

In Austrian, German, Swiss, and Israeli cultures working hard is motivated by an inner feeling of national obligation (Kanungo & Wright, 1983; Becker & Fritzche, 1987). The ethic of hard work growing from a feeling of national obligation is also prominent in Far East countries (Hamilton & Biggart, 1988; Hofstede & Bond, 1988). Security motivation is highest among African, Arab and Latin American countries (Almaney, 1981; Jones, 1988). Security and social motivation rank the highest among Latin Europeans, Far East, and Near East countries. We can compare national cultures to the "Type A" and "Type B" personalities of individual people. Type A people are aggressive, goal-oriented, competitive and under constant time pressure. Type B people are relaxed, easygoing and less task-oriented. Anglo, Germanic, and Nordic cultures tend to be Type A, and the other countries tend to be Type B. Stress among employees is more evident in Type A countries. Symptoms of stress include high blood pressure, stomach ulcers, migraine headaches, nervousness and heart disease.

Western workers tend to view people in isolated fragments, and behavior and thought are separately evaluated. This is seen in Western legal systems where people cannot be punished for thinking undesirable thoughts. But they are liable for carrying out undesirable actions. In some non-Western countries, however, no distinction is made between behavior and thought. And "wrong thoughts," even though no action follows, is adequate grounds for public rebuke. The synthesis of behavior and thought is seen in the many non-Western clients who seek help for crimes of attitude. Merely telling these clients that they are alright or worthy persons is seldom adequate therapy. They must be assisted to find a way to make amends with the "injured" person who was the subject of their errant thoughts. Non-Western workers are motivated by positive thoughts and relationships more than economic rewards or self-actualization. Their positive self-esteem does not come from success on the job; it comes from success in relationships with their significant other persons, who may be co-workers.

Leadership

Douglas McGregor (1957), William Ouchi (1982), Rensis Likert (1967), and Robert Blake and Jane Mouton (1964) are authors of popular leadership theories. McGregor's *Theory X versus Theory Y,* Ouchi's *Theory Z,* Likert's *four systems* and Blake and Mouton's *Managerial Grid* advocate subordinate participation with management decisions, with participation initiated by the manager. The autocratic or dictatorial style of management is described as being "top down" and absolute, analogous to the parent who rules a family with an iron hand. Power and control are usually centralized, and the degree of trust in others tends to be low. According to McGregor, this style of management is based on Theory X, the belief that people are basically lazy and need to be continually supervised. Theory X assumes that most people dislike work and will avoid it if possible, that most people lack job responsibility and exhibit little initiative, and that they work to survive. Thus, the manager must coerce, control and, occasionally, punish subordinates to get them to work. Theory Y assumes that most people enjoy work and are not inherently lazy. On the contrary, they are self-directed, and under proper conditions they will accept and seek responsibility. The Theory Y manager's role is to develop employees' potential.

Ouchi's Theory Z model is characterized by lifetime employment, nonspecialized careers, individual responsibility, concern for the total person, less formal control systems, consensus decision making, and slower rates of promotion. The model, which is based on effective Japanese management systems, has as its primary goal the desire to foster close, trusting, cooperative relationships within the work place. While it is unclear what criteria should be used to select this approach, there is some evidence that Theory Z firms are successful in improving productivity and employee morale. The key observation made by researchers is that this management approach can create a stable and cohesive work environment in which employee needs for inclusion, independence and minimal control are met (Ouchi & Johnson, 1978; Contino & Lorusso, 1982).

Likert uses the term "supportive management" to describe his four systems of management styles. System 1 is "exploitive-authoritative," an autocratic style. System 2, called "benevolent/authoriative," is a benovolent-dictator type of manager. System 3 is referred to as "consultative" management; and System 4 is "participation-group" or democratic. Other management theorists have used similar concepts to describe various styles of management and leaders who change styles based on situational factors. David Stephens (1981) observed that there is no reason to believe North Americans (and other Anglo persons) are innately Theory Y in orientation and citizens of other countries are innately Theory X. The autocratic style of leadership is a function of traditional family hierarchy, extreme social class differences, and lack of long-term formal training in participative management—conditions which characterize Third-World nations.

According to Shaker Zahra (1982), autocratic behavior is the predominant model in most underdeveloped nations; many of them are Moslim. Workers in these countries tend not to display initiative because of negative management control systems, few economic rewards and little recognition for jobs done well. A low level of creativity and a great amount of job mediocrity are the result of managerial practices and social class structural restraints. Stephens (1981) observed that the extreme social class differences between Latin managers and their subordinates partially accounts for their autocratic leadership style. It is socially unacceptable for Latin managers to include lower socioeconomic persons in the administrative decision-making process.

The Managerial Grid charts the extent to which managers are concerned for people and production. The five managerial types are: 1,9 managers who are low in concern for production but high in concern for people; 9,1 managers who are high in concern for production but low in concern for people; 9,9 managers who try to get work accomplished from committed personnel in a climate of trust and respect; 1,1 managers who have low concern for productivity and low concern for human relationships; and 5,5 managers who are middle of the road in terms of production and human relationships.

Rabindra Kanungo and Richard Wright (1983) conducted a study of British, French, Canadian, and Japanese managers. The results of the study revealed significant differences between cultures. The British managers placed greater importance on individual achievement and autonomy than the French. The French managers placed greater emphasis on organizationally controlled and interpersonally mediated job factors than the British. The French had stronger needs for security and self-esteem. British, Canadian, and Japanese managers were similar to each other. Kanungo and Wright were surprised by the latter finding — they had expected the Japanese to have job attitude profiles more closely resembling those of the French. Few Asian cultures fit the Western intrinsic-extrinsic paradigm. Asian worker self-sacrifice for the good of the organization is generally a source of intrinsic reward and fulfillment (Sengoku, 1985). To the extent this is true, the Confucianist work ethic does not fit Western models.

Perhaps success or failure has more to do with leadership style than any other variable. George England and Raymond Lee (1974) studied the relationship between managerial values and success in the United States, Japan, India, and Australia. They concluded:

> Successful managers tend to emphasize pragmatic dynamic achievement-oriented values, while less successful managers prefer static and passive values, the latter forming a framework descriptive of organizational stasis rather than organizational flux. More successful managers favor an achievement orientation and prefer an active role in interaction with other individuals useful in achieving the managers' organizational goals. They value a dynamic environment and are willing to take risks to achieve organizationally valued goals. Relatively less successful managers have values associated with a static, protected environment in which they take relatively passive roles and often enjoy extended seniority and security in their organizational positions (p. 416).

There is a new spirit among managers throughout the world who dare to innovate and deviate from traditional leadership styles. The rigid culture encapsulated conformist is gradually losing ground to managers who believe that the most appropriate style of leadership depends on the organization situation. According to Fred Fiedler's *contingency* (or *situational*) *model* (1967), the leader's situation is determined by three variables: leader-member relationship, task structure and leader power position. But leaders cannot choose their styles at will; what is acceptable depends to a large degree on the cultural conditioning of the subordinates. Regardless of how much formal power and authority an organization confers on its managers, *usable power* and *usable authority* are granted by their subordinates. Managers in Anglo and Nordic countries are more likely to deviate from traditional leadership styles than those in other countries.

Unlike Western managers, who generally are expected to initiate new actions, managers in some developing countries have the primary function of maintaining the status quo. They are usually not rewarded for initiating change. Thus, they entrench themselves in their positions and encourage their subordinates to do likewise. Even the "work" of Western-oriented professional helpers may clash with the folkways and mores of traditional Third-World cultures, especially if the helping modality is rational, secular, and future-oriented. As managers of the helping process, these practitioners are linear in their thinking. They conceive of client problems as having a clear beginning and a conceivable non-status-quo end, with intermediate changes between. This approach is a stark contrast to the Hindu and Buddhist belief that life continues in an endless circle. Certainly, if societal norms and philosophies of life can influence leadership styles, then they should also be considered when selecting therapeutic intervention strategies.

The leadership styles appropriate for international situations leave little room for the myopic or rigid personality (Chang, 1985). Each situation will influence a manager's perspective and techniques of leadership. The most logical method of analyzing the leadership process is an interactional one which takes into account the interaction of these basic factors: the leader, the organization, and the environment. Multidimensional leadership is necessarily a dynamic interaction process involving the manager with his or her own personality, the organization with its particular needs and cultural characteristics, and the environment in which the workers and organization exist. Good leadership includes accomplishing tasks by making the organization's objective coincide with the goals and interest of its members. When all things are considered, managerial competence is very important in determining a leader's success. An effective organization, in an Asian sense, runs itself and the leader is accepted as a part of the team. Lao-Tse (1944) advised:

A leader is best
When people barely know he exists,
Not so good when people obey and acclaim him,
Worse when they despise him.
"Fail to honor people,
They fail to honor you";
But of a good leader, who talks little,
When his work is done, his aim fulfilled,
They will say, "We did this ourselves."

Throughout the ages, the art of human leadership has held a basic fascination for people in many fields. There has been speculation by historians, philosophers, and management specialists concerning the qualities or conditions that have endowed some persons, though not countless others, with successful leadership capabilities. Both those in authority and those under it strive to diagnose by careful dissection the discarded purposes and organizational goals that result when international leadership is unproductive.

It is counterproductive for practitioners to "treat all foreign workers alike." For example, Mexican workers are not Argentines; Catholics are not Protestants; men are not women; and socialists are not capitalists. There are some human characteristics that all people share (for example, physical needs for food and shelter), there are some characteristics that people share with certain other people (for example, language and trade), and there are some characteristics that people share with no other groups (for example, unique racial or ethnic historical conditions). The secret to helping workers from various cultures is knowing the similarities and differences between ethnic groups. The following illustration shows how some of the concepts discussed earlier may or may not fit Mexican workers.

WORKERS IN MEXICO

After World War II, the pace of Mexican migration into the United States increased significantly, and by 1984 more than 9 million of the United States' 15.9 million Hispanic people were of Mexican descent. Despite Mexico's close proximity to the United States and the fact that nearly 4 million Mexican citizens visit the United States annually, the country and its people are often viewed inaccurately and negatively. Misperceptions and stereotypes such as Mexico is a flat, hot, dry country and its citizens are lazy are commonplace. In reality, Mexico's topography includes mountains, jungles and fertile valleys; and Mexicans tend to be hard-working people characterized by a strong work ethic.

Perceptions of Mexico as a bankrupt nation are also inaccurate. In 1985 Mexico's economic output was the fifteenth highest in the world. Furthermore, Mexico is the United States' third-largest trading partner and its most important oil supplier. Like all countries, Mexico is an extremely diverse nation; its complexity is evident in its history, economy, social life and foreign relations. What is normal and functional behavior in one country may be abnormal and dysfunctional in another. It is imperative that we not define reality according to a monocultural value system. Many foreign companies, including those from the United States, have important investments in Mexico. Most Mexican subsidiaries of U.S. corporations rank high in payment of wages and fringe benefits. They are also leaders in providing training opportunities. Foreign executives have found that it is important to maintain close personal contacts with government officials and to maintain a good public image in the labor-relations field. These factors have coalesced to make U.S. companies choice places for employment among Mexican nationals. Now, let's consider specific management styles befitting Mexico's cultural, business, and work climate.

Leadership Styles

As we have seen, leadership consists of the total pattern of a leader's actions as well as how these actions are perceived by employees. The leadership style represents an individual's philosophy, skills, and attitudes. Theory X type leaders (who coerce and control employees), Y leaders (mainly concerned with the development of employees' job potential) and Z-style leaders (a hybrid of X and Y) are seen in varying degrees in Mexico but most Mexican leaders are X types. They centralize power and decision making in themselves while at the same time assuming full responsibility and authority. Few Mexican managers are participative leaders. The participative leader and his or her subordinates act as a single social unit. However, the general trend in multinational companies located in Mexico is toward wider use of participative practices. It is questionable whether Theory Z-type organizations—distinguished by lifetime employment, specialized careers, individual responsibility, concern for the total person, consensus decision making, informal administrative control systems and slow rates of promotion—will soon catch on in Mexico. The reason for this skepticism is the currently unfavorable economic climate in Mexico.

Job Satisfaction

As in other countries, job satisfaction in Mexico is positively correlated with age and high occupational status and negatively correlated with high turnover, absenteeism, and organization size. However, there is little correlation between job satisfaction and productivity. Mexican workers have a long history of being productive in unpleasant, menial jobs in order to keep a job and earn enough for subsistence. It is not what they produce but rather having something to produce that results in satisfaction. When there is a positive relationship between job satisfaction and productivity in Mexico, it is likely to be job performance that results in satisfaction rather than productivity.

New Trends

In many instances, increased urbanization has meant a decline in community life and the absence of meaningful social activities. Each year, more Mexican workers find themselves trapped in impersonal technostructures which once were only characteristic of Western people. Gradually, the desire to meet, exchange ideas and develop close relationships is being unfulfilled. Traditional organizations are not providing the mechanisms for closeness. If the number of Mexican workers exhibiting sociopathologies is an indication, there is a growing hunger for intimacy, relatedness, care, affection, and understanding which the major institutes of employment, religion, and family are not providing. Better jobs and more pay will not meet these needs. Both Western and non-Western workers are trapped in the miracles of change. With increased reliance on science and technology, bureaucratization and computerization, a dehumanized culture is growing worldwide. Within this culture the individual does not seem to have much worth. A deterministic-behavioristic view prevails in which workers are merely cogs in a larger machine. Furthermore, increased mobility compounds this situation. Workers follow jobs instead of friends, and this detaches them from permanent significant relationships which provide positive identity and wholesome values. There is ample evidence that more, not fewer, Third-World workers will become afflicted with conditions associated with job burnout.

DIFFERENT STYLES OF DEALING

The North American socialization process produces independent, free-wheeling business executives — many of whom are perceived throughout the world as unpredictable, illogical, and insensitive (Heikal, 1980; Herzberg, 1984; Graham, 1985). American executives have a lot of discretion when making business deals. Conversely, non-Western decision making is usually a group consensus process which leaves little room for individual action. Consensus is achieved through an elaborate, time-consuming process that unnerves most Westerners. Interestingly, these differences show up in preferences for styles of helping in therapy.

Traditional Asians consider it presumptuous and offensive for an individual to accept sole responsibility for making decisions for other people. Furthermore, when making decisions, Asians use indirect language and try to maintain rather neutral facial expressions. The locus of decision making and responsibility is asymmetrical; the individual is subjected to the will of the group. This is counter to the typical Western symmetrical locus of decision making in which one individual makes a decision and other persons accept responsibility for carrying it out. The Confucian ethic demands unanimity through compromise on almost every issue until a consensus is reached. No one must ever be completely defeated, because to do so will cause them to lose face. In fact, compared with Western styles of decision making, most Third-World peoples exhibit asymmetrical behavior (Applebaum, 1984; Hofstede, 1984; Neff, 1985; Sengoku, 1985).

U.S. business executives are characterized by foreign executives as being obsessed with punctuality, action oriented, inclined to develop shallow interpersonal relationships with their business colleagues, and extremely self-centered. U.S. therapists are characterized this way, too. These behaviors are opposite of those exhibited by executives and professional helpers in most other countries. The peoples of northern Europe are the closest to kindred souls an American can find abroad—and they are not extremely close kin. When North American executives encounter persons in developing nations who do not display "proper" deference, they often become hostile. Organization consultants tell of an American manager of an engineering company with operations in Nigeria. The poor fellow spent several days in jail for shouting insults at and exchanging blows with his Nigerian co-workers. When the precipitating events were sorted out, it was clear that the problem was largely poor cross-cultural communication. The Nigerians displayed brusque behavior— culturally acceptable in their country—that the American interpreted as an insult.

The British place a high value on the rights of the individual against collective power (Gospel, 1988). Conversely, the West Germans subordinate the individual to the collective. The British place great faith in the ability of the individual to shape the direction of his or her government, while West Germans place considerably less faith in the efficacy of the individual in government. The British exhibit relatively more interpersonal trust than the Germans who exhibit more aggressiveness. Once these characteristics are known, it is not surprising that British workers are slightly more individualistic than Germans. Also, British executives are more likely to welcome new ideas or innovations, whereas Germans prefer to maintain the status quo. Strategic administrative decisions are made by top management in both countries, but operational and personnel decisions are made at a lower organizational level in Britain than in Germany (Kanungo & Wright, 1983).

U.S. managers discover that they must deal differently with co-workers and subordinates in Germany than in Britain. German managers tend to delegate less to subordinates than British managers do. British managers attach greater importance to employee rewards and benefits, recruiting, training, and promoting workers; German companies place greater reliance on rules, procedures, and proven routines. One of the first fallacies U.S. managers trip over when dealing with the British is the assumption that "they are just like us." Americans and British share a common language and heritage, but they are not the same. Another fallacy is to think of the British as a homogeneous population; they are actually a polyglot of cultures. Nor are the British as motivated by money as their American counterparts. Many British people still consider America the lost colony and at times have difficulty "lowering" themselves to the American level. They also enjoy their privacy. For example, the question "What do you do?" is considered an invasion of privacy by many British citizens. Instead of being "small talk" or an "icebreaker," the question is as much an invasion of privacy as asking an American "What is your age?" or "How much money do you earn?"

German managers, like U.S. managers, tend to have experience in more than one firm and are specialists within the same industry. They are slow to reach decisions; committees make most German managerial decisions. Unlike most U.S. managers, the Germans are concerned with the precision of written agreements when other staff members are present. Furthermore, they are sensitive to being compared unfavorably with the French and the British (Kanungo & Wright, 1983). While their demeanor may be stoic, it is a mistake to believe that Germans do not have a sense of humor. Like most Europeans, their sense of humor is often extremely localized. Loud or indiscriminate joviality is not well received in Europe.

Japanese managers are even more different from U.S. managers. Their style of dealing evolves around problem identification, harmonious decision making and saving face (Kanungo & Wright, 1983). The Japanese action-orientation typically is accompanied by a need to be very deliberate in negotiations so that they can move in on the next project with few loose ends. Japanese executives enter negotiations to ratify already reached agreements, while U.S. executives view negotiation sessions as opportunities to further define the deal. The Japanese are loyal to their employers. They are more concerned about the success of their company than their own individual well-being. They resent being put in a position of having to admit failure or inefficacy. Unlike most U.S. executives, they are ill at ease working with abrasive, egotistical or harsh individuals. Americans who feel uncomfortable with silence during negotiations tend to fill in the gaps with chitchat; Japanese prefer silence.

The Asian use of "yes" and "no" may cause confusion due to differences in the grammatical structure between English and many Asian languages. A "yes" to a negative question in the Asian grammatical syntax means a "no" in English. For example, a manager asks his Asian colleague, "Haven't you finished the report?" His colleague answers "yes," meaning, "Yes, I have not finished the report." One of the techniques used by traditional Asians to avoid confrontation is to blame themselves for the other person's mistake. The correct behavior for the second person is to say, "No, it is not your fault." This requires a degree of honesty and humility that non-Eastern managers frequently find difficult.

PROTOCOL

Few executives throughout the world share the U.S. way of doing business in a hurry (McCaffrey & Hafner, 1985; Snowden, 1985; Bristline, 1986; Smedley & Zimmerer, 1986). From a non-U.S. perspective, time is not "lost" when it is used to get to know business acquaintances. Unlike the Western concept of linear time, many nations (particularly those in Latin America and Africa) have adopted the concept of cyclical or circular time. It cannot be lost, it merely continues into the future. Executives and professional helpers in most nations prefer to do business slowly and with friends, not strangers. In addition, most of the nations of the world deal in long-term, personal business relationships. In China this is called *guanxi*, a network of friends who do business with each other. They eat, drink, and play together. This type of long-term personal commitment occurs to a lesser extent among North American business executives.

Anglo Americans in particular prefer to restrict gift-giving to conditions that minimize incurring social obligations. Consequently, they customarily give gifts to commemorate special events such as birthdays, anniversaries and religious festivals. In most other cultures social reciprocities involving gifts is commonplace. Gifts are almost always given to business associates. In most Latin American, African, and Far East countries gifts are obligatory in business dealings. In the United States we mistakenly call this "bribery" or "extortion." Great care must be taken to give the right gifts. Usually, they are not of great monetary value. In the Far East the gifts must be neither so personal as to embarrass the recipients nor so expensive as to cause them to lose face. Appropriate gifts include liquor, corporate mementos, and candy (but liquor is taboo in Islamic countries and should never be given as a gift). African executives favor small monetary gifts. In Europe gift-giving is more of a courtesy than an obligation. Flowers (except red roses, chrysanthemums, and white flowers) are an acceptable gift for the host's wife, and toys are okay for his children.

Now for a brief overview of other selected generalized business-related customs and courtesies that can cause stress to outsiders. (See the Appendix for additional examples of customs and courtesies.) These generalizations should not be substituted for *getting* to know each client personally. They may or may not fit the generations.

Arabs

- Wives are not taken to business entertainment functions. Almost all executives are men.
- Moslims do not pass food with their left hand. This is their "toilet" hand.
- Long waits before appointments are typical and interruptions are frequent.
- It is an insult to refuse hospitable offers.
- Acknowledge persons of senior rank and status first.
- Don't inquire about a man's wife and daughters.
- Don't publicly criticize a colleague.
- At a meeting sit as near as possible to the person they want to do business with.
- "Yes" or "no" often means "maybe" or even the opposite.
- Meetings normally end with an offer of coffee or tea, and future meetings are arranged at this time.

Europeans

- In many European countries, coffee and dessert may come before drinks.
- There are few female executives in European corporations.
- When there are several people in a room you enter, make a little bow and then go around to each person and shake their hands.

Latin Europeans, more so than other Europeans, are paradoxes to U.S. visitors. Unlike most U.S. citizens who are products of the Protestant work ethic, Latin Europeans have a Catholic ethic which de-emphasizes the work ethic and places more value on the family. The demeanor of the French in particular puzzles unenlightened Americans. The French are generally argumentative, friendly, sardonic, and humorous. Americans are likely to be humorous but seldom will they be humorous and sardonic. But it is the French worker's view of his or her job as not having value for its own sake that is of more interest to us in this chapter. Work has value for an individual's social image among family and friends. Other points about the French are the following:

- Intense competition is seen as antagonistic, power-hungry behavior.
- The French place little value on working overtime; they have the longest paid vacations in the world.
- They are individualistic but not boastful. Boasting is considered a sign of weakness or immaturity.
- The French are extremely status conscious; they are categorized according to job and social origin. Yet, they are hard to impress and impatient with people who try.
- They are punctual in attending business meetings and social activities.

Latin Americans

- Latin Americans are frequently late to meetings, but they expect North Americans to be on time.
- They avoid the use of first names until a friendship is established.
- The pace of business is slow.
- As in Europe, in Latin America it is proper to bow when entering a room with several people present and then to shake their hands.
- When conducting business, one should dress conservatively.
- Latin American women are liberated in many countries, but few of them are business executives. *Macho-oriented* males will not want to

conduct business with women. In many Latin American countries, it is common for men and women to be in separate rooms even during informal gatherings.

- Latin American business executives tend to let chance or fate guide their destiny. That is, they adopt the philosophy, "What will be will be," and they are willing to accept the outcome. Therefore, they take more risks than their American colleagues.
- Most business is conducted on the *manana* concept—an indefinite future. Sometimes, a Latin American will promise to do something at a particular time while knowing that he or she will not be on time. This is not perceived by the promisor as lying. Rather, it is perceived as making the other party happy at the time of the promise.
- Decisions are made at the top echelon of corporations, and they are usually finalized in person, not by letter or telephone.

Africans

- Business meetings usually begin with general talk that can last for a long time.
- Interpersonal relationships evolve around sincerity, trust and friendship. Friends visit each other at any time; they do not have to wait for formal invitations or office appointments. However, business is almost always discussed in an office, restaurant or bar but not in the home.
- Ethnic identity is a major factor in who gets a job and what kind. Kinship is the primary basis for an individual's duties, rights, marriage, inheritance and succession.
- Although time is a flexible concept throughout most of the African continent, managers in the various countries are usually "on time" when meeting with foreigners. They expect foreigners to be on time too.
- African managers usually model their behavior after managers from the European country that colonized theirs. There are clear replications of British and French management styles, for example.
- While they occupy very few corporate and government managerial positions, African women are liberated in many other areas. In fact, there is a long history of African women being involved in tribal leadership. Even so, many African men have great difficulty dealing with women in formal organization positions of authority.

Japanese

- Sentences are frequently left unfinished so that the other person may finish them in his or her own mind.
- The Japanese listener will make noises of understanding and encouragement. *"Hai"* is a common word used to convey "yes" or "I understand" or "I'm listening."
- They avoid praising their products or services; they let their literature or a go-between discuss them.
- They seldom take their spouse to a business dinner.

Chinese

- Avoid self-centered conversations using the word "I."
- They don't single out a colleague as having unique qualities.
- Women expect to be treated as equals.
- Family names are given first. Teng Tsien-mo should be addressed "Mr. Teng." (This is true in Korea, too.)
- They use proper contacts to arrange meetings, and avoid letters and telephone calls to make deals.

BURNOUT

Workers throughout the world are amazingly adaptive organisms. However, under conditions of physical and psychological stress survival adjustments can be impeded, and ultimately, if stress is extreme, people will die. *Stress* refers to any assault or demand placed on a person or system. Perhaps what I have described are conditions of modern living, or as Louis Kaplan (1959) observed: "Despite the fact that they spend a large proportion of their time among other people, this relationship is often impersonal and mechanical. Many people are merely cogs in a working world where no one really cares for them as persons.... The high rate of personal and social maladjustment found among social isolates in our large cities testifies to the intensity of the strain under which these people live" (p. 200). The longer people are on the job, the less they self-disclose. Slowly, a light seems to go out in their eyes.

The deadening effect of mindless, sterile role conformity and the inevitable negative effect of workers trying to hide their feelings of frustration, anger, and inadequacy should not be minimized. Therapists are discovering with alarming scientific proof that one of the reasons why most workers fail to self-actualize, why they fail to fulfill many of their potentialities as persons, why they frequently become ill, is because the daily patterns of existence among employees is characterized by impersonality, by playing rigidly prescribed roles, by self-manipulation and manipulation of others. Inability to find a way to relieve the incipient job-related stress leads to *burnout* — the syndrome of emotional exhaustion and cynicism that occurs after long hours of physical and psychological strain.

What does burnout mean? Dictionary definitions say that it means failing, wearing out, and becoming exhausted from excessive demands on our energy, strength and resources. After studying several human services organizations, Cary Cherniss (1968) defined burnout as psychological withdrawal from work in response to excessive stress or dissatisfaction with job-related activities. This is not much different from Christina Maslach's observation (1977) that burnout is the loss of concern for the people with whom one is working in response to stress. We could define it in terms of the extent to which people have become separated or withdrawn from the original meaning or purpose of their work, and the degree to which they are alienated from supervisors, co-workers, and the company. All of these definitions were poetically and cogently summarized by Herbert Freudenberger (1980): "Under the strain of living in our complex world, people's inner resources are consumed as if by fire, leaving a great emptiness inside, although their outer shells may be more or less unchanged" (p. xv).

Myths and Stereotypes

It is ironical and sad that managers — individuals trained to diagnose and prescribe for others — often behave in unnecessarily stressful ways. As a whole, managers throughout the world pay little attention to their own burning out. Furthermore, they spend less time with burned-out subordinates, and when counseling them seem to have little to say. They tend to repress the thought of burnout. Paraphrasing Emily Mumford and James Skipper (1967): Without being aware of how much they demand of themselves, such persons can experience a disturbing sense of personal discomfort when they face the burned-out worker. Burnout is a painful reminder of the realistic limits of the science of management and the skills of professional helpers, as well as a reminder of human mortality. Non-Western unskilled workers burn out for the same reasons that Western workers burn out: low pay, long hours, inadequate fringe benefits and high task-quotas. With little chance for job advancement, some workers frequently switch jobs in order to enhance their salaries by a few more pennies an hour. In short, being underpaid and overworked is a stressful condition. Perhaps in the end, unskilled workers burn out for the same reason that most workers burn out: There is inadequate financial and emotional compensation for their demanding jobs. In this regard, most Japanese workers are well off. But this gain is frequently offset by employer demands for high job performance (Sengoku, 1985).

In *Staff Burnout*, Cherniss (1980) gave four reasons why burnout is an important issue. First, it negatively affects a worker's team morale and individual well-being. Second, it negatively affects the quality of job performance. Third, it impacts negatively on administrative functioning. Fourth, it is an important issue even if it is not experienced by workers; some of their relatives and friends are likely to have burned out. By now it should be clear that the issue of burnout has more than economic dimensions. Sure, lost wages and profit are important considerations. However, of foremost consideration are the wasted human lives. Money can be replaced, but human beings are not replaceable. Management can get others to do their jobs, but they cannot replace burned-out workers because of the uniqueness of each person. Only recently have graduate schools with helping-oriented programs focused on skills for working with burned-out persons.

But I am not talking about isolated individuals who suffer burnout in the solitude of themselves. On the contrary, burnout affects the significant other persons of the individuals afflicted with it. Increased urbanization and job mechanization have meant a decline in non-Western community life and the absence of meaningful social activities. Each year more non-Western workers find themselves trapped in impersonal technostructures in which their desire to meet, exchange ideas and develop close relationships are unfulfilled (Pines & Aronson, 1981; Maslach, 1982). Most places of employment seem to have lost their ability to provide ways of finding these satisfactions. The traditional cultures of developing countries still provide the mechanisms for closeness. But if the growing number of people in developing countries who exhibit social pathologies is an indicator, then there is a tremendous undercurrent hunger for intimacy, relatedness, care, affection, and understanding that the traditional institutions of employment and family are no longer providing. In short, practitioners have paid too little attention to changing world conditions.

Erich Fromm (1968) called attention to the need of people to develop wholesome personalities through socialization. The personality, he noted, is shaped by the way in which persons relate to each other, and this relationship is determined by the socioeconomic and political structure of their nation. The shift to modern technology takes a heavy toll in developing nations. Socialization is disrupted and mental illnesses increase, but adequate mental health services are not available.

Helpers Are Workers, Too

I do not want us to dismiss too quickly the "burden" that many helpers carry who have burned-out clients. Besides, helpers burn out too. Helpers who burn out imagine themselves as somehow being responsible for the decisions of others. Anguish, abandonment and despair are natural responses to these unrealistic societal responsibilities. Most practitioners who accept this type of responsibility cannot help but feel a profound sense of guilt (even anxiety) when they choose destinies for others. "Who can then prove that I am the proper person to impose, by my own choice, my conception of man upon mankind?" Sartre (1965) asked. "If a voice speaks to me, it is still I myself who must decide whether the voice is or is not that of an angel" (p. 293). Burning out is sometimes the result of finding out that we hear neither angels nor devils, only human voices. Too many helpers forget that they do not own the client's problems.

An important theme of helping, one which most helpers can identify with and find comfort in, is the notion that they are mere mortal people — some good, some bad: "The world is made up of people, but the people of the world forget this. It is hard to believe that, like ourselves, other people are born of women, reared by parents, teased by brothers, . . . consoled by wives, . . . flattered by grandchildren, and buried by parsons and priests with the blessing of the church and the tears of those left behind. . . . It is easier to speak of fate, and destiny, and waves of the future than to see the ways we determine our own fate, right now and in the immediate past and future" (Menninger, 1942).

Numerous researchers have dealt with ways to combat burnout. First, people must avoid false cures such as the use of the defense mechanism of denial as a way of avoiding pain. Denial is not always bad, but once it becomes obsessive and crosses over the pain threshold into dulling and deadening the senses, it works against us. If practitioners continue to deaden themselves, they create havoc in their lives; the problem will only get worse. Camouflage does not make the burnout go away. No matter what form it takes, denial does not solve problems. Another form of denial is to become other-directed. The afflicted person suspends his own motivating forces and abdicates his responsibility by acquiescing to the will of others. When people become other-directed, they deny their own importance and mold themselves according to externally imposed standards. This is how many practitioners behave.

There are two reliable cures for burnout: closeness and being inner-directed. Before helpees can achieve closeness with others, they have to achieve it with themselves. People who burn out seldom spend enough time with themselves in a constructive manner. Closeness is anywhere and with anyone one chooses. Inner-directedness is not being selfish. Rather, it is taking time out for one's own self. The purpose, of course, is to do things that are good for our renewal. People in the helping professions should watch for signs of burnout even when things appear to be going well with their clients. It is too easy for non-Western workers to become martyrs who defy their own gratification. Helpers should watch for tiredness before it becomes extreme exhaustion. Attention should be paid to physical symptoms such as colds or nagging pains in the back. Also, helpees should monitor themselves for shifts in attitude, especially towards self-doubt or pity.

Many people who choose to enter helping professions usually have a sense of altruistic mission. They are compassionate and caring, which makes them especially vulnerable to the excessive demands that are made on them. Frequently, they remain unaware of their vulnerability. It is then that burnout is likely to occur. Above all else, they are oblivious to burnout signs of growing rigid, increasing negativism and cynicism. There are ample examples of helpers who believe that they must be congruent and in control of themselves at all times. Other people, they think, may be incongruent and out of control, but not them. Some helpers even believe that assisting others to self-actualize is enough reward to keep themselves going. Third-World women, in particular, tend to behave this way. This kind of vicarious identification with the successes of others is seldom not enough over the long run. Then there are helpers who believe that they must give most of their time to their job and virtually little to their own family. I call this the "show-must-go-on" attitude, even at the expense of one's own health and happiness.

Finally, there are helpers who believe that if they do their jobs well, then they always will be appreciated and adequately rewarded.

The stereotype of the most effective people being the persons who push their own needs in the background is the fuel that when ignited can burn up an individual's energies and dreams. There is a tendency within Third-World countries to minimize the importance of self-love. In Aristotle's time, it was generally accepted that we should be our own best friend, and our best friend is someone who wishes for our well-being. This is the kind of self-love a person should feel in his or her own behalf. Only if people have strong positive feelings for themselves are they then able to have these feelings for others. But people who gratify their appetites and emotions in self-destructive ways lack the qualities necessary for assisting others to show restraint. In this regard we can learn much from Eastern and African religions and philosophies.

The person burning out may be irritable, angry, resistant to change or listless. Fatigue is a frequent symptom that many Third-World workers in particular experience because of a painful erosion of their traditional values. Other social symptoms include high resistance to going to work, a sense of failure, guilt and blame, frequent clock-watching, dread of contact with supervisors, avoiding discussions of work with friends, reverting to rules and regulations, and self-preoccupation. Socio-psychological disorders are not less real or less painful than physical injuries. There are many well-documented physical reactions to psychological stress—including migraine headaches, nausea, belching, diarrhea, dryness of the mouth, excessive salivation, heartburn, ulcers, asthma, and rhinitis. As non-Western people become more like Westerners, they will have proportionately more of these disorders. We might be able to learn how to deal with this situation by observing traditional curers.

Burnout among Western and non-Western managers is especially high and the reasons are obvious. Supervising people on a continuous basis is emotionally and physically draining. This is compounded by the fact that in all work situations there are circumstances beyond the manager's control. It takes an extremely well-adjusted individual to be able to distinguish between failure to help a subordinate achieve a certain goal and failure as a person. The end result of therapy may not be what either the helper or the helpee who seeks relief from burnout wants.

Certainly we always try to eliminate suffering and especially pain. But it is not the task of therapy merely to reduce mental and physical suffering. One may be inclined to do this because one assumes that the elimination of suffering is an essential or even *the* essential drive of man, as psychoanalysis proclaims in the pleasure principle. But placing this in the foreground would often *not* help the patient. The idea of the pleasure principle, particularly when applied to normal life, overlooks the enormous significance of tension for self-realization in its highest forms. Pleasure, in the sense of relief from tension, may be a necessary respite. But it is a phenomenon of standstill. One can achieve the right attitude toward the problem of the elimination of suffering in patients and in normal individuals only if one considers its significance for self-realization and its relationship to the value of health. If the patient is to make the choice we have mentioned, he may still suffer but may *no longer feel sick,* i.e. though somewhat disordered and stricken by certain anxiety (Goldstein, 1959).

Finally, it is important for helpers not to delude themselves into thinking that they can change clients. M. Esther Harding (1965) was correct: "We cannot change anyone else; we can change only ourselves, and then usually only when the elements that are in need of reform have become conscious through their reflection in someone else" (p. 75). Helpers who are dealing with job-related issues are fighting a battle of credibility on at least three fronts: first, against the pressure of society for 100 percent success, second, against the needs of clients for 100 percent success and, third, against their own internal pressure for 100 percent success. Unlike a television or movie script, professional helpers are not 100 percent successful. Helping is still more of an art than a science. A job environment merely adds to the difficulty of performing the art of helping.

In summary, workers of every country bring to therapy culturally unique ways of interacting. The usefulness of Western approaches depends on the situation. Competent helpers are individuals who are able to make sense of ethnic and national diversity, have connections with relevant client country therapy resources, and are flexible. In summary, they exercise common sense when dealing with other people. But even with this a helper may be unable to solve a client's job-related problems, which in turn may impact negatively on non-job-related activities.

Chapter 6

CROSS–NATIONAL COMMUNICATION

B roadly speaking, communication can be defined as a process by
which a person sends a message—verbal or nonverbal or behavioral
stimuli—to someone with the conscious intent of evoking a response. In
reality, "one cannot *not* communicate" (Watzlawick et al., 1967, p. 49).
All human behavior is potentially a communication. We are concerned
in this book with only behavior that is informative. By this I mean any
behavior, intentional or unintentional, interpreted by another person.
Most of what is communicated is not interpreted as it was intended.
Thus, *effective communication* is the process in which the receiver interprets the message in the same way intended by the sender. This is
extremely difficult to do across cultures. An unknown author summarized the difficulty thusly: "I know you believe you understand what you
think I said, but I am not sure you realize that what you heard is not what
I meant!"

The overarching element of the helper-helpee communication process
is empathy. Clients are influenced to follow a therapeutic regimen when
their helpers project empathic credibility. Whether they come of their
own free will or are coerced, most clients enter the social services arena
with preconceived notions of what is interpersonally satisfying. Consequently, unless through communication helpers are able to establish
rapport with clients, much of their skills will be unused or inappropriately
used. We cannot separate communication from culture. There have been
numerous attempts to explain the importance of *intercultural communication,*
transcultural communication and *interracial communication* (Rich, 1974; Heikal,
1980; Kim, 1984; Gudykunst & Ting-Toomey, 1988). I am adding yet
another term *cross-national communication* to the list. By this term I refer
to a subset of intercultural communication across societal boundaries
between individuals who differ in ethnicity.

There are at least five barriers to accurate cross-national communication (Barna, 1970). First, language differences impede accurate communication. Second, nonverbal communication is frequently less articulate

123

and more emotional. Third, cultural stereotypes distort meanings. Fourth, most people tend to evaluate what others say and do as either good or bad. Fifth, a high level of anxiety, which characterizes cross-national interactions, tends to distort meanings. The most effective helpers are skilled in intercultural communication (Schroeder & Ibrahim, 1982; Sundberg, 1981; Arrendondo-Dowd & Gonsalves, 1980).

THE COMMUNICATION PROCESS

By the very nature of their training, all professional helpers should be concerned with helping clients. However, helping is a complex task that requires an understanding of human relations. Verbal and nonverbal communications are integral parts in both the definition and treatment of illnesses.

> Verbal and nonverbal influences interact in ways previously unsuspected in processes intimately involved in illnesses. The study of this interaction discloses the profound effect of the two signalling systems in the life of feeling and of bodily processes, normal and pathological. Ulcers of the stomach seem clear manifestations of illnesses; tears and blushing are not so named. The second signalling system, verbal processes, regulates bodily functions as when someone weeps in recounting a loss. The name "illness," on the other hand, poorly differentiates ulcers from tears: This is one of the many errors of the symbolic process (Lewis, 1972).

Communication constitutes the basic process of human interaction. Most definitions of human communication include explicit or implicit references to a dynamic, irreversible process. Equally important, it is a symbolic process that allows humans to transcend their physical limitations. That is, through communication (symbolic interaction) humans are able to recall their past, analyze their present, and predict their future. Without symbolization each of us would be trapped in our own skin, unable to communicate our personal experiences to others. Through communication, illnesses are described, cures are discovered, and rehabilitation plans are devised. Usually, the helpee must send the first message in a helper-helpee communication: "Help me, I can't solve my problem." Most people are hesitant to admit they need help, and it is only after being told that they are in need of help by their significant-other persons do they adopt the helpee role. Maladjustment implies exemption from normal social role responsibilities, a condition that must be changed, a desire to "get well," and an obligation to cooperate with the helper. There are many factors that provide a context for helper-helpee communication, including environment, culture, social roles, and power relationships.

Environment. We need only to look around us in order to see how the physical environment affects the quality of the helper-helpee interaction. Consider, for example, the differences between an inner-city slum and an affluent suburb, mountains and seashores, chemically polluted and nonpolluted communities. The manner in which helpers utilize office space can influence client perceptions. Proper lighting, ventilation, and temperature are also components in putting clients at ease. Environments are equivalent to nonverbal statements about health care—they cause practitioners and clients to feel fearful or relaxed, cheerful or sad, claustrophobic or free.

Culture. Culture preference or bias is a major problem in interaction. As discussed in earlier chapters, members of different cultures not only speak different languages, they also live in different worlds. Inability to understand and communicate with culturally different people will render helpers unable to be optimally effective treating all clients (Hecht & Ribeau, 1984). Mediterranean, African, Asian, and Caribbean peoples have a preference for right hemisphere of the brain activities, while Western Europeans are left-hemisphere peoples (Trotter, 1979). The former group is characterized by emotionalism and spiritualism, and the latter group is oriented toward intellectualism and rationality. Also, Latinos, Africans, Arabs, and Asians have been described as being *polychronic* — they do many things at the same time, are circular in behavior, repetitive in speech, and time is not of essence. Western Europeans are characterized as being *monochronic* — linear in thinking, sequential in behavior, clock-oriented, and work-oriented.

Social roles. Shakespeare said it very well in *As You Like It:* "All the world's a stage/ And all men and women merely players/ They have their exits and their entrances,/ And one man in his time plays many parts." Some individuals forget that "helper" is a role and not themselves. Relatedly, "client" is a role and not the essence of the individual so labeled. Inflexible role players are unable to change when situations require role adaptation.

Power. It is no secret that professional helpers have power over clients. In some situations, helpers who are authoritarian and dominating tend to be less helpful than their colleagues who are democratic and encourage client initiative. Authoritarian helper messages to clients follow the classic power flow interaction process: (1) communication flows more readily laterally between helpers or between clients than either downward from helpers to clients or upward from clients to helpers; (2) more communication goes from helpers to clients than from clients to helpers; (3) clients are more cautious than helpers about the messages they send; (4) helpers and clients incorrectly assume the extent they are being understood by each other; (5) clients distort the messages they receive from helpers; and (6) both helpers and clients tend to avoid talking to each other.

Part of the helper's dilemma is that he or she must be sufficiently detached from clients to exercise sound judgment and at the same time have enough concern for clients to provide sensitive, empathic care. It is possible for a helper to suppress on the conscious level emotional responses while working with clients, but this detachment does not remove the stress and concern hidden in the unconscious domain of the mind. The pathological process of detachment which tends to produce mature helpers also tends to produce cynical clinicians. The therapeutic relationship evolves around technical skills, impartiality and the ability to communicate with clients. In our imperfect world, we tend to expect perfection from individuals to whom we entrust our secrets.

A Delicate Relationship

The helper-helpee relationship necessarily is based on acceptance, expectation, support, and stimulation. "Acceptance" means to unconditionally give oneself to and to receive another person. The helper who accepts a client is communicating "I will apply my knowledge to help you, and, as I do this, I will try to meet your needs, try to understand you, and try to respect your right to retain your own identity." In most instances, these nurturing qualities are not easily taught or freely applied. Yet, the ability to accept a client is the beginning of the helping relationship.

"Expectation" means the projection that responsive behavior will occur. Helpers expect their clients to follow the therapy plan, while clients expect their helpers to devise the best possible health plan for them. Usually, helpers are quite explicit and direct in their expectations. Clients tend to be less direct and to rely more on nonverbal behavior to express themselves. For some helpers, the support and stimulus needed to continue working with a client comes from positive interactions. For others, it comes from fees received. For yet others, it is a combination of rehabilitation ànd fees. Clients, on the other hand, tend to receive their support and stimulus from positive rehabilitation and interpersonal relationships, mainly with family members.

Effective helpers are able to project to a client an image of genuine concern, empathy, and technical skills. Even this may not be sufficient to dissolve a client's fears and anxieties. There is something inherently disconcerting about having to seek professional help. Although talking may not allay a client's fears and anxieties, it can certainly pave the way for this to occur. Most frequently the client will begin the initial interview by telling the helper what he or she thinks the problem to be. However, there are many instances when a client will remain silent or inarticulate or talk about nonrelated issues. As the client tells his or her problem, glibly or haltingly, the helper should communicate that he or she not only understands but also empathizes. Failure to do this will result in the termination of the relationship.

> Ethnocentrism makes it difficult for providers to communicate with many minority patients. And lack of awareness of a patient's cultural preferences and style of interaction often generates antagonisms which lead to curtailed or aborted treatment. A classic example is found in a confrontation between an Anglo physician and a traditional South Texas Chicano. After the physician laughed at the Chicano's diagnosis that his wife's complaint resulted from witchcraft, the physician ordered the lady to undress. "This I could not stand, that my wife should be naked with this man. We never returned, of course, and my wife was treated by a folk healer. Maybe Anglos let doctors stare at their wives' bodies and fool around with them, but not me. And the fool didn't even know about susto [magically induced fright]. He is lucky I did not reduce his arrogance right there" (Weaver & Garrett, 1978 p. 697).

Clients tend to take their cues from helpers. Insensitivity to a client's beliefs and fears may result in premature termination of the consultation. Most clients need time to talk, to listen and to learn about scientific health care beliefs and practices. Relatedly, to tell clients and their relatives not to be embarrassed or feel guilty because they do not fully understand an illness may inadvertently suggest that they *should* experience these feelings. When feelings are expressed and received the distance between helper and helpee is spanned. As the helper-helpee relationship unfolds, the scientific background of the helper comes to the center of the interaction. Both verbally and nonverbally, an effective helper will communicate expertise. For most non-Western clients this means being exposed to new ways of defining and treating their health problems. Unfortunately, new ways are not always easy to accept. When the client is nourished and sustained by contact with the helper, the relationship is not only good but also helpful. Mental health students would do well to remember that most clients are like the Philosopher in James Stephens' *The Crock of Gold* (1946), who said, "I have learned that the head does not hear anything until the heart has listened, and that what the heart knows today the head will understand tomorrow" (p. 128). Helping clients to tell what ails them requires more than a receptive listener.

VERBAL COMMUNICATION

Verbal communication is the most important component of helper-helpee interaction. It consists of words uttered by individuals in an effort to transmit data, to solve problems or to merely acknowledge their own existence. Words play a major part in our lives and therefore deserve considerable scrutiny. The rookie police officer learns that words have the power to transform seemingly lifeless and unrelated individuals into a screaming, jeering, and destructive mob. In retrospect, words have the power to mold thoughts, canalize feelings, and set behavior in motion.

Research studies focusing on gender differences conclude that Western females are more accurate senders of messages than males (Buck, 1984). And the receiving ability is higher in females than males regardless of ethnic group (Hall, 1976; Mayo & Henley, 1981). Comparing college students from Taiwan, the Peoples Republic of China, and the United States, Ross Buck and Wan-Cheng Teng (1987) corroborated the receiving tendency but not the sending tendency among males and females. Communication accuracy was slightly higher for males in their study. This suggests that social learning rather than biological differences between the sexes may account for communication accuracy. In most countries females are more expressive than males because of cultural conditioning.

People of similar cultures agree that certain sounds, grunts, and gibberings made with their tongues, teeth, throats, lungs, and lips systematically stand for specified things or conditions. All people utter sounds in hope that the person who receives them will be in common agreement about their meaning. Indeed, words are what make us human; their value is transcendent. At the same time, words are full of human relations traps. Their meanings can be distorted and, when this occurs, a client may experience physical pain and psychological misery beyond all reason. In extreme cases, clients' distortion of a helper's words have cost them their health and, in some cases, their lives.

The language of a culture describes and determines the identity of the individual (Giles & Edwards, 1983). The European languages, as an illustration, ascribe private identity to individuals. These languages have only one pronoun for the first and second person, such as "I," "Thou," while in Japanese, for example, there is no single word equivalent for "I" or "Thou." The Japanese first- and second-person pronouns are expressed differently, depending on the situation of the moment: whether one is speaking with a male or female; whether the other person is on a higher or lower social level; whether one is speaking in public or private; whether one is writing or speaking. Thus, identity is public, based on a series of interrelationships. In Asian and African cultures the self is a collective or group identity. The self does not create but instead is created by social situations.

Another related issue is the accuracy of language used by persons outside a culture to describe it. Consider how the word "African" is used. The reference group "Africans" is technically correct. Socially and culturally, the term is a nondescript generalization. And that is how I use the term in this book. Africa is a continent. A citizen of Nigeria who is a member of the Ibo tribe is not the same as a Kenyan, Egyptian or South African—all who also may be classified as "Africans." In Swahili language there are three main racial-social groups: *Mafrika* (Black Africans); *Mhindi* (Asians and Indians); and *Mzungu* (Europeans or all white persons). In Japanese there are two broad groups of people: *Nihon jin* (the Japanese) and *Gai jin* (Westerners or white foreigner). There are no specific words for other peoples.

Words are helpful, harmful or neutral in their effect. To use an analogy, words are like a sharp ax—invaluable for cutting through barriers but also capable of injuring the people behind the barriers. For this reason, numerous writers have advised helpers that words and their meanings will to a great extent determine how successful or unsuccessful they will be in relating to their clients. On the one hand, the use of professional jargon is often a major factor that subverts effective communication even when an attempt is made to develop a helping relationship. On the other hand, the use of precise psychological terms may be equally as confusing and alarming. The client who is told that she has a "translucent self," even when other terms are appended, may still come away with the idea that she has a terrible disease. Simple terminology should be used and, if the client does not understand, he or she should be given the opportunity to ask questions.

By now it should be clear that it is hard work to communicate with persons from other cultures. Practitioners frequently observe that helpees verbally say one thing or nothing while their bodies communicate the opposite (Davis & Skupier, 1982). It is customary, for instance, for Asians to sense another person's feelings rather than for the person with the feelings to express them verbally (Marshall, 1979). There is ample research which notes that a considerable amount of communication is the outgrowth of nonverbal behavior and not words (Watzlawick et al., 1967; Mehrabian, 1972; Davis & Skupien, 1982; Wolfgang, 1985; Kim, 1985).

NONVERBAL COMMUNICATION

Only about 30 percent of what is communicated in conversation is verbal (Birdwhistell, 1970). Even so, nonverbal communication should never be considered a total substitute for words unless the client is deaf. Nonverbal communication is commonly called "body language." Technically, it is the science of *kinesics* (Hall, 1959). This science includes the study of reflexive and nonreflexive movements of a part or all of the body used by a person to communicate a message. There are several kinds of body language that people use, including the following.

Gestures and clusters of gestures. There are approximately 100,000 discrete gestures that have meaning to people around the world. These gestures are produced by facial expressions, postures, movements of the arms, hands, fingers, feet, legs, and so forth. Gestures are essential in face-to-face communication because they accentuate words. It is now accepted in psychology that facial expressions of emotions are universal (Ekman & Friesen, 1986; Ekman et al., 1987). Agreement in judgment of facial expressions of emotions was very high among subjects in Estonia, Germany, Greece, Hong Kong, Italy, Japan, Scotland, Sumatra, Turkey and the United States (Ekman et al., 1987). But it is important to remember that although facial expressions of emotion are universal in evoked muscular displays for particular emotions, they are also culturally variable in terms of display rules. Practitioners need to know the culturally acceptable rules of clients for showing a particular emotion.

Different cultures teach their members to move their body trunks differently (Curt, 1980). That is, Nordic Anglo and Asian cultures move their body trunks as if they were one unit. Conversely, non-Nordic cultures— particularly Latino and African cultures—move their trunks as if they were made up of several parts. These differences are noticeable in dance. Anglos tend to dance with rigid, methodical motions, while Latins and Africans tend to dance with more fluid, free-flowing movement. Neither culture is more rhythmical; they merely learn to express themselves differently.

In the United States, a common way to call a waiter or waitress is to point upward with the forefinger. In Asia, this is how people call a dog or another animal. To get the attention of a waiter in Japan, one should extend the arm upward, palm down and flutter the fingers; in the Middle East, clap your hands; and, in Africa, gently knock on the table. Americans hold a thumb up as a gesture meaning "OK"; in Japan it means money; in Ghana and Iran it is a vulgar gesture, equivalent to raising the middle finger in the United States. Nodding the head implies agreement in the United States, but a slight upward nod means "no" in Greece. In Brazil, it is a sign of seduction when a man nods to a woman.

It is a common practice to pat children on the head in the United States. In Malaysia and other Islamic countries, the head is believed to be the center of intellectual and spiritual powers and should not be patted. Shaking the head left and right means "no" in most countries of the world. But among some Arabs and in parts of Bulgaria, Greece, Turkey and Yugoslavia, a person says "no" by tossing the head to the side. In traditional Chinese cultures, people sometimes stick out their tongue to indicate surprise, widen their eyes to show anger, and scratch their ears and cheeks to express happiness.

Manner of speaking. The tone of an individual's voice and the placing of oral emphasis are closely related to gestures. Specifically, the manner of speaking includes the quality, volume, pitch, and duration of speech. Relatedly, how a message is delivered will favorably or unfavorably influence the recipients. There are mixed results in emotional speech. An emotional speaker is likely to be judged by Western standards as being assertive, self-assured and tough-minded; while a calm, objective speaker is likely to be seen as more trustworthy, honest and people-oriented (Pearce & Conklin, 1971; Scherer et al., 1973). However, the helper's ability to correctly use his or her voice to communicate understanding is only half the communication problem. The client must be able to decode the message (Hall, 1980).

Zones of territory. Edward Hall (1959) coined the word *proxemics* to describe human zones of spatial territory and how they are used. Zones of movement increase as intimacy decreases. That is, the more space available without other persons present, the more movement is likely to occur. Each culture has zones of appropriate distance. That is, at the near or far distances more attention is paid to the speaker's physical appearance, while at the intermediate distance more attention is paid to the content of the speech (Albert & Dabbs, 1970; Heslin & Patterson, 1982).

In informal gatherings, a distance of six to eighteen inches is considered too close for the average North American male, whereas this distance does not cause discomfort for the average North American female. In one study, middle-class Whites stood further apart during interpersonal interactions than lower-class African or Puerto Ricans (Aiello & Jones, 1971). In another study, Mexican Americans stood closer together than Anglos or African Americans (Baxter, 1970). Among lower-class African Americans, Anglos and Puerto Ricans, females of all ethnic groups stood closer together than males (Jones, 1971). When our zones of territory are invaded or we in turn invade the territory of others, we communicate our discomfort or apologize for our intrusion.

The nature of most helping necessitates that helpers invade the intimate zones of clients—even when such an invasion is uncomfortable. Physical comfort zones vary from country to country, and the space allowed for interactions is also important. In informal gatherings, people of Anglo countries tend to require more territory than those of non-Anglo countries. South Americans stand much closer than North Americans. During a conversation between a North American and a South American, the rhetoric of nonverbal communication is attraction-repulsion. In a typical conversation, the South American moves into proper conversation distance, and the North American backs away to a more comfortable distance. Arabs stand even closer than South Americans. Many Americans are literally pushed around the room by people from countries in which closer contact is acceptable. Researchers have identified Latin Americans, Africans, Arabs, and Southern Europeans as "contact" cultures; and Asians, Pakistanis, Indians, and Northern Europeans as "noncontact" cultures. In the former cultures, people face each other more directly; there is a progressive decline in the frequency of contact from Central America to South America. The most extreme differences exist between Colombians and Costa Ricans.

Eye contact. Most North Americans are taught not to stare at other people (Kelley & True, 1980). Instead, they learn to acknowledge another person's presence through deliberate and polite inattention. That is, they look only long enough to make it clear that they see the other person and then look away. Through body language individuals conditioned to respond in this manner say, "I know you are here, but I will not intrude on your privacy or embarrass you with my stare." Therapists are taught to stare at clients—even if it embarrasses them. In most Third-World countries, continuously looking someone in the eyes is considered rude behavior. As in North America, good taste requires looking at someone only long enough to establish contact and then to looking away. In some Far East countries, it is impolite to look at the other person at all during conversation. And in England, the polite listener stares attentively at the speaker and blinks occasionally to signal interest. In Israel, it is common for an individual to stare at the other person from head to toe. The lack of eye contact, the blinking of eyes, and staring at the total body are all subject to misinterpretation by culturally uninformed or insensitive persons. Lack of eye contact may be incorrectly perceived as a lack of interest, blinking may be misinterpreted as a gesture of intimacy, and head-to-toe staring could be taken as a precursor to physical aggression.

Touching. The sense of touch conveys acceptance or rejection, warmth or coldness, positive or negative feelings (Baron & Dixon, 1984; Suiter & Goodyear, 1985; Driscoll et al., 1988; Willison & Masson, 1988). Much of the helper's contact with clients does not require touching. But the touch of a helper *can* be meaningful. Sensitive hands can be soothing to a client, help relieve tension and fear, instill confidence and courage, and communicate understanding and a desire to help. In terms of body movement, Hispanics touch each other more than Anglos or African Americans (Baxter, 1970).

There is much more physical contact between members of the same sex in Asian, Arab, and Latin American countries than in North America. In Mexico men greet each other with an *abrazo* (embrace), and women frequently kiss. Touching—hugging, patting each other on the back, etc.—are important ways of communicating in Mexico. At least one study concluded that Hispanic fathers touch their sons less than Anglo and African American fathers touch their sons (Pollack & Menacker, 1971). These studies have lead to several recommendations for helpers who have Hispanic clients: (1) Do not attempt to maintain eye contact with Hispanic helpees who consistently avoid it; forcing eye contact may be interpreted by the helpee as a loss of respect or impropriety of the helper. (2) Chairs should be placed less than two feet apart between the helper and the helpee. (3) Placing an arm on the shoulder of an Hispanic male client or shaking hands may increase his discomfort. These recommendations seem to be relevant for Africans and African Americans too.

Listening. Effective communication does not occur unless effective listening also occurs. Interviews are designed to get and give information. It is during the interview that listening skills become crucial to diagnosis. In order to conduct a good interview, practitioners must familiarize themselves with the purposes of specific interviews and methods of conducting effective interviews, including things to look for during the interview.

Movement. Most practitioners learn how to give verbal feedback and elicit client conversation but are not systematically taught to use movement and the arts (music, dance, drama and visual arts) in therapy. Africans, Latin Europeans, and Latin Americans use movement and the arts as modes of communication. Kofi Gbekobu (1984) pointed out that to Africans the arts, similar to religious beliefs and practices, are part of the whole life. According to Curt Sachs (1937), art is the recreation of things heard and seen, and give form and substance to intangible and irrational perceptions. But to be therapeutically helpful, practitioners must learn to fit how people move and say and do things into a total social and cultural context (Turner, 1969; Allan, 1987). Inability to do this will cause the helper to misinterpret a client's movement, to attribute meaning that was not intended. This caution notwithstanding, it is true that African Americans in particular, more frequently than do non-Blacks, perceive the environment and respond to it with movement (Pasteur & Toldson, 1982; Hanna, 1984).

EFFECTIVE COMMUNICATION

One of the most effective ways to help clients to determine their own problem resolution is to communicate effectively with them. Effective communication means that the helper will:

1. **Understand the roles of each player in the drama of the helping relationship.** It usually is quite obvious what the role of the person with the problem is to be: he or she becomes the individual to be helped. However, in contrast to the role of the client, the role of the helper is not always clear. Questions that a client may ask are "What do you expect of me?" "What are your limits?" In other words, "Where does your role end and my role begin?" Once the client has answers to these questions, he or

she can effectively interact with the helper. Without answers to these questions, the client will not know what to expect in the helping relationship and probably will refuse to commit himself or herself to the process.

2. **Listen to what others say.** Although total silence is not recommended in the interaction with a helpee, neither is nonstop talking recommended. Talking is one way of relieving anxiety, but excessive talking creates anxiety in the person to whom one is speaking. Effective listening requires paying careful attention to not only the spoken words but also the speaker's body language. A helper may obtain a great deal of information by observing the helpee's facial expressions and body movement. The helper should also pay attention to how the helpee talks, i.e., inflections and pauses.

3. **Organize one's thoughts and make sense of the many perceptions that may be running through the client's mind.** Some of these thoughts may be "I am uncomfortable with what he is saying." "She is asking me to do something I am afraid to do." "That is not what I want to do." "What will my friends think of this?" "I am embarrassed talking about this." "Will my family accept me?" It is imperative that the helper learn to sort out and deal with the disquieting feelings of the moment and carefully discuss them with the helpee. It is not uncommon for people under stress to jump from one subject to another. Therefore, it is helpful for clients to learn to state their feelings and make their points clearly and coherently.

4. **Wait for reaction once something has been presented to the helpee.** This is more effective than skipping from one concern to another. Waiting for a reaction means more than listening to the words. It also means, where possible, observing the person's body reaction.

5. **Keep an open mind.** This means more than being receptive to the helpee's ideas. It means being willing to question one's own values and perceptions. Because an individual is a professional does not mean that he or she automatically knows what is best for a client. Besides, it is the client's life.

6. **Make sure of the communication.** Once an agreement has been made regarding the subject under discussion, every attempt should be made to ensure that the client's understanding and the helper's understanding are the same. The best helping strategies will crumble if all parties are not operating from the same reference points.

Now I will briefly critique some of the communication tips students are given in Western-oriented graduate programs. Cross-national observations and suggestions are presented to provide a broader cultural overview. Persons in helping roles across cultures are able to engage in behaviors that are considered inappropriate within a particular culture. This is in essence professional idiosyncratic behavior. In simple power dynamic terms, helpers are able with impunity to give little thought to how their behavior will be interpreted by clients, while clients tend to spend an inordinate amount of time worrying about how their behavior will be interpreted by helpers. Therefore, many of the tips and techniques which follow may be alright for helpers but will create considerable stress in clients from certain cultures. Insensitive helpers engaging in these behaviors and encouraging clients to do likewise may inadvertently create cognitive dissonance within clients.

To Convey Interest, The Helper Should Move His or Her Chair As Close As Possible To The Helpee And Smile When Appropriate.

A key challenge in cross-national helping is to appropriately display interest. To correctly convey interest, the helper must know which culture he or she is moving the chair closer to (McFadden, 1981; Turner & Giles, 1981; Ponterotto, 1987). In most helper-helpee relationships the customary behavior of the interacting individuals are typically more formal than informal. For instance, in Mexico and other Latin American countries helpers may be expected to sit closer to clients and smile when appropriate. In other countries, like Great Britain and Israel, this behavior is inappropriate. Custom therefore determines intimate, personal, social, and public distances. In this situation Latin American cultures prescribe four to six inches between the helper and the helpee, while in Great Britain and Israel the appropriate public distance is six to eight inches.

In most countries proxemics are based on the degree of respect, authority and friendship. In European cultures there is considerably more distance between people with high status and those without than in the United States. High-status Western male helpers in particular may sometimes maintain greater distance between themselves and helpees. In Africa moving one's chair closer to the helpee, and especially with a smile, is perceived as a highly positive gesture. This establishes the social chemistry which creates confidence in the helper. Africans are less sensitive to personal space than Germanic peoples and the Soviets who tend to keep "proper" distance and conservatively smile. Asians would keep a proper public distance and smile frequently.

A caveat is in order. The smile does not always give accurate informa-

tion to the receiver (Bugental et al., 1971), and there are definite differences in how facial expressions are used across cultures (Ishii, 1973). The
Japanese smile of embarrassment is such an example. Many of the
conclusions drawn from research using Western subjects do not apply to
non-Western cultures. Facial expressions can be used to mask feelings or
deceive other people about our feelings (Mehrabian, 1972; Ekman &
Friesen, 1974; Schulz & Barefoot, 1974).

If Helpees Are Upset, The Helper Should Show Support And Concern By Gently Touching Them.

Touching implies interpersonal involvement, but the meaning of touch
can be very ambiguous. One researcher observed that the counselor's
touching did not make clients perceive him to be more empathic or
warm (Pattison, 1973), while another researcher found that patients in a
hospital touched by psychiatric nurses believed the helpers were empathic
and warm (Aguilera, 1967). Touching that may be perceived to be pleasant to one individual may be unpleasant to another. Differences in
ethnicity, age, and gender greatly affect the meaning given to touch. In
the right cultural setting touch is able to make people feel more positively about the toucher (Fisher et al., 1976), and it can also help recipients talk about themselves (Aguilera, 1967; Pattison, 1974).

In many situations where the helpee is upset and the helper touches
him to demonstrate support, this is appropriate behavior. The value
systems in southern Europe, Africa, and Latin American countries encourage personal contact. But touching is not encouraged in Israel or Asian,
northern European and Middle East countries. In the Far East touching
may be extremely disruptive when dealing with an older person. Elders
traditionally are respected and touching them is a disrespectful act. If an
elder client initiates the contact it is not considered disrespectful. Generally,
touching by strangers, especially strangers from another country, is
stress producing.

As noted earlier, in most Third-World countries people of the same
sex touch a lot and stand close together. But people of the opposite sex
seldom touch and they stand further apart than Anglos. Asian women
may touch foreign women during business interactions to express close
feelings, but they would not touch a foreign man. Arab men also will
touch each other often. Traditional Japanese men and women seldom

touch in public. Nor are the British and Scandinavians considered touchers. It is inappropriate to touch a person's head in Thailand or Singapore.

The Head Nod Is The Most Common Nonverbal Cue For Encouragement.

The nonverbal context provides the background in which verbal messages can be interpreted. Both verbal and nonverbal communications occur within the environment and cultural pattern of a society. The head nod can be done the same way in different cultures for different meanings. It may have a common meaning in Western and Western colonized countries such as Africa and India. However, in the Far East, for example, there is a high probability that a head nod by a Western person will be misinterpreted. In most Germanic countries gestures and slight body movements can be disconcerting to the observer. Yet in other countries, particularly Latin American and Latin European, gesturing is an integral aspect of self-expression.

Nonverbal expressions per se are not associated with positive or negative meanings. They are used negatively in Latin America and do not cue encouragement. In India a slight twist of the head which North Americans interpret as "no" means "yes" or "agreed." In Israel nodding the head would be rude and disrespectful to a speaker. It informs the speaker that the listener is self-centered and selfish. This in turn demeans the speaker, especially an older person. Thus, each culture has unique and explicit nonverbal styles that are used to ensure cultural norms. Human behavior and nonverbal communication are interwoven to form complex cultural patterns.

If The Helpee Has Just Had An Exhilarating Experience, The Helper Should Smile and Convey Enthusiasm By An Animated Voice Tone.

Depending on several factors, trying to help a client who has just had an exhilarating experience by smiling at her and conveying enthusiasm by an animated tone of voice may or may not be effective. This behavior is likely to be effective with African clients but ineffective with Asians where smiles are common, especially in stressful situations. Asians frequently smile or giggle when they are embarrassed or told negative things. It is important for the helper to be able to ascertain the difference between a smile of happiness and a smile to suppress uncomfortable and negative feelings. Also, Asians are tuned to relatively even, clear, but not loud conversation. Most Asians expect people to conduct themselves with restraint and refrain from loud behavior. Asian clients, most of whose communication styles are subtle and reserved, are often described by non-Asian practitioners as being "passive," "unemotional," "non-expressive," "uncaring," and "resistant" (Root et al., 1986). Silence is a sign of respect for elders or authority figures.

Like Asians, Portuguese people seldom engage in loud, animated behavior. Most Africans and Latinos however are very animated during conversation. They visibly communicate with their entire bodies. Arabs also tend to express their feelings with little inhibition. In a conversation among equals, Arab men talk in loud voices—a sign of strength and sincerity. The British and Germans are much more restrained. They do not favor a helper conveying enthusiasm by an animated voice tone. To the British such behavior may display arrogance, preponderance, and insensitivity. In Israel and Mexico this kind of behavior is likely to be considered overbearing and unbecoming an educated person's demeanor.

The Helper Generally Does Not Direct
The Focus Or Content of The Helpee's Talk.

In societies where the helpee is expected to aggressively seek the truth, there is no viable alternative to direct interventions. In these countries helpers are proactive rather than reactive. Anything else is perceived as a lack of clear helping. This is especially true in Africa and Latin America. The helping process is perceived as helpers asking questions and helpees listening attentively and responding appropriately. In Latin America, for example, the *peon-patron* relationship obligates the role players to behave in ways to reflect their relative status differences. In most traditional societies where social mobility is greatly limited, symmetrical-obligatory patterns are culturally functional. Consequently, authority figures (including professional helpers) command respect by virtue of their position, influence, age and so forth.

Authoritarianism in Latin American cultures facilitates compliance to authority. This includes accepting advice and directives from authority figures, but it does not mean being submissive to them. Impersonal authority figures, individuals whose authority resides only in their formal titles, will be challenged by Latin Americans if they demand action. Individualism is an important aspect of Latino cultures. Authority figures are expected to set limits and offer advice, but individuals must make up their own minds (Ruiz, 1982). Tradition requires persons in authority to manage in a caring way. Most Third-World clients expect helpers to give them guidance, structure, and advice without in-depth probing of family problems. They prefer concrete solutions to their immediate problems. They are uncomfortable with ambiguity and prolonged conversation focusing on future goals or childhood experiences perceived within their cultures as improper or embarrassing (Lefley & Bestman, 1984).

Most Helpees Are More Concerned With The Specific Skills Of Helpers Than Their Physical Appearance, Particularly Clothing.

Richard Heslin and Miles Patterson (1982) concluded that "clothes can give force and credibility to one's words" (p. 69). The effect of appearance often is strongest at the initial encounter, particularly between racially different persons; and less important when trust is established (Hendrick et al., 1972; Grantham, 1973; Gudykunst, 1985). Helpers who dress casually and maintain a familiar or condescending attitude toward clients are frowned upon in many countries. Authority figures are expected to look and act their role. In Britain and the Germanic countries, not dressing well is associated with low social status. Like the Europeans, Third-World peoples in major cities tend to dress conservatively in business settings. Clothing, jewelry and hairstyle have social meanings. Upper-class individuals pay special attention to their dress and coiffure. Israelis, Asians, and Africans, however, pay little attention to dress and coiffure as long as the helper has the needed skills. Generally, all cultures take into consideration the personality of the helper, e.g., openness, resilience, etc. Helpers who are nondefensive, relaxed, and self-confident are better received than those who are defensive, rigid, and unsure of themselves, regardless of how well dressed.

Probably The Most Important Use Of The Eyes In A Helping Situation Is Direct Eye Contact. Looking Directly At Someone Suggests Honesty and Concern.

To the Germanic peoples direct eye contact may not only express honesty and concern, but it can also mean rebellion or defiance. Asians are taught deference to authority by directing the eyes away from the authority figure. In many Latin American, Latin European, and Asian countries a person who looks a subordinate in the eye is perceived as being judgmental and punitive, while someone who looks his or her superior in the eye is believed to be hostile—or even mentally unbalanced. Israelis and Arabs are the opposite. They prefer eye contact. "The eyes are the windows of the soul," they believe. The Soviets also use direct eye contact in interpersonal relationships. Yet, in Africa direct eye contact is very disrespectful; it connotes dominance and aggressiveness. Usually, the Third-World listener will look downward and listen carefully without any cues for agreement or approval.

Open Arms Are Associated With Accessibility To Communication, At Least For Seated People. A Helper With Arms Across The Chest Presents A Visual Message Of Defensiveness Or A Visual Message Of Being Closed Off.

It is generally accepted in the helping professions that helpers in an open body position (limbs outward) are evaluated more positively by clients than those in a closed body position, and they establish greater trust than helpers who interact from a closed position (McGinley et al., 1975). It is worth noting that most of the studies of posture have been conducted with Western Anglo subjects. Even so, in almost every culture open arms are associated with accessibility. And a helper with closed arms across his or her chest presents a message of defensiveness. In Great Britain, Israel and Africa, in particular, closed arms connote power and authority to the helpee. Open arms are less clear. For example, among Asians an extended arm is a familiar sign of action; during excitement an extended arm is a prelude to speech, implying something of importance that ought to be heard. Standing with one's arms folded, head down and looking at the ground would be interpreted as arrogance, hostility or defiance in Western countries, but in some Third-World countries, particularly those in the Caribbean and the Far East, this body language communicates humility and respect.

Crossing One's Leg In The Opposite Direction To The Helpee's Suggests Distance Or Opposition.

In Turkey it is impolite for women to cross their legs if facing someone. In most Anglo countries crossing one's leg means little for males and is considered quite "ladylike" for females. Western men, as a general rule, do not consistently cross their legs. To the Swedes and French, crossing one's legs in an opposite direction to the helpee may not necessarily suggest distance or opposition. The Swedes are very businesslike in their disposition. There is a mass conformity to regulation, and generally in the business world crossing one's legs is a formal way of presenting one's self. To the French it is a common posture. One of the correct ways to sit in France is to have the legs crossed with one knee over the other. It should be noted empathically though that this type of posture will not be acceptable to the Arabs, because to them it is an insult to see the sole of the other person's feet. They would prefer both feet on the ground. However, given the cultures of the Greeks and Israelis this may not matter very much. In Africa, crossing one's leg in front of an elder person is considered rude. Most Asians and the Soviets have a tradition of not crossing their legs in formal situations.

Rigidity Of Posture Can Communicate An Unintended Attitude Of Dislike To The Helpee.

Among Arabs, Latin Americans, Africans, and Israelis rigidity of posture may be seen as a dislike to the helpee. It would not necessarily be interpreted this way by the French, Germanic peoples, and Asians. Sitting in a reclining position may project poor child rearing to northern Europeans. Some Asians may interpret rigid posture as a sign of proper physical balance and spiritual development. To make a favorable impression in Japan or Korea, a helper will often sit with his or her feet squarely on the ground, with shoulders slightly rounded. There are scientific indications that a helper who mimics a client's behavior (leaning forward, sitting erect, crossing arms, and so forth) shows congruence with him (Schelfler, 1972; Bates, 1976; Trout & Rosenfield, 1980; Matsumoto & Kudoh, 1987; Hermansson et al., 1988). Indeed, mimicking the client's behavior may be more therapeutic than the ritualistic posture of a helper. Practitioners who are congruent with their clients have more rapport with them than their colleagues who do not mimic clients (Heslin & Patterson, 1982).

If A Helper Says "I Really Understand You" In A Dispassionate Way, The Helpee Will Not Only Disbelieve The Message But Will Also Question The Helper's Sincerity.

Asians seldom publicly question authority. They judge actions by the manner in which they are performed. How something is done (form) is more important than what is done. Thus, an Asian client is likely to ask himself or herself the following questions about the helper: "Did he (she) show proper behavior?" "Was the behavior done in a non-confrontive manner?" Asians, Arabs and Latinos are concerned with "saving face' '—not being shamed and humiliated. Besides, these peoples are high context cultures; that is, they are inherently vague in their communications but not how they communicate. Germanic, British and Scandinavian peoples are low context—information is specific and words have specific meanings. The British, Scandinavian, and Germanic people are for the most part publicly dispassionate; their behaviors tend not to be animated. Israelis, Asians, Africans, Italians, and Latin Americans are likely to question the sincerity of a dispassionate speaker.

If A Helpee Is Continuously Late For A Meeting With The Helper, The Helper Will Question The Helpee's Sincerity.

This statement is not true in all countries. Higher-status male persons in Western cultures seldom wait for low-status persons, have larger spaces around them, are free to touch others, look anywhere they want and as long as they wish, and smile only when something is funny to them (Esser et al., 1965; Firestone, 1970; Henley, 1977). This behavior is dysfunctional in many helping situations. In international human relations we must understand that punctuality on the part of the helpee is not always important. The helper must be on time and usually a little early. In most Latin American and African countries clients tend to show up later than the time designated, but they expect their helpers to be on time. This really creates mixed emotions on behalf of the Western-oriented helper. Care must be taken to not assume that client lateness (e.g., "African time," "Mexican time," "Indian time") also connotes lack of desire to be helped. It usually does not.

A Helper Who Talks About Himself Or Herself To A Helpee Detracts From The Therapeutic Relationship. It Is Inappropriate For A Helper To Disclose Information About His Or Her Family To A Helpee.

This myth is perpetrated by therapists who work with extremely maladjusted clients. This is not necessarily a therapeutic relationship between "healthy" people of different cultures. Much depends also on how close the relationship is between the helper and helpee (LeVine & Franco, 1981; Neimeyer & Fong, 1983; Hendrick, 1988). Excessive self-centered conversations using the word "I" should be avoided, however. Client self-disclosure usually occurs in Asian countries after a friendship is established. Asians put an unusual emphasis on getting to know their business partners. In fact, most non-Western people like to establish friendship and trust before conducting business. Reticence to share minimal information about one's family and self is considered aloof or rude behavior, or both.

Being genuine or authentic does not mean that helpers should exercise complete freedom of expression, either verbally or behaviorally. Situational variables such as client sensitivity, expectations, and awareness influence the amount of disclosure appropriate by the helper. The key to self-disclosure is the word "appropriate." The primary reason for the helping relationship is to assist the helpee to more clearly understand herself or himself and resolve conflicts. A helper's self-disclosure is inappropriate if it takes the helpee's attention away from her or his own personal situation. Helpful self-disclosure is curvilinear—too much or too little decreases helpee self-disclosure.

Most Third-World clients prefer to start a therapeutic relationship on personal terms with the helper. They will inquire about such things as his or her childhood, family, favorite foods, hobbies and music. Through disclosure the trust necessary for a therapeutic relationship is built. Once trust is established, these clients will maintain a personal commitment, even loyalty, to the helper. It is common for Third-World clients to offer gifts to their helpers. This is not necessarily manipulation but, instead, an expression of gratitude and generosity (Sandoval & De La Roza, 1986). Refusing the gift is likely to be interpreted by the clients as rejection.

In summary, depending on the relationship that has been established between the helper and helpee, a helper talking about himself or herself may or may not be detracting from the therapeutic relationship. Although some people are private and take great care in saying the right thing at the right time, they often relax or are less rigid and reserved when they get to know the helper.

The Gender Of The Helper Does Not Matter
As Much As His Or Her Professional Skills.

In some countries gender matters a great deal, but times are changing (O'Malley & Richardson, 1985). In China and the Anglo-speaking countries women expect to be treated as equals in professional settings. Women are less liberated in most Third-World countries because of traditional patterns of economic survival and religious practices. A helper should take into consideration local customs when dealing with clients of the opposite sex. For example, in Israeli, African, Latin, and Arab cultures a woman's "place" is still considered to be in the home.

It Is Appropriate For The Helper To
Call Helpees By Their First Name.

Perhaps nothing can destroy a helping relationship faster than incorrectly addressing people. While appropriate in the United States, Israel and Australia, first names and nicknames are inappropriate forms of address in most countries. In Asian, Latin European, Latin American, and Arab countries formal address is common, e.g., Senor Juan, Mrs. Lee. Using first names usually shows disrespect or familiarity. First names are used for friends, children and youth; otherwise, Mr., Mrs., Miss or some other appropriate title is used before the family name. In Brazil almost every male Brazilian is called *dotor* (doctor) as an expression of respect and affection. It would be extremely disrespectful for a client not to call a professional helper doctor. As a general rule of thumb, one should never use the first name of other persons unless asked by them to do so. Formal rules of etiquette are proper, and male helpers must be especially careful to not be overly friendly with female clients.

Research indicates that few mental health practitioners have mastered the ability to communicate with culturally different clients. Helpers who cannot or will not correctly communicate with clients from foreign cultures pose a great threat to world populations. Sadly, these helpers misread and misdiagnose client problems. Unless practitioners understand diverse populations, they will intervene at the wrong time or with the wrong family members. Above all else, the practitioner must help the client to effectively use scientific knowledge and therapy modalities. This is best done with communication that the client understands. Help is only help when it is perceived as such. Little good is likely to be accomplished if a helper uses unexplained jargon or ignores indigenous ways of communicating.

Chapter 7

EFFECTIVE HELPING

It is prudent for helpers not to delude themselves into believing that they are free of prejudices and consequently treat all people the same. *Helpers do have favorites.* In fact, we are all prejudiced for or against someone or something. To say that we are not will render us unable to compensate for these feelings. It is human for helpers to have preferences. Some practitioners are uncomfortable around ethnic minorities; others prefer not to have women or older persons as clients. Still others have little desire to help people from other countries. Many helpers fear persons or groups they do not know. Nor should helpers try to "treat all clients alike." People *are* different and therefore require different treatment. To ignore a client's (or helper's) color, for example, perpetuates "the illusion of color blindness" (Thomas & Sillen, 1972; Gibbs, 1985; Thomas, 1985). Color, ethnic identity and gender are important cultural factors. But great care must be taken to place these characteristics in proportion to their effects on a particular helpee.

HISTORICAL CHANGES

From time to time historians have argued with much fervor that human nature changes greatly from century to century. While ego-inflating, this is not true. Our "savage" ancestors who roamed half naked through Europe, Africa, South America, and Asia had just as much innate intelligence as we have. While the centuries have added to our inventions, our innate intelligence has undergone little change. In short, the tools our minds work with have improved considerably, but not our minds. For example, Cro-Magnon people who inhibited Europe for approximately 25,000 years and became extinct approximately 10,000 years ago had stone implements and drew pictures of the animals they hunted. Most anthropologists believe that the cranial capacity of Cro-Magnons and their drawings imply people who were at least our intellectual equals.

It is also foolish to dwell excessively on the "great race" theory; that is, the belief that different races differ significantly in terms of intellectual ability. Rather, there are ample reasons to assume that the various races are approximately equal in native endowments of the mind. For one thing, there are no pure races—all nations are mixed races. Furthermore, the so-called "advanced" or "developed" cultures were recently backward, while the so-called "underdeveloped" or "developing" cultures were once the advanced nations. This does not mean that the peoples of African, Asian or Latin American stocks have degenerated biologically during the last 2,000 years. Instead, it shows that unless nations continuously maintain and, where necessary, improve technological aspects of their cultures, they will undergo technological stagnation.

Consider the following illustrations: The Spaniards used gunpowder (invented by the Chinese) to destroy the Aztec civilization. The Japanese have only recently borrowed technological aspects of Western civilization, and they have regained the world prominence they lost thousands of years ago. These illustrations do not have much to do with biological inferiority or superiority; they reflect cultural conditions. The decline of Greek, Roman and African cultures, or the German shift from intellectualism of the early nineteenth century to militarism in the early twentieth century are additional illustrations. Change is the only constant condition characterizing societies. Science and technology are two of the principal causes of the constantly accelerating rate of change.

Finally, it is foolish to perpetuate the notion that different social classes differ with respect to traits of human nature, especially intelligence. Such a notion is erroneous and elitist. Historically, members of the underclasses have been defined as inferior to the top classes in morality and mentality. In Western thought we owe much of this kind of thinking to Aristotle and Plato, who argued that slaves and the common people were as much below the ruling class in native intelligence as non-humans are below human beings. Similar ideas have been perpetuated throughout the centuries, and today it is commonplace to hear poverty-stricken people referred to as "animals," "brutes" and "inferior." Along with this mythology goes the belief that affluent, upper-class people are very intelligent. The illogic concludes that the latter group is affluent and successful because of high intelligence, whereas the former group is poor and unsuccessful because of low intelligence. Missing in this explanation are the opportunity structures which facilitate or impede achievement of social and economic aspirations.

It is not merely a brain or an isolated set of nervous tissues but, instead, a whole person that comes to the therapeutic setting. For this reason, student trainees are told that they must understand the "whole client." Each client enters into a helping relationship with functional and dysfunctional behaviors, with misinformation as well as accurate knowledge, with loosely formulated and tightly formulated goals. In addition, he or she may be ill-nourished or well-fed, energetic or listless, placid or tense. It is this extremely complex mass of characteristics that confront the helper. In essence, every helpee is limited by both heredity and environment. Broadly speaking, heredity determines whether a client will learn, and environment determines what he or she will learn. The human tragedy to be culled from history is that humans have yet to build a world that is more human than savage.

UNDESIRABLE HELPER BEHAVIOR

Seldom are helpers neutral in their feelings about people with whom they help. Moreover, helpers tend to be aware of the prejudices of others but not their own. Being culturally conditioned, our attitudes, feelings and values make objective thinking difficult. Not even college classes and on-the-job training can completely eradicate earlier conditioning. For this reason, it is both behavior and beliefs that comprise major obstacles to helping individuals from other cultures. Because most helpers define themselves as being well-adjusted and nonjudgmental, they frequently are shocked, embarrassed or even hostile when their prejudices are exposed. Helpers who are most different from helpees in terms of culture generally have more difficulty communicating empathy, congruence, respect, and acceptance than helpers who share or understand the helpee's cultural perspective (Atkinson, 1983; Pedersen, 1985; Pedersen & Lefley, 1986; Ponterotto et al., 1988). To be more specific, helpers who understand the social and psychological backgrounds of clients are better able to work with them than helpers who lack this knowledge.

Psychological understanding is easier to achieve with people from one's own cultural background (Kohut, 1959). But as I have stated earlier, generalizations about race or ethnicity and effective helping should be made with great caution. The literature on this subject is inconclusive. Several studies suggest that racial barriers make the development of cross-cultural helping improbable (Parham & Helms, 1981; Atkinson, 1983; Sanchez & Atkinson, 1983; Morten, 1984; Pomales et al.,

1986). Yet, other studies conclude that well-trained, empathic helpers can cross over ethnic differences (Devore, 1985; Ponterotto et al., 1986; Atkinson & Schein, 1986; Parker, 1987). The literature pertaining to gender in the helping process documents a consistently lowered estimation of women's abilities and behavior (Johnson, 1981). Sexism exists on both sides of the helping relationship. Research is unclear about whether male or female helpers are more effective with clients of their own gender (Lambert, 1981; Sundal-Hansen, 1985; Suiter & Goodyear, 1985; O'Malley & Richardson, 1985). Berta Williams (1974) concluded that age, race and gender are not critically important variables in the development of trust, which precedes self-disclosure. As long as we are talking about Western clients, it seems probable that ethnic and gender similarities are not crucial qualities if helpers are linguistically compatible with helpees, empathic and well-trained. In non-Western cultures where one's kinship and gender greatly determine role-appropriate behavior, the ethnicity and gender of a helper may be of paramount importance. Youngsook Kim Harvey (1981), a female Korean nurse-therapist, described such a situation:

> I recall a Polish American patient with a marked accent and serious psychiatric problems who, irate at discovering me in attendance, bellowed out that he wanted no "chink" nurse. To him, a man already indignant and feeling betrayed by American medicine, I was the symbolic last straw that broke the camel's back. My foreignness was an insult that aggravated his condition.... Another difficulty I experienced as an immigrant was that of not being taken seriously by patients and, sometimes, by colleagues as well.... I had to struggle to be treated as an adult, let alone as a therapist (p. 115).

Negative attitudes, stereotypes, prejudices, and ethnocentrism are four major interrelated barriers that impede the understanding necessary to achieve successful cross-cultural helping. *Attitudes* are psychological states that predispose individuals to behave in a given manner when they encounter a specific object or situation. Most people become defensive and feel threatened when interacting with "foreigners."

Stereotypes are attitudinal sets in which an individual assigns positive or negative attributes to another person on the basis of the category or group to which he or she belongs (Blalock, 1982; Feagin, 1984). For example, negative stereotypes might lead to the belief that the people in a developing country are uncivilized or of lower intelligence. Conversely, media stereotypes might foster the belief that the people of Western industrialized countries are highly civilized and quite intelligent. There is a tendency for helpers to look for pathological behaviors in clients from other cultures while overlooking pathologies in their own culture (King, 1978). Helpers who behave in this manner were described by C. Gilbert Wrenn (1962, 1985) as being *culturally encapsulated.* Encapsulation is the process of substituting symbiotic model stereotypes for real-world conditions and ignoring cultural variations among clients.

Professional encapsulation is characterized by four basic processes (Wrenn, 1962; Kagan, 1964). First, helpers define reality within a monocultural perspective which is substituted for reality. Second, helpers become insensitive to cultural variations among people and assume that they are all alike. Third, these assumptions are accepted without proof and resist contradictory evidence. In fact, alternative religious and political views in particular are perceived as threatening. Fourth, helping techniques are adopted which reinforce the monocultural view. Encapsulated helpers are prone to blame clients from other cultures for their problem situations (Pederson, 1981). This sometimes is called *blaming the victim.* Joseph Townsend (1979) cited four "traits" involved in stereotyping clients:

1. [Stereotypes] are exaggerated to dichotomize between the in-group and the out-group.
2. They are maintained through selective perception.
3. They erect high thresholds for "crossing."
4. They persist despite the flow of personnel across boundaries and despite campaigns to alter them (p. 208).

Stereotypes have the tendency to become realized through the self-fulfilling prophecy process. That is, definitions or descriptions of people which initially are neither true nor false are accepted as being true; the individuals involved act accordingly and prophecy is fulfilled (Pedersen, 1981). There is a danger that helpers from middle-class and upper-class backgrounds will negatively stereotype lower-class clients (Sladen, 1982; Vontress, 1982). An example of misuses of stereotypes occurs when helpers conclude that all lower-class Latinos are slow and emotional, while all lower-class Asians are academically smart and polite. Low-income people can live *in* the slums but not be *of* the slums. Physical appearance—structural neglect and decline, low levels of sanitation, overcrowding—belie the people. Most poor people are not recipients of welfare. True, they rarely get their names in the news as outstanding representatives of their race or ethnic group. But equally true is the fact that as a whole they are law-abiding, upwardly aspiring persons. An even more grievous error of similarity is the assumption that Western approaches to helping are universal and without modification can be applied successfully to all cultures.

Prejudices or prejudgments are attitudinal sets that predispose individuals to behave in certain ways toward people solely because of their group membership (Foster, 1982). For example, countless Americans living abroad avoid eating in non-American restaurants because they attribute an inferior or unacceptable quality to the foods of the host country. This type of reasoning has resulted in corporations exporting American foods and hotel accommodations to countries with large numbers of American visitors. Indeed, fortunes have been made catering to such prejudices. Professional helpers hold attitudes similar to the general population in which they live (Millikan, 1965; Millikan & Patterson, 1967; Bloombaum et al., 1968). Or in the words of William Smith et al. (1978): "It is often naively assumed that 'professionals have miraculously cleansed' themselves of racial and class biases . . . [however], they have the same cultural stereotypes, fears, and concerns about individuals of different cultures and races as the rest of the population" (pp. 148–149). Indeed, helpers may not even like or respect some of their helpees (Harrison & Carek, 1966).

Ethnocentrism, the belief that one's own group is superior to all others, is the major source of cross-cultural problems (LeVine & Campbell, 1972; Eyton & Neuwirth, 1984). Ethnocentrism makes it difficult to communicate with colleagues and clients from other cultures who are believed to be inferior. Failure to acknowledge an individual's equality leads to antagonisms which curtail or abort the interaction. A classic example is found in a confrontation between an American executive and his African colleague. The American not only ridiculed his co-worker's belief in evil spirits but also assumed that the individual, despite his Ph.D. degree in clinical psychology from a prestigious American university, was "backward" in his comprehension of psychological issues and helping techniques. Helpers caught up in ethnocentric beliefs of their superiority and the other ethnic groups' inferiority cannot effectively counsel clients from other cultures. These "helpers" are too much a part of the transcultural problem to effect a solution. Their implicit or explicit bias shows up as demeaning, dehumanizing, and patronizing behaviors and communication. Attitudes notwithstanding, it is the *behavior* generated by attitudes and beliefs that determines the success of a cross-cultural interaction, and this includes the following.

Courtesy. Courtesy is using socially acceptable manners in specific situations. In short, it is showing respect for other people. By extending social courtesies, we publicly acknowledge the other person's dignity.

Cooperation. Cooperation is working harmoniously with others. To cooperate with citizens of other countries, we must be willing to interact with people whose life-styles differ from our own. It is not easy to push our cultural conditioning into the background in order to work with culturally different persons. Contrary to a popular notion, many people in other countries would rather give help than receive it. Social embarrassment and humiliation cut across all nationality, social class and ethnic backgrounds. For this reason, cross-national cooperation is an act of global survival which leads to the reciprocity needed to bridge culture distances.

Consistency. Consistency is acting the same way in similar situations. Capricious or contradictory behaviors will confuse clients. For example, if a helper's behavior does not correspond with his words, he will be behaving like the white person an old American Indian described: "What you do speaks so loudly that I cannot hear what you are saying."

Tact. Tact is doing or saying what is appropriate and nonoffensive in a given situation. Unfortunately, some individuals confuse sarcasm and tact which are really polar opposites. Even when hidden in humor, sarcasm can be damaging to cross-cultural interactions. Caustic comments about a client's country or fellow citizens may get a laugh at a party, but the price of the laughter is usually a loss of respect for the person and his country.

Unfortunately, few helpers are trained to assist peoples of other countries resolve personal problems. Many professional helpers believe that docility, punctuality, and unquestioned obedience are the characteristics of all Third-World clients (Herr, 1987). Third-World clients who deviate from this stereotype are labeled "weird" or "abnormal." The most assiduous aspect of labeling clients is associating them with the salvageable people all too readily thrown away by insensitive helpers. Some helpers are similar to malnourished athletes. They might look healthy to untrained eyes, but in reality they are sick and decaying inside. Equally important, their helping modalities often do not fit peoples of other cultures. Because of the way they look, smell, talk or behave, some helpees frustrate or irritate helpers. Individuals who do not fit the constantly shifting and highly subjective normative characteristics of "good clients" are less likely to receive help than those who have them.

UNDESIRABLE CLIENTS

Undesirable clients can be placed in one of the following categories: socially undesirable, attitudinally undesirable, physically undesirable, circumstantially undesirable and incidentally undesirable (Papper, 1970). *Socially undesirable* helpees include individuals who are members of another country or ethnic group, or those who are crude in behavior. *Attitudinally undesirable* helpees are individuals who are ungrateful or arrogant: those who believe they "know it all." *Physically undesirable* helpees include individuals who have identifiable physical illnesses, especially chronic illnesses. Sometimes helpees are *circumstantially undesirable* because of situations totally apart from them and beyond their control. Examples of circumstantially undesirable helpees are nonviolent persons whose country is linked with militaristic or terrorist acts against the helper's country. James Groves (1974) placed undesirable or hateful helpees into four classes: dependent clingers, entitled demanders, manipulative help-rejectors and self-destructive deniers.

> Clingers escalate from mild and appropriate requests for reassurance to repeated perfervid, incarcerating cries for explanation, affection, analgesics, sedatives and all forms of attention imaginative.... Demanders resemble clingers in the profundity of their neediness, but they differ in that—rather than flattery and unconscious seduction—they use intimidation, devaluation and guilt-induction to place the doctor in the role of the inexhaustible supply depot.... Help-rejectors, or "crocks," are familiar to every practicing physician. Like clingers and demanders, they appear to have a quenchless need for emotional supplies. Unlike clingers, they are not seductive and grateful; unlike demanders, they are not overtly hostile. They actually seem the opposite of entitled; they appear to feel that no regimen will help.... Self-destructive deniers display unconsciously self-murderous behaviors, such as continued drinking of a patient with esophageal varices and hepatic failure (p. 305).

Effective helpers are able to manage their negative beliefs. This is not to imply that they are completely objective and treat all helpees equally, but they minimize unfair treatment and maximize fair treatment. Getting to know culturally different persons might alter a helper's negative attitude toward them, and he or she will be better able to respond therapeutically to them. While it would be ideal, a helper need not like clients in order to help them. Understanding and empathy can occur without condemning or liking the helpee.

There is no truly homogeneous group of helpers. Within each field of specialization there are noticeable differences in life-styles, aspirations, education and abilities. Having a professional degree or title and proficiency in a helping modality are not per se absolute determinants of intercultural and cross-cultural competence. Nor do differences in age, gender, color, social class, ethnic background or language automatically result in helping abilities or deficiencies. Part of education for professional competence is learning the limitation of one's presumptions.

> In daily life it happens all the time that we presume that the psychology of other people is the same as ours. We suppose that what is pleasing or desirable to us is the same to others and that what seems bad to us must also seem bad to them. It is only recently that our courts of law have nerved themselves to admit the psychological relativity of guilt in pronouncing sentence.... And we still attribute to the other fellow all the evil and inferior qualities that we do not like to recognize in ourselves, and therefore have to criticize and attack him, when all that has happened is that an inferior "soul" has emigrated from one person to another. The world is still full of *betes noires* and scapegoats, just as it formerly teemed with witches and werewolves (Jung, 1968, pp. 64–65).

Helping is complicated by the fact that each helper is a complex personality. A helper's psychological needs, values and prejudices determine his or her approach to clients. Despite a certain amount of variability, both helpers and helpees develop fairly stable, stereotyped ways of dealing with each other. Some helpers are oversensitive when interacting with culturally different clients and see insult where none was intended. Long before entering their professions, these persons become cynical and disillusioned about themselves, their chosen profession and culturally different people. Thus, they enter the helping relationship bitter, hostile and with little expectation of being culturally sensitive. In this instance, it is the helper, not the helpee, who is undesirable.

Helpers in all cultures must be able to give of themselves and to receive from their helpees. The act of unconditional acceptance communicates to helpees, "I acknowledge your existence, but I will not cause you to lose your identity." Acceptance does not mean feeling *like* other persons, because no two persons live in the same cognitive world. The behavior of each helpee is not determined solely by his or her cultural environment but also by the environment created by the helper. By trying, helpers usually can understand and accept people who are culturally different. Prejudice is not an innocuous children's game. Words can hurt—they can set in motion behaviors that socially, emotionally and economically harm people.

An optimum helper-helpee relationship involves two people freely responding to each other. This does not mean that the relationship will always be pleasant. Rather, it is an encounter in which both parties feel free to say "I agree" or "I disagree." There are many reasons an open, honest interaction can be beneficial to both parties. However, there are some obvious risks in caring about helpees who are culturally different. They might withdraw, not follow through on promises, complain easily or move to another community. That is, they might not solve their problems; they might even get worse. But these are the same risks found in culturally similar helper-helpee situations.

The temporary nature of most helping relationships can be heart-breaking for the helper and the helpee. This is compounded by the fact that sometimes helpees develop negative concepts of themselves that no helper can assist them to alter. To care under this condition is to become frustrated by the inability to succeed. Some helpers are afraid to care because they might be rejected. Upwardly mobile African American helpers, for example, who identify with their White colleagues are frequently unwilling to help other minorities. These black Anglo-Saxons are determined to prove that they are better than other minorities. Their self-hatred is intensified when they are treated like the people they reject. Gordon Allport (1954) clearly demonstrated that members of an oppressed group tend not only to both despise and reject their own group but also hate themselves for being a member of it.

Because a major aspect of an individual's behavior is an outgrowth of his or her self-concept, it is disappointing when helpers lower a helpee's self-image. In some instances, helpees try to steel themselves against further rejection by being uncooperative. They test their helpers to see if they too will turn against them. Specifically, these helpees ask helpers to give more of themselves than is humanly possible, thereby trying to justify their own negative acts. Throughout these trials helpers should try to not be hostile to individuals whose behaviors are irritating, attacking or demanding. Helpers who respond by verbally attacking, degrading or emotionally destroying a client are not being helpful. Upon close examination, even the most hateful helpees do not wish to behave that way. They simply have not internalized other, less caustic behaviors.

Records and Reputation

Almost every adult helpee has an academic record, an employment record and a social reputation—all of which precede and follow him or her. Academic records mainly consist of school grades, while employment records chronicle the jobs and positions one has held. Social reputations are an imprecise mixture of anecdotal records and rumors. Seldom do records or reputations acknowledge unequal opportunities, myths and stereotypes and other circumstances beyond the control of the helpee. If taken at face value, some practitioners will be horrified at the mere thought of helping certain individuals.

A review of related studies provides evidence that minorities are diagnosed differently than majority group clients, and they receive less preferred forms of treatment than majority group clients (Atkinson et al., 1978). Even the diagnostic tests used by Western helpers contain what Nancy Freeberg (1969) called "unspecified biases." These biases include: (1) formats that are entirely verbal at a relatively high reading rate, without the complement of pictorial information; (2) the content favors Western middle-class concepts, language or experiences; (3) most of the formal measures are lengthy; (4) oral presentation is seldom used; (5) tests are designed to be administered to large, highly structured groups; and (6) they have tight time restrictions, which is consonant with the Western perception of time-bound activities. Helpers need to use multisource, multimethod, and multilevel assessment instruments (Sundberg, 1981; Lonner & Sunberg, 1985; Patterson, 1985).

Without a doubt, some of the helpees described in this book are handicapped by their own and their helper's low expectations of them. Despite thousands of volumes detailing environmental blockages faced by certain kinds of helpees, many helpers continue to look mainly at accomplishments instead of potential. Far too many professional helpers cling to the myth that some individuals (e.g., alcoholics, the lower class, foreigners) are not salvageable. There is a strong temptation to accept an individual's records or reputation as gospel. By so doing, we are relieved of the tiresome burden of individualizing our behavior for people we think we do not like or cannot salvage. To quote Carl Jung (1957):

> There is and can be no self-knowledge based on theoretical assumptions, for the object of self-knowledge is an individual—a relative expectation and an irregular phenomenon. Hence it is not the universal and the regular that characterize the individual, but rather the unique. He

is not to be understood as a recurrent unit but as something unique and singular. . . . At the same time man, as member of a species, can and must be described as a statistical unit; otherwise nothing general could be said about him. . . . The individual, however, as an irrational datum, is the true and authentic carrier of reality, the *concrete* man as opposed to the unreal ideal or normal man to whom the scientific statements refer (p. 20).

It is of utmost importance that those involved in the helping relationship always keep in mind the injunction to avoid labeling, stereotyping, generalizing, categorizing, and rationalizing the unique human being who defies the reduction and simplification provided by his or her records and reputation. Quantified data certainly have their place and can provide us with varied and invaluable heuristic tools to use in our roles as helpers, but we must be willing and prepared to discard these tools when they do not fit or when they cease to lend understanding of the individuals with whom we are helping. That is true of the data I present, too.

The best way to learn what people are like is to observe their behavior, listen to their conversation, and let them tell us about themselves. It is a rare experience for a helpee to talk with somebody who, instead of criticizing, listens without judging. It is even rarer for individuals in trouble to talk with somebody who does not admonish them but listens in an effort to better understand and help them. The major difference between an effective helper and an ineffective one is that the former listens with a sensitive ear and the latter with a deaf ear. When an individual asks for help, he or she usually needs to be assured of being understood and respected. The helping encounter is most effective between *people* rather than between *concepts* and *theories.* Most helpees want to be able to tell their story in their own way and in their own time. Equally important, they want to be heard. True, they may ramble, digress, seem to be incoherent and at times bring in extraneous details, but they want to tell it. They do not want practitioners to put words in their mouths, prejudge them or try to make their problems insignificant. In short, they want to achieve self-growth, a positive self-concept.

Because they possess language and high intelligence, humans are able to think about their bodies, their behavior and the impression they make on other persons. Only the human being is able to become an object to himself or herself. The notion of self grows out of interaction and communication with other persons. For this reason, the self is a social product. Three conditions are necessary for the formation of a self-concept. Charles Horton Cooley (1902) explained this process in his concept of "the looking-glass self": an individual gets a reflected view of herself from the actions of others toward her. First, the individual must imagine how she is judged by her significant others. These judgments may be implicit, as when she interprets her mother's frown as a sign of disapproval; or they may explicit, as when a friend tells her she is ugly, dumb or not wanted.

The second condition for the formation of a self-concept is the individual's ability to judge her reflection of self against a set of norms that she and others hold in reference to how she should behave and what characteristics she should have. We have seen many illustrations of this on preceding pages. Finally, if she meets or exceeds these standards, she is likely to feel proud; if she does not, she is likely to feel ashamed. The social self therefore refers to the way a person perceives herself in relation to significant others. Consequently, self-concept is the organization of qualities that an individual attributes to herself or himself in varying situations. Clients who believe that they are weak, bad or stupid, for example, will behave accordingly. Their behavior is largely determined by their mental pictures of themselves. Once a negative picture is drawn, it is difficult to erase. Arthur Jersild (1952) described such a situation:

> When a person resists learning that may be beneficial to him, he is, in effect, trying to protect or shield an unhealthy condition. But more broadly speaking, he is not actually protecting something unhealthy as such; he is trying to safeguard his picture of himself, his self-concept, the illusions concerning himself which he has built and which give him trouble (p. 114).

In the early days of scientific helping modalities, much time and energy were devoted to seeking the best technique of helping. Implicit in this approach was the belief that what clients learned was a direct consequence of the techniques used by helpers. Only lately have practitioners begun to realize that technique or method as such is only one variable in complex learning patterns that have attitudinal as well as instructional determinants. In summary, therapy is related to clients' readiness to learn about themselves and new ways of behaving. This in turn depends on the clients' cultural norms.

Whichever Western modality discussed in this book that one uses, the common task is to remove blocks and immobility and to encourage and teach new modes of responding and acting (Ivey, 1981). However, different clients require different therapeutic outcomes. It is also important to reiterate that a helping modality can harm clients if utilized in an inappropriate manner. The ineffectiveness of some helpers is seen in studies which document that approximately 50 percent of American ethnic minority group clients—Hispanics, Asian Americans, African Americans and Native Americans—terminate counseling after the first interview, compared with a 30 percent rate for Anglo clients (Sue et al., 1974; Sue & McKinney, 1975; Sue, 1977). It is likely the dropout rate is even higher among non-Western clients with Western-oriented helpers.

Derald Sue (1981) noted that Western helping interventions, particularly counseling, hold the following basic assumptions. Helpers often expect helpees to be verbally, emotionally and behaviorally expressive. Helping is perceived as being most effective through a one-on-one activity that encourages helpees to tell intimate aspects of their lives while the helper listens and responds. The helpee is expected to be the primary active participant. There is a clear distinction between mental and physical illness or health. This approach to helping is in clear conflict with most Third-World processes of helping.

BEYOND TELLING

It is true that helpers have a degree of power over clients. Helpers who are authoritarian and dominating tend to be less helpful in some cultures than their colleagues who are democratic and encourage client initiative. Yet, in many cultures, the authoritarian approach is the most effective. Part of the helpers' dilemma is that they must be sufficiently detached from clients to exercise sound judgment and at the same time have enough concern to provide sensitive, empathic care. It is possible for professional helpers to suppress on a conscious level emotional responses while counseling and assisting clients, but this detachment does not remove the stress and concern hidden in the unconscious domain of their minds. Helping clients to tell what they feel requires more than a receptive listener and it is more than collecting predetermined data (Cormier et al., 1984). Helpers who believe that the predetermined interview schedule is the only effective method of eliciting pertinent data should learn from the experiences of Helen Perlman (1957):

It has long been said in casework, reiterated against the sometime practice of subjecting the client to a barrage of ready-made questions, that the client "should be allowed to tell his story in his own way." Particularly at the beginning this is true, because the client may feel an urgency to do just that, to pour out what *he* sees and thinks and feels because it is his problem and because he has lived with it and mulled it within himself for days or perhaps months. Moreover, it is "his own way" that gives both caseworker and client not just the objective facts of the problem, but the grasp of its significance. To the client who is ready and able to "give out" with what troubles him, the caseworker's nods and murmurs of understanding—any of those nonverbal ways by which we indicate response—may be all the client needs in his first experience of telling and being heard out (p. 142).

Not all clients can easily talk about their problems. Comments such as "I imagine that this is not easy for you to talk about" and "Go on, I'm listening" may be enough encouragement for some reticent persons. Others will need direct questions to help them focus their conversation. Accurate information is not the result of passive listening; it is the by-product of interpretive talking and active listening. Effective listening is demanding; most people have to work hard at listening to hear what others are trying to say. Few people know exactly how they feel about their problems until they have communicated sufficient data to another person. To tell someone what and how they feel is in itself a relief for many clients, but telling is not enough. Problem resolution must follow if the helping relationship is to be complete. This is likely to occur when the client's questions pertaining to his or her problem are amply discussed. The words of Paul Tournier (1957) sum up the process of helping persons with problems to communicate: "Through information I can understand a case, only through communication shall I be able to understand a person" (p. 25).

Distressed individuals may only be aware of internal discomforts. Providing opportunities for them to tell how they feel is usually the first step in isolating negative feeling and related behaviors. They may have previously communicated internal discomforts by arguing with, laughing at or avoiding contact with other persons. Talking about negative feelings can provide a better view of them and, hopefully, a better chance for managing them. While allowing a helpee to "tell" is a valuable technique in resolving problems, it is only a first step. Telling should be related to some end and not merely an end in itself. Again, I say: *Solutions must be sought.*

In their unsuccessful effort to fulfill their needs, no matter what behavior they choose, all [distressed persons] have a common characteristic: They deny the reality of the world around them. Some break the law, denying the rules of society; some claim their neighbors are plotting against them, denying the improbability of such behavior. Some are afraid of crowded places, close quarters, airplanes, or elevators, yet they freely admit the irrationality of their fears. Millions drink to blot out the inadequacy they feel but that need not exist if they could learn to be different. . . . Therapy will be successful when they are able to give up denying the world and to recognize that reality not only exists but that they must fulfill their needs within its framework (Glasser, 1965, p. 6).

Problem identification consists of three operations: fact-finding, analysis of facts, and implementation of action steps. To achieve greater effectiveness, helpees must be fully involved in efforts to solve their problems. It is possible for professionals to define the problems and prescribe the solutions, but this weakens their clients' self-responsibility. After all, clients own the problems; their helpers do not. In summary, the following principles are crucial to problem identification:

1. **A problem can be solved only if the necessary resources are available.** A helper may want to understand helpees from other countries but be unable to do so because he or she does not have adequate resources, e.g., reading materials. Most helpers are unable to learn about people from other cultures because of missing or inadequate resources. In any puzzle, if pieces are missing, one cannot see the whole picture.

2. **Many clients do not know how they feel about their situation until they communicate their feelings to someone.** They may be vaguely aware of internal discomforts but totally unaware of their implications. Providing clients an opportunity to tell how they feel is usually the first step to isolating negative feelings. Some clients will communicate internal discomforts in a childlike manner by striking, laughing at or ignoring others. As we have seen, allowing clients to "tell it like it is" is not the end of the process, however. The helping relationship should have purpose beyond relating unpleasant feelings. If solutions are not sought, talking will serve only to frustrate clients further.

A distinction should be made between thinking *about* a problem and thinking *through* a problem. In the first instance, little more than free association of ideas takes place. In the second instance, more purposeful things occur: problem is acknowledged, its implications are examined and solutions are contemplated. Thinking through a problem is physically as well as mentally stimulating. The heart beats faster and perspiration may break out. The whole person gets caught up in thinking through a problem. Helpers must not push clients to hurry this process. The helper who chides a client, "If you really wanted to, you would make the necessary adjustments" is insensitive to the complexities of problem identification and altering established behavior.

3. **Clients who want to change may not know how or may feel threatened by the thought of changing.** Some persons become obsessed with the fear that they will be publicly embarrassed or lose what little security they have if they behave differently. They might know how to behave differently but are unsure what will happen to them if they stop playing the role of helpless, dependent persons. Indeed, some families structure their lives around taking care of dysfunctional members. There is no denying the vulnerability inherent in trying new behavior. When helpees expose themselves this way, they may indeed lose something.

4. **It is imperative that helpers focus on problems they can help clients think through.** Helpers should do the job they are paid to do: focus on the problems their training implies or delineates. It is helpful to focus on immediate crisis situations or the single most important issue at the moment but not to become a participant in a client's flight. Experienced helpers know when and where to refer clients when they are unable to help them.

Outside Looking In

Today, more than ever, clients need sensitive helpers. Without being able to see others as they see themselves, to dispel fears of personal and cultural inferiority, and to effectively communicate, helping will turn into a socially and psychologically destructive battlefield. If helpers are unable to put themselves in the minds of their helpees, there will be little help for distressed persons. To quote Karl Menninger (1930):

> When a trout rising to a fly gets hooked on a line and finds himself unable to swim about freely, he begins with a fight which results in struggles and splashes and sometimes an escape. Often, of course, the situation is too tough for him. Sometimes he masters his difficulties; sometimes they are too much for him. His struggles are all that the world sees and it naturally misunderstands them. It is hard for a free fish to understand what is happening to a hooked one (p. 3).

It is precisely this understanding that forms the foundation of the helping relationship; that is, for a psychologically mature human being to counsel, care for, or administer therapy to another human being in conflict or feeling uncomfortable with himself or herself, other persons, the environment, or any combination of these.

As noted earlier, the ability of helpers to achieve and maintain a condition of objectivity when dealing with helpees' problems is important in the helping process. Helpers who get wrapped up in their own inner world will not be able to perceive clearly the feelings of others. The challenge to helpers is awesome: they must feel with others but not to the point of losing their own identity. Control of one's own feelings requires putting aside feelings that may be vital fibers of one's personality. Even when helpees resist these efforts, the helper must do so in such a way as to communicate, "If I do not understand or agree with your perceptions, I will not force my beliefs on you." Facts alone are relatively ineffective in altering deep-seated stress. Besides, facts include accounts and events seen and felt by the distressed person. For this reason, helpees must be allowed and, if necessary, encouraged to express their feelings so that they and the helper are focusing on the same issues.

In summary, the dynamics of problem solving are threefold. First, the facts that surround the problem must be understood. Facts frequently consist of objective reality and subjective reactions to it. Second, the facts must be thought through. They must be probed into, reorganized and turned over in order for the client to grasp as much of the total configuration as possible. Third, a plan must be devised that will result in some type of adjustment. Fact-finding is more complex than many authors suggest. Not all professional helpers are taught to effectively elicit information—how to talk, to listen and to provide feedback. However, this does not mean that there are only a few professionals who can communicate effectively with people from other cultures. There are many who do so, but most of them are self-taught. Something as important as cross-cultural communication should not be left to intuition or chance. It should be a part of all college curricula and in-service training programs.

Numerous studies have concluded that a large number of "foreign" helpees receive insufficient information about their conditions and coping skills. For example, many persons terminate agency relationships without ever having understood what their helpers decided were their needs, why certain procedures were followed, what, if anything, their failures consisted of and what the reasons for them were. The rights of clients include the right to courteous, prompt, and the best treatment. They also include the right to know what is wrong, why, and what can be done about it. A case could be built that this ignorance is a by-product of the helping mystique. That is, professional and lay helpers typically are perceived as being men and women whose training and predilections place them in a special service category. To put it even more bluntly, there is a tendency for clients to be in awe of individuals who help them. The intangible dimension of the helping process is one reason, but attention must be given to other reasons communication breaks down.

There are many reasons for an individual's failure to communicate pertinent information. Some helpees make no effort to communicate information about their situations. In other instances, helpers fail to request needed information, particularly that which would give them basic understanding of the helpee's culture. Since human communication is a two-way process, both helpers and clients distort messages. Some individuals forget information that had been clearly communicated to them. Furthermore, research demonstrating that people who understand their problems adjust more quickly than those who do not is sparse. From this narrow perspective one could conclude that clients' understanding of their problems is unimportant. However, if a goal of helping is to educate or inform people, then it is important for clients to understand what is happening to them. In the end, the quality of the information helpers are able to give is directly proportional to the quality of information they solicit. Additional tips for facilitating the communication process are as follows:

1. Respect the family. In most instances, the family is very much involved in decisions made by a helpee. The final decision may be made by the client, but only after considering the feelings of other family members.

2. Call people by their right names. In Spanish, for example, each person has two last names. The first last name is the father's family name, and the second last name is the mother's family name. Use both last names so as not to insult the client. Also, use the correct pronunciation of names.

3. Try to understand local customs.

4. Analyze your feelings about various cultures.

5. Avoid patronizing or condescending approaches.

6. When given information, do not merely ask if clients understand what you have said. Ask them to tell you what they think you have said.

The most successful helpers are linguistically compatible with their clients, empathic and well-trained. This means that the initial edge held by a helper from the same ethnic group as the client will be lost if he or she cannot go beyond physical identity and ethnicity. A helper does not have to be from the same culture as helpees in order to assist them.

The Challenge

The helping task is formidable. Aggrieved or ailing persons must be given the best chance of resolving their problems and the least chance of disillusionment. This, of course, is the perennial problem of all helpers regardless of the modality used. Helpers must be able to humanely manage the living and console the dying. Clearly, considerable human relations skills are needed to perform these tasks. People seeking help should not be judged as good or bad persons. Whatever their situation, if we agree to help, we should suspend value judgments. If our personal values and helping modalities are unalterably in conflict with a helpee's behavior or condition, then we should refer him or her to someone else. Useful help is not likely to come from helpers with hang-ups about the helpee's ethnicity or environmental condition. For example, a White racist should not counsel a Black worker who complains about job discrimination. Self-knowledge is an important characteristic of a helper. According to Maurice Nicoll (1964):

> No one as he is mechanically—that is, as formed by life and its influences— can enter into and understand another, and, from that, give help, unless he already knows from his own self-observation, self-study and insight and work on himself, what is in the other person. Only through self-knowledge is knowledge of others practically possible. . . . One of the greatest evils of human relationships is that people make no attempt to enter into another's position but merely criticize one another without any restraint and do not possess any inner check to this mechanical criticism owing to the absence of any insight into themselves and their own glaring crudities, faults and shortcomings (pp. 149–150).

Beyond the usual injunctions to be nonjudgmental and empathic, there are several reasons why it is difficult to behave this way: The actions of helpees frequently make it difficult to be understanding; it is seldom easy or natural for most of us to be understanding persons; and there are times when helpers are offended by the behavior of a helpee. These factors reinforce the need for self-awareness. The more we know and understand our own values, prejudices and aspirations, the better able we are to cope with another person's problems in a therapeutic manner.

According to Carl Rogers (1961), the helping relationship is a professional challenge: "To be faced by a troubled conflicted person who is seeking and expecting help has always constituted a great challenge to me. Do I have the knowledge, the resources, the psychological strength, the physical strength—do I have whatever it takes to be of help to such an individual?" (p. 31). Central to the helping process is *respect* for the helpee. Thus, a helping relationship can become the focal point for experiencing the world as a totality through recognition of the other. But we may find even more than this through what Martin Buber (1966) called the *I–Thou relationship:* "Creatures are placed in my way so that I, and the fellow creatures, by means of them and with them find the ways to God" (p. 132). The opposite of the loving, revealing I–Thou relationship is the I–It relationship, which is dehumanizing and destructive. Helpees whom we do not like become It; they are treated as objects rather than subjects. According to Anthony Storr (1961):

> To incorporate another person is to swallow him up, to overwhelm him, and to destroy him; and thus to treat him ultimately as less than a whole person. To identify with another person is to lose one's self, to submerge one's own identity in that of the other, to be overwhelmed, and hence to treat oneself ultimately as less than a whole person. To pass judgment, in Jung's sense, is to place oneself in an attitude of superiority; to agree offhandedly is to place oneself in an attitude of inferiority. . . . The personality can cease to exist in two ways—either by destroying the other, or being absorbed by the other—and maturity in interpersonal relationships demands that neither oneself nor the other shall disappear, but that each shall contribute to the affirmation and realization of the other's personality (pp. 41–43).

The major task of professional helpers is to help clients adjust to their problems. This means guiding them to information pertaining to their attitudes about themselves and other people. Effectively listening as the client speaks is one of the most valuable tools available to a helper. We have seen that what at first glance appears to be a natural process is in fact a deceptively difficult art that must be learned. It seems easy, but effective listening requires helpers to put aside their own personal needs to talk, explore things and solve personal problems in order to assist someone else. Most conversations are barely listened to. For most people, hearing is natural but listening is not. Attending to the verbal and nonverbal communications of clients is an art or a skill that most helpers learn on the job, if they learn it at all. The sensitive helper knows that all clients need more than a quick solution. A successful interview can provide the client with a rare opportunity to be heard in a noncritical setting.

Whether we are involved in a helping relationship as professionals or as friends and confidants, it is inevitable that at some point in the relationship the issue of making choices will arise. The right kind of choosing is essential to bringing about a change in an individual. Helping relationships in which choosing is continually delayed or postponed by the helper and avoided by the helpee are not helpful. Rollo May (1953) defined the choosing of values as the central concern and goal toward which a person must move if he or she is to grow and eventually become integrated as a human being. "The human being not only *can* make such choices of values and goals," May wrote, "but he is the animal who *must* do so if he is to attain integration. For the value—the goal he moves toward—serves him as a psychological center, a kind of core of integration which draws together his powers as the core of a magnet draws the magnet's lines of force together" (p. 174). Knowing what one feels and what one wants are the foundation blocks of change. The mark of mature persons is that their living is integrated into self-chosen goals. Someone must help ailing and aggrieved people to choose and achieve healthy goals.

In order to help clients achieve their goals, optimally effective helpers are first able to take care of themselves. The people being helped can comprehend the "wholeness" or "togetherness" in these persons. Each success for a client is a personal success for the helper. In the words of Robert Carkhuff (1969): "In a real sense then, the helping process is a process of personal emergence and/or re-emergence. It is a process in which each barrier looms higher than the last, but one in which the rewarding experiences of surmounting previous hurdles increases the probability of future successes. If the helper is not committed to his own physical, emotional and intellectual development, he cannot enable another to find fulfillment in any or all of these realms of functioning" (p. 31). The author of this book does not agree with Carkhuff's last assertion. Professional helpers can effectively help clients without taking care of their own needs. However, the price is quite high; burnout usually occurs. While I do not wish burnout for anyone, there is something ennobling about burning out while trying to help other people.

A HUMANISTIC APPROACH

All definitions of help are based on subjective values—something tangible or intangible discovered in a relationship between a helper and a helpee in which the helper aids the helpee in achieving a measure of self-fulfillment. In actuality, help is something that a person discovers for himself or herself. Each person must accept and act on helpful information with the knowledge that the ultimate responsibility belongs to him or her. In the final analysis, help cannot be given to clients; it can only be offered. The helping relationship has qualities that are the same whether it is between social worker or therapist and client, counselor and counselee, or teacher and student. The psychological equilibrium underlying the occupational roles resides at a much deeper, more fundamental level. This is true for both the helper and the helpee. In Chapter 1, I postulated that effective help at the emotional level is initiated not so much by technique or special knowledge of the different professions but, rather, by positive attitudes of the helper. Specifically, research findings suggest that experienced helpers who have self-insight have a better conception of what constitutes a helping relationship than their colleagues who have mastered the theoretical concepts but have little insight (Stain, 1964; Combs, 1969). In many instances, the man or woman in the street can describe a good helping relationship about as well as the so-called experts.

Some practitioners see the helping process as one in which they make intricate diagnoses of clients and then use a wide variety of helping methods on them. Still other practitioners define all helpees as being sick and themselves as being well. These are not really helping relationships. On the contrary, they are controlling relationships. When the client becomes an object rather than the subject, he or she is no longer the person who acts but instead becomes the person acted upon. Conceptually, a thin line separates wanting to help another person from wanting to change him or her to conform with our expectations. There is an underlying assumption in the helping professions that trained persons can make a significant contribution to the lives of others if their training has instilled a commitment of effectively using oneself in the helping process. The primary technique or instrument in the helping relationship is the ability of the helper to become an instrument to be used by the helpee to achieve basic needs that must be met (at least from the helpee's perception) and to achieve some measure of self-fulfillment.

This means that the helpee will become more realistic, self-directing and self-confident.

One of the most important things about helping in cross-national settings is that the great majority of clients do not seem to want to be helped. At least they do not appear to want to be helped by Western standards. Many clients who ask for help are afraid of it and may try to make sure that no real helping takes place. There are many ways of asking for help. For example, excessive smiling in public may be a plea for help. Consequently, helpers must be aware of these subtle pleas and be prepared to enter into a growth-producing rather than punitive relationships with the helpee. Alienated clients are in a narrowly constructed psychological box—built for them by their relatives and other community members—from which they can seldom escape. Behaving like any normal person would in such a box, they become hostile toward people who constantly demand a higher degree of restraint and control than other persons seem to exhibit; hostile toward professional helpers who clutter the box with technical terms and elaborate procedures; and hostile toward themselves for being born. Most clients sense these feelings and try to get out of their predicament. Usually, community forces shut the psychological box with the clients still inside.

Important Values

Carl Rogers (1958) defined the helping relationship as "a relationship in which at least one of the parties has the intent of promoting the growth, development, maturity, improved functioning, improved coping within. . . the other" (p. 6). The characteristics that distinguish a helping relationship from an unhelpful one are related primarily to the attitudes of the helper and the perceptions of the client. Determining what is helpful and what is not depends to a great extent on who is perceiving the situation. In other words, a client might not see a situation in the same way as the helper. An example of this would be the case of a fight between two students. A counselor may see two students fighting, with one obviously receiving much physical abuse. On the one hand, the counselor also may perceive that the helpful thing to do is to intervene and stop the fight. On the other hand, the student being beaten might much rather take the physical abuse than face the verbal abuse of his fellows, who in all probability will make fun of him for having to be saved by the counselor. Social humiliation can be a much greater pain than physical punishment.

Certain values in a helping relationship must be observed by helpers if the relationship is to be productive in the long run:

1. The belief that human life and well-being are to be valued above all else.

2. The belief that each person is the master of his or her own destiny with the right to control it in his or her own interest and in his or her own way as long as the exercise of this control does not infringe on the rights of other people.

3. The belief that the dignity and worth of each person shall be respected at all times and under all conditions.

4. The belief in the right of all people to think their own thoughts and speak their own minds.

I will not attempt to provide a how-to-do-it approach with clearly outlined steps to follow. While lists are presented, they are mainly to summarize various thoughts. Helping relationships do not allow a rigid structure. Therefore, I present a "be-it-yourself" approach, since helpers need an attitude of "being for others." From this perspective, it is more important for the practitioner to be aware than to be an expert. To be aware and to care about the world, values and life-styles of clients is a significant aspect of the helping relationship in which helpers try to promote positive intrapersonal and intergroup relationships.

Rogers (1958) further stated that a helping relationship is one "in which one of the participants intends that there should come about in one or both parties more appreciation of, more expression of, more functional use of the latent inner resources of the individual" (p. 6). Relatedly, the job of the helper as seen by Alan Keith-Lucas (1972) is to provide a situation and an experience in which a choice is possible. Ideally, through the helping relationship the fears that restrain clients can to some extent be resolved, and they can find the courage to make a commitment to a course of action and learn some of the practical skills necessary to make this decision a reality. Arthur Combs (1969) stated that "the helper's basic beliefs and values rather than his grand schemes, methods, techniques or years of training are the real determiners of whether or not the helper will be effective or ineffective" (p. 3).

Questions for Helpers

In a classic article entitled "The Characteristics of a Helping Relationship," Rogers (1958) asked a series of questions that he felt revealed characteristics of a helping relationship. If helpers can answer these questions in the affirmative, especially concerning most of their interactions with culturally different clients, then it is likely that they will be or are helpful to all clients.

Can I be in some way which will be perceived by the other person as trustworthy, as dependable or consistent in some deep sense? (p. 12).

This is more than being rigidly consistent. It means being honest and congruent with our feelings so that we are a unified or integrated person.

Can I be expressive enough as a person that what I am will be communicated unambiguously? (p. 12).

If we are unaware of our own feelings, a double message can be given which will confuse the situation and cause the relationship to be marred by the ambiguous communication.

Can I let myself experience positive attitudes toward this other person— attitudes of warmth, caring, liking, interest, respect? (p. 12).

A professional attitude of aloofness is sometimes unhelpful; it can create a barrier or distance which protects scientific objectivity at the expense of establishing a helping relationship.

Can I receive him as he is? Can I communicate this attitude? Or can I only receive him conditionally, acceptance of some aspects of his feelings and silently or openly disapproving of other aspects? (pp. 13–14).

The helper is usually threatened when he or she cannot accept certain parts of the client. The helper must be able to accept those characteristics of the client that he or she chooses not to accept in himself or herself.

Can I act with sufficient sensitivity in the relationship that my behavior will not be perceived as a threat? (p. 14).

If the client is as free as possible from external threats, then he or she may be able to experience and to deal with internal feelings that are threatening.

From this perspective four subtle attitudinal characteristics are necessary for constructive personality change to occur. (1) The helper manifests empathic understanding of the client. (2) The helper manifests unconditional positive regard toward the client. (3) The helper is genuine or congruent, that is, his or her words match his or her feelings. (4) The helper's responses match the client's statements in the intensity of affective expression. These four conditions must be communicated to the helpee. In an effort to conceptualize this process, Rogers (1961) formulated what he called a *process equation of a successful helping relationship:* Genuineness plus empathy plus unconditional positive regard for the client equals successful therapy for the client (G + E + UPR = Success). The helper can convey genuineness, empathy and unconditional positive regard through four statements including the feelings and actions that accompany them: "This is it," "I know that it must hurt," "I am here to help you if you want me and can use me" and "You don't have to face this alone." These statements contain reality, empathy, and support or acceptance. To be effective, reality and empathy must be conveyed to the client.

> Reality without empathy is harsh and unhelpful. Empathy about something that is not real is clearly meaningless and can only lead the client to what we have called non-choice. Reality and empathy together need support, both material and psychological, if decisions are to be carried out. Support in carrying out unreal plans is obviously a waste of time (Keith-Lucas, 1972, p. 88).

Let us look now at three characteristics of a helping relationship: genuineness, empathy and acceptance.

Genuineness

To be genuine in a helper-helpee relationship requires the helper to be aware of his or her own inner feelings. If these inner feelings are consistent with the expressed behavior, then it can be said that he or she is genuine and congruent. It is this quality of realness and honesty that allows the client needing help to keep a steady focus on reality. Sometimes it may seem that reality is too brutal for the helpee. Granted, the truth is not always painless; as the old saying goes, "The truth shall make ye free—but first it shall make ye miserable." It is also important to note that being open and honest is not a license to be brutal. A helpful, as opposed to a destructive, relationship is very much like the differences between a fatal and a therapeutic dose of a painkiller—it is only a matter of degree. In the process of attempting to be transparently real, it is wise for helpers to evaluate their failures, their reasons for being less than honest with clients. To protect clients from the truth about their situation or skills is to make a very serious judgment about them. It is to say that they are not capable of facing their real problems. Conversely, if the helpers only provided honesty in the relationship, it probably would not be very helpful. Empathic understanding is also needed.

Empathy

Empathic understanding is literally an understanding of the emotions and feelings of another, not by the cognitive process but by a projection of one's personality into the personality of the other. It is a sort of vicarious experience of the feelings of the other to the degree that the helper actually feels some of the pain the person is suffering. Empathy requires the helper to leave temporarily his or her own life space and to try to think, act and feel as if the life space of the other were the helper's own. We often forget that most people heal themselves spontaneously without the assistance of professional helpers (Prince, 1976). Drawing on their unique history, community resources, and intrapsychic energy they manage quite well without outsiders. Most people who seek help outside their family are reluctant to disclose to a stranger the sense of failure they have about not being able to cope with their problems. A sensitive helper realizes that part of his or her job is to create a relationship in which the client conceptualizes the problem in a minimally defensive way. Such a relationship is characterized by the helper's understanding, interest, tact, maturity, and skills (Strupp, 1973). Central to this condition is empathic understanding.

> Man can no more survive psychologically in a psychological milieu that does not respond empathically to him, than he can survive physically in an atmosphere that contains no oxygen. . . . The [helper's] behavior vis-a-vis his patient should be the expected average one—i.e., the behavior of a psychologically perceptive person vis-a-vis someone who is suffering and has entrusted himself to him for help (Kohut, 1977, p. 253).

Cross-cultural helping involves two culturally dissimilar persons in a therapeutic interaction. An optimally effective cross-cultural interaction occurs when the helper understands the client's problems from the client's perspective including his or her beliefs, values and assumptions about reality and truth (Arrendondo, 1983; Ibrahim, 1984). But it is not enough for helpers to be aware of the clients' perspective; helpers must be aware of and accept their own cultural reality (Paradis, 1981; Sue et al., 1982; Ibrahim, 1985). Only then is empathy going to be more than a buzzword.

While most researchers conclude that empathy is the foundation upon which effective helping is built, this view is not unanimous (Mitchell et al., 1977). On the whole, the data support the centrality of empathy in the helping process (Elliott et al., 1982; Gladstein, 1983; Carkhuff, 1983; Egan, 1985; Elliott, 1985; Gelson & Carter, 1985). In fact, Frederick Fiedler (1950, 1951) found empathy to be present in the "ideal" therapeutic relationships established by psychoanalytic, Adlerian, and Rogerian therapists. In this regard, they are quite similar. The art of helping consists largely of judiciously and sensitively applying a given technique in a warm and understanding manner (Strupp, 1977). To be optimally effective, Ivey (1981) suggests that the empathy provided must be suitable for the client:

> Empathic qualities manifest themselves differently in different cultures. Touching is appropriate in many South American cultures but could represent intrusive and unwanted "warmth" in the North. Concreteness is highly desired in Western culture, but may be less relevant to the more subtle Asian cultures. The Japanese and English concepts of the word "love" are an important illustration of this point. It would be argued that love represents the highest of the facilitative conditions. There is no direct translation for the word "love" in Japanese. The closest word is "anan" which describes a fondness, but also includes dimensions of dependency. In the United States, love implies a non-dependent, more equal relationship (p. 295).

Some clients need more warmth than others; some clients need a genuine helper, others do not; some need closeness, while others need more distance.

Empathic understanding does no good unless it is communicated to the client—to let him or her know that someone has a deep understanding of his or her predicament. This kind of understanding allows clients to expand and clarify their own self-understanding. One way of communicating this kind of understanding is through empathic listening. Empathic listening is not mere tolerance; a helper, for instance, has to really care and feel the emotions attached to the helpee's words. The following four points express what empathic listening means.

1. Empathic listening means trying to see the situation the way the other person sees it.

2. Empathic listening means one must enter actively and imaginatively into the other person's situation and try to understand a frame of reference different from one's own.

3. Empathic listening does not mean maintaining a polite silence while we rehearse what we are going to say when we get a chance.

4. Empathic listening does not mean waiting alertly for the flaws in the other person's argument so that we can correct her or him (Drause & Hendrickson, 1972).

Once helpers are behaving genuinely and have empathic understanding toward the client, the next step, which often occurs simultaneously, is acceptance.

Acceptance

Acceptance of the client means that the helper will feel and show unconditional positive regard for him or her. It is worth repeating that Rogerians believe helpers must be congruent or consistent in both their feelings and expressions of acceptance for clients. If helpers do not really accept clients yet attempt to express acceptance, they will be giving a double message: acceptance and rejection. In such a case, the best that can happen is that clients will perceive these helpers to be phonies. The worst that can happen is that clients' esteem will be damaged. Double messages occur when feelings do not coincide with words. For instance, a helper's words may say, "I accept you and respect your feelings," but his nonverbal messages of rejection reflect more deeply held feelings and are difficult to correct because he does not have as much control over them as over words.

The basic reason for demonstrating acceptance is to build a relationship based upon trust and openness, to establish a situation in which the client is able to gain respect for self, and to develop an atmosphere through which the client can come to respect others. The essential process involved in this aspect of the relationship is caring and support given through respect. In a sense, the helpee will perceive the helper's attitude of caring as an either/or thing: either the helper does or does not care for him. This may be an oversimplification, but if the helpee perceives it in this manner, then the consequences of that perception are real. In searching for the accepting relationship, it would be wise to remember the following Zen poem:

> *It is too clear and so hard to see*
> *A man once searched for fire with a lighted lantern.*
> *Had he known what fire was,*
> *He could have cooked his rice much sooner.*

The quality of care received by clients who are culturally different than their helpers depends on whether a trusting relationship is established. Unfortunately, minority-status clients generally receive inferior care (Sue and Sue, 1977; Anderson, 1978). Clients in particular who are non-White and lower class tend to be poorly served in mental health situations by North American helpers (Wolfgang, 1975; Pedersen et. al., 1976; Davis, 1978). These issues were succinctly presented by Marvin Westwood (1983) and Carole Christensen (1985) who focused on Canadian helpers and helpees. They concluded that accurate empathy is possible only when helpers understand themselves and possess adequate knowledge about their clients. Stated another way, in addition to understanding the client's cultural conditioning, practitioners must be aware of their own "cultural baggage" (Paradis, 1981; Sue et al., 1982; Ibrahim, 1985).

Summary

Empathy has been identified as the single most important dimension in establishing a helping relationship, especially with ethnic minorities (McFadden, 1981; Ridley, 1984; Ponterotto, 1987). Hence, this aspect of Western modalities is particularly applicable to most Third-World clients. Missing in many articles about empathic exchanges are helpers' grasp of Third-World clients' need to find ways to overcome the dehumanizing conditions in which they are born. Excluding behavior-oriented therapies, Western therapies tend to be post-dictive; they explain the why of behavior but seldom tell clients how to change. But a behavioral approach is useless if the helper does not understand what constitutes reward and punishment for particular clients.

Similar to psychotherapists, person-centered helpers generally behave as a blank screen or reflector of the client's problems and perceptions. Instead of a blank screen, most Third-World clients prefer helpers who are willing to disclose something personal about themselves (see Chapter 6). By getting to know the person with whom they are going to transact the most intimate business (exchanging money, time, and secrets for guidance), Third-World clients are better able to establish trust and rapport (Stikes, 1972). Few Third-World people do business with strangers, especially therapeutic business.

Of particular irritation to some Third-World clients is the person-centered helper's tendency to reflect back or paraphrase the helpee's sentences. This practice can be misinterpreted as condescending or patronizing. Valuing economy of words, many Third-World clients dislike having to reply to a helper's queries such as "Do you mean . . . ?" "Am I correct in assuming . . . ?" "Are you . . . ?" One irritated client blurted out after the helper asked his tenth "Do you mean . . . ?" question: "What's the matter, can't you hear or understand what I'm saying?" Sometimes helpers get so caught up in adhering to the rigidly prescribed rituals of their craft that they do not allow clients to tell their secrets in their own way and at the time of their choice. This is hardly an example of accepting the client on his or her terms. There is some evidence that action-oriented helping modalities are more successful than humanistic approaches when working with Africans, Hispanics, and Asians (Sue & Sue, 1972; Abad et al., 1974; Smith, 1978).

The person-centered or humanistic approach to helping focuses on the whole person and the full range of his or her interactions. Care concerning people is a predominant theme. There is recognition that the subjective aspect of living is crucial, with emphasis on awareness of both self and not-self. Value and meaning are key concepts. Attention is devoted to intentions, purposes and choices. There is an underlying emphasis on the positive—on self-actualization which transcends immediate circumstances. There is more concern for the present and future than for causative factors of the past. Finally, in humanistic helping there is flexibility in techniques and research methods. But none of this has destroyed or reduced the importance of psychodynamic and behavior modalities. We do not have a paucity of modalities—only a paucity of creative theorists who can conceptualize better ways to adapt Western modalities to non-Western cultures.

APPENDIX
A SAMPLE OF CUSTOMS AND COURTESIES

A knowledge of a country's customs and courtesies will help practitioners to better help its citizens. The following sample provides such data.

ANGLO COUNTRIES

The Anglo countries speak English, which is a West Germanic language. Present-day English has been traced directly from the speech of the Anglo-Saxons. British English and the American language are the two major types of English spoken throughout the world. The largest English-speaking countries are England, Ireland, the United States, Canada, Australia, New Zealand, India, and South Africa.

United Kingdom

The British Isles are a group of islands located off the northwest coast of mainland Europe and separated from the continent by the English Channel, the Strait of Dover, and the North Sea. At the closest point, the British coast is 22 miles (35 kilometers) from France. Great Britain is the largest island of Europe and the seventh largest island in the world. England occupies the southern and eastern parts of Great Britain. The terrain of England has lakelands, woodlands, moors, and agricultural land. The large industrial cities are mainly in the north and the Midlands. Scotland lies north of England, with Lowlands dividing the farming region of the southern Uplands from the barren mountainous Highlands of the north. Wales borders England to the west and is almost entirely hilly and mountainous. Northern Ireland is the other large island of the United Kingdom. It occupies the northeast corner of Ireland and consists of a lowland region surrounding an area of peat bogs.

179

If you want to be polite in the United Kingdom, one of the first things you must do is be careful how you use the words "English" and "England." There are English people in the United Kingdom, but there are Scots, Welsh, and Irish living there, too. And there is an England, and Scotland, Wales, and Ireland. Don't refer to individuals by the wrong ethnic group, or areas of the nation by the wrong name. When in doubt about what to call citizens of the United Kingdom, the term "British" is acceptable.

Generally, British people are more reserved and formal in interpersonal relations than Americans. It takes longer for them to feel comfortable addressing each other or strangers on a first-name basis. Unlike Americans who frequently strike up conversations with strangers on public vehicles, the British rarely initiate casual conversations with strangers. But if you need help or directions, they will assist you in whatever way they can.

Nonaggressive handshakes are customary when greeting British people. But backslapping is impolite and so too are intimate gestures such as putting an arm around the shoulders of new acquaintances. Demonstrative hand gestures should be used judiciously. It is acceptable to call your friends by their first names, but titles should be used when you want to show special respect. Women's liberation notwithstanding, many British men still hold doors open for women and stand when women enter the room. When crossing your legs, cross one knee directly over the other. A handkerchief should be used when sneezing. And it is a sign of rudeness to yawn without covering your mouth and asking to be excused.

While slow to establish close relationships, once they become your friends, the British are very gregarious persons. However, it may be a long time before you are invited to their homes. Britons value and guard their privacy. And the home is the last bastion of privacy in this tiny nation. Fifty million people crammed into a land smaller than the state of Oregon learn to cherish their space. This does not mean that they do not enjoy socializing at home. Instead, it indicates their need to be highly selective in terms of who to socialize with.

In general, the British do not give public displays of affection, anger, or other strong emotions. And they disapprove of individuals to do so. People who engage in public displays are considered rude and lacking in etiquette. This is also true of humor. Understatement is preferred to exaggeration and vulgarity. The British humor that you see on the "telly" (television set) reflects this life-style. Even the dress of adults tends to be conservative. Yet, there is the other side of the British which is seen in the trend dress and behavior of the youth.

Australia

Australia, the world's smallest continent but one of the largest nations, is located below the Southeast Asian archipelago and is bounded on the east by the Pacific Ocean and on the west by the Indian Ocean. Most of the continent is a low, irregular plateau. The center is generally flat, barren, and arid. In the southeastern quarter of the country are 500,000 square miles of fertile plain. Average elevation is slightly more than 900 feet above sea level. The 12,000 miles of coastline is regular, major exceptions being the Gulf of Carpentaria on the northern coast and the great Australian Bight on the southern coast. The Great Barrier Reef, the longest coral reef in the world, stretches 1,200 miles off the east coast of Queensland.

The mountains lie roughly parallel to the east coast, in the center of the continent, and in western Australia. Chief of the eastern group are the Great Dividing Range, which runs from north to south almost the entire length of the coast, and the Australian Alps, extending as a continuation for about 300 miles through New South Wales and Victoria in the southeast. The highest point in Australia is the summit of Mt. Kosciusko in the southeast—7,314 feet.

The coastal region is well watered by rivers, although many are short, swift, and unnavigable. The greatest of the rivers is the Murray—1,609 miles long, forming the major part of the boundary between New South Wales and Victoria before entering the sea in South Australia, southeast of Abelaide. Its chief tributaries are the Darling, the Murrumbidgee, and the Lachlan. Many other rivers become mere trickles in the dry season. Availability of water is the dominant factor in settlement; one-third of the continent is desert and another third consists of marginal grazing areas.

Australians are gregarious, easygoing people, except when religion and politics are discussed. And men tend to keep their emotions to themselves. Most Australians prefer to be called by their first names and greeted with a handshake. However, it is polite for a man to shake hands with a woman only if she offers her hand. Also, it is acceptable to greet people at a distance with a wave. Outward signs of emotion such as hugging are avoided in most instances. Nor should men wink at women.

When yawning, an individual should cover his or her mouth and say "excuse me." Hitchhikers do not use the American sign of a clinched fist with a raised thumb, because to Australians this is a vulgar gesture. Punctuality is important in Australia and so too is eye contact when conversing. Speakers who are natural in their delivery while standing erect and using modest gestures are accorded the greatest respect.

Business is conducted in Australia in much the same way as it is in the United States. Appointments are made as far in advance as possible and is expected that callers will be punctual. When addressing Australians, personal titles should be used. Dress tends to be a little more relaxed in Australia due to the climate; however, business attire is expected on appointments. After-hours socializing is a part of the business scene and demonstrates the extremely warm hospitality Australians give to visitors.

Canada

Canada is over 9.9 million square kilometers (3.97 million sq. mi.) in area and is the second-largest country in the world. Canada shares an 8,892-kilometer (5,335 mi.) border with the United States, unfortified for more than a century. There are five major geographic regions:

- The Appalachian region encompasses the Atlantic provinces and part of southeastern Quebec and consists of rounded hills and rolling plains.
- The St. Lawrence lowlands consist of fertile, low-lying plains bordering the Great Lakes and the St. Lawrence River in southern Quebec and Ontario.
- The Canadian shield is an area of pre-Cambrian rock extending from Labrador to the Artic islands and covering most of eastern and central Canada. The northern area of the shield is a moss-covered, treeless plains with permanently frozen subsoil. The shield is thickly forested in the south.
- The interior plains extend from the U.S. border to the Artic Ocean. In the south they are unforested and form the breadbasket of Canada. North of the prairies, the plains are forested and contain large deposits of oil, gas, and potash.
- The Cordilleran region is a strip of mountainous terrain about 500 miles wide that includes most of British Columbia, the Yukon, and part of western Alberta.

Most Canadians—French, English, Indian, and Eskimo—are very

friendly. However, persons who visit French and English Canadians should observe formal rules of etiquette. For example, it is expected that a man on a bus will give his seat to a woman or an elderly person, or that he will open his door for a woman. However, men must be careful to not be overly friendly with women who they do not know. The people of Western Canada and Quebec are generally more open and friendly than the people of Ontario.

Because of its many different cultures, Canada has many acceptable greetings. But in almost all instances the handshake is common. The French embrace close friends. In all provinces one should never use the first names of older persons unless asked by them to do so. When addressing acquaintances in French, it is proper to use the polite *"vous"* pronoun instead of the personal *"tu,"* which is reserved for close friends. Speakers should be straightforward in their remarks, direct their comments to the whole group rather than singling out individuals, and maintain eye contact.

India

India dominates the South Asian subcontinent geographically. It has common borders with Bangladesh, Burma, Pakistan, China, Nepal, and Bhutan; Sri Lanka lies beyond a narrow strait off India's southern tip. India has three main topographical areas: (1) The sparsely populated Himalayan Mountains, extending along much of the northern border. (2) The heavily populated Gangetic Plain, a well-watered and fertile area in the north. (3) The peninsula, including the Decan Plateau, which is generally of moderate elevation.

Traditional values of modesty and humility are very important to most Indian people, particularly women. Public displays of affection are considered impolite, and females are taught to not wink or whistle in public. In fact, it is impolite for males to whistle in public. Backslapping is rude behavior. Most Indians believe love is divine, and therefore couples should express their love and affection only in privacy. Women cover their heads when entering sacred places. Normally, Indian women do not shake hands. Instead, the *namaste* (bending gently with palms together below the chin) is the common greeting. Men seldom touch women in formal or informal gatherings. Educated Indian women do shake hands with Westerners as a courtesy. It is proper to use the right hand for the *salaam* gesture of greeting and farewell. And it is polite to ask permission before taking leave of others. Beckoning is done with the palm turned down, and pointing is often done with the chin.

Business is usually conducted at a much more leisurely pace than Americans are used to. An exchange of pleasantries and a cup of tea are preludes to most business conversations. American business travelers need to be aware of, and sensitive to, the hospitality associated with doing business in India. A few basic religious beliefs and social customs merit brief mention. Hindus revere the cow and thus do not eat beef. Many Hindus are in fact vegetarian, although their religion does not forbid the consumption of other forms of flesh. Alcohol is consumed (if at all) in moderation by Hindus, and orthodox Moslims do not drink alcohol at all. Moslims are forbidden by their religion to eat pork.

GERMANIC COUNTRIES

The major language of Germanic countries is German. And the German-speaking nations are Germany, Austria, and Switzerland. The descendants of Germanic peoples are credited with destroying the Roman Empire. From the second to the eleventh century, various Germanic peoples invaded and conquered great parts of Western Europe. In modern Germanic countries class consciousness, formality, and an obsession with etiquette are common characteristics.

West Germany

The Federal Republic of Germany is located in the middle of Europe and has borders with Denmark in the north; The Netherlands, Belgium, France and Luxembourg in the west; Austria and Switzerland in the south; and Czechoslovakia and the German Democratic Republic (East Germany) in the east. There are more than 60 million people living on only 95,975 square miles of land.

Similar to the United States, there are regional customs throughout Germany. Cultural survival depends on your ability to become acquainted with local people, their laws, and customs. The Germans can be characterized as great respecters of law and order at home and in public. And they expect visitors from other countries to be respectful of German laws and customs, too.

Germans do a lot of handshaking but not in an excessive amount as many Americans think they do. It is proper to shake hands when you are first introduced. However, if the other person is a woman, wait until she makes the first move to extend her hand. An even safer behavior is to wait for your German hosts—male and females—to make the first move. If they shake hands, you should shake too. If they give a casual wave, you should give a casual wave.

Titles are important in Germany, particularly when addressing professional persons and public officials. Thus, as an illustration, it is correct to say, "Herr Doktor; Herr Burgermeister," "Herr Professor," "Herr Major" and "Herr Schmidt" when addressing distinguished males. The terms "Frau" (FROW) and "Fraulein" (FROY-line) are prefixes used before the same words for married and unmarried females, respectfully.

Austria

Austria is a mountainous country, with the Alps and their approaches dominating the southern and western provinces. The eastern provinces and Vienna are located in the Danube River basin.

Although German is the native language of Austria, Austria and Germany have different heritages, customs, and values. Austrians are proud of their country and life-style and have a relaxed attitude. In fact, Austrians are nearer to English, French, and Italians in manners than to Germans.

While business practices and etiquette are not basically different from American usage, it also is wise to observe certain unwritten rules of conduct and thus avoid offending Austrian sensibilities. When making appointments with prospective buyers or distributors, it is courteous to offer to meet them wherever is most convenient to them. Appointments for such visits should be made in writing or by telephone well in advance. Austrians tend to be tradition-conscious and attach much importance to titles and recognition implied through the use of such titles. While Austrians are generally well disposed toward Americans, they expect understanding for their ways of doing things.

Switzerland

In the alpine highlands of Western Europe, Switzerland is bounded by the Federal Republic of Germany, Austria, Liechtenstein, Italy, and France. Its position has been described as the crossroads of northern and southern Europe. Switzerland, where many rivers originate, forms the great European watershed. The Rhine flows to the North Sea; the Inn feeds the Danube; the Rhine empties into the Mediterranean; and the Ticino, which runs through Lake Maggiore, is the source of the River Po.

The Alps mountain chain runs roughly east and west through the southern part of the country and constitutes about 60 percent of Switzerland's area. The Jura Mountains, an outspur of the Alps, stretch from the southwest to the northwest and occupy about 10 percent of the territory. The remaining 30 percent comprises the lowlands—actually a plateau between the two ranges—where the larger cities and the industrial sections of Switzerland are concentrated.

The Swiss prize punctuality, thrift, independence and hard work. Like other Germanic Europeans, they also value family privacy. When invited to a Swiss home, you should carry an impersonal gift such as candy or flowers. A handshake is appropriate for men and women. When being introduced, it is appropriate to say, "My pleasure" or "Pleased to meet you." Family names and titles, for men and women, should be used except among close friends.

When entering crowded public places, greetings are exchanged, even among strangers. It is acceptable to wave to friends across the street. Men frequently tip their hat when greeting others. It is acceptable to cross your legs but is unacceptable to stretch them out. Generally, a relaxed but composed posture is best. It is rude for men to put their hands in their pockets during conversation. Neither men nor women should chew gum in public.

NORDIC COUNTRIES

Although Nordic and Germanic countries are separate, they share a common culture base. The Nordic peoples of Sweden, Denmark, Norway, and Finland speak North Germanic languages, which have been traced to the Vikings who traveled throughout Europe during the eighth through the tenth centuries. Nordics speak Swedish, Danish, and Norwegian languages.

SWEDEN

Sweden covers more than 170,000 square acres and has three natural regions. The northern part (*Norrland*) takes in more than half of Sweden, and the northern part of this region lies above the Artic Circle, "The

Land of the Midnight Sun." The land is characterized by high mountains, thick forests, moors, and rapid rivers. Central Sweden is a hilly plateau. Southern Sweden is low and level. Most of Sweden's population resides in this region. Half of Sweden's surface is covered with forests. The country also has plentiful supplies of water. Approximately 100,000 lakes are connected in a lacework of waterways, with many large rivers flowing from the northwestern landscapes. The seasons there are extreme. The winters are dark, cold, and snowy; the summers are warm with long days and short, bright nights. In the far south is Skane, which is the granary of Sweden. This province is flat and fertile agricultural land. Most of Sweden's population live in cities and towns, especially in the three major urban regions of Stockholm, Goteborg, and Malmo.

When greeting Swedes it is common practice to say "Hello" or "How do you do" followed by a handshake. It is polite to shake hands with elderly persons on each meeting. At a distance it is acceptable to acknowledge people by nodding the head or, if close friends, raising a hand. Also, unless close friends, people address each other by their last name preceded by Miss, Mrs., or Mr. Many men, particularly those of the older generation, lift their hats to women when they pass on the street. A gentleman always removes his hat, even in cold weather, when talking to a woman unless she gives him permission to keep it on.

The Swedes are a most correct and punctual people. They take great care to try to say the right thing at the right time. Strangers will find most Swedes extremely rigid, but once they get to know them (for example, at a party after a few drinks), the impression often changes. The once-rigid, reserved Swedes talk to friends about almost anything and everything with frankness. Family and other personal matters which are usually kept private become the topics of conversation. Formally and informally, the Swedes prefer direct eye contact and do not put their hands in their pockets when speaking to others. And gestures such as embracing and putting one's arm around the back of another is not common, except among close friends. Of course, excessive gesturing is to be avoided.

If a precise time is given for a business meeting or social activity, it is meant to be interpreted precisely. As a people, the Swedes have made a virtue of punctuality. Swedes are traditionally formal and well organized. Some observers say that the Swedes are overorganized. An example is seen in the mass conformity to laws and regulations. They have been socialized to follow a series of public instructions such as "keep off the grass," "stand to the right," "don't walk," "don't litter." Foreigners with less discipline are amazed to see scores of persons waiting to cross an entirely clear street daring not to do so until the light changes. Not only do Swedes obey their societal rules and regulations but they also expect their guests to obey them too.

Festivals and holidays are very much a part of Swedish life. Even though most Swedes are casual church attenders, festivals and holidays are celebrated within the context of religious tradition. Foreigners who are unfamiliar with the various Swedish traditional festivities are also likely to be unfamiliar with the country's culture.

Denmark

Located strategically at the mouth of the Baltic Sea, Denmark consists of the Jutland Peninsula, projecting north from the Federal Republic of Germany, and about 406 islands, of which 100 are inhabited. The straits between these islands connect the Baltic and the North Sea. Denmark proper and the 17 Faroe Islands (540 sq. mi.) cover an area slightly smaller than Vermont and New Hampshire combined. Greenland is the largest island in the world (857,159 sq. mi.), 84 percent of which lies under a permanent ice cap. Greenland's population is roughly 53,000.

The Danish people are outgoing and casual but they adhere to strict and formal rules of etiquette during interpersonal interactions. Casual clothes are acceptable for most occasions, but it is customary for women to wear dresses and men to wear coats and ties to dinner, meetings, indoor concerts, and church. The handshake is the most common form of greeting. It is polite for men to remove their hats when in buildings and to tip them to women. One should always say "please" and "thank you" when passing and receiving things, especially food. It is impolite for guests to leave the table or ask to be excused before the hostess rises. Furthermore, before leaving the dinner table, guests should thank the hostess for the food and compliment her on the meal.

Netherlands

The Netherlands is bordered by the North Sea, Belgium, and the Federal Republic of Germany. The country is low and flat except in the southeast, where some hills rise to 304 meters (1,000 ft.) above sea level. Because roughly one-third of the remaining land is below sea level, the

Dutch have had to build their famous dikes to reclaim land from the sea. The Netherlands is still often called Holland, which was the largest Dutch province and incorporated the country's three largest and most prosperous cities—Amsterdam, The Hague, and Rotterdam. The original province is divided into Noord-Holland and Zuid-Holland.

Netherlanders commonly call their nation "Holland" and refer to themselves as "Dutch." And they define correct social behavior as being dignified, proper, and decorus while at the same time being comfortable and enjoy the people present. Dutch business executives, for example, go to great lengths to be courteous and earnest. Most Dutch people do not use first names until a firm friendship has been formed. The Dutch tend to be slow to befriend foreigners. But once formed, friendships are highly valued. The Dutch greet people they recognize by wishing them a good morning—*goeden morgen* (hoo-dun MAWR-hun)—or a good day— *goeden dag* (hoo-dun DAHK). Friends are greeted with a hearty handshake.

Most Dutch also believe that it is important to be on time. Therefore, if you are late for an appointment, it is expected that you will offer an apology as soon as you arrive. It is customary to give flowers to friends. It is not customary to touch another person, except when shaking hands or when touching a friend's shoulder. Public hugging and embracing are impolite except among close friends and relatives. When yawning, you should cover your mouth or, better yet, suppress it. Pointing to the forehead with a finger is an insult. Nor should you talk to people while chewing gum or with your hands in pockets. When eating, the hands should always be above the table, without resting the elbow on it.

LATIN EUROPEAN COUNTRIES

Latin Europe is comprised of France, Belgium, Spain, and Portugal. The language of these countries is derived from Latin, a member of the Indo-European family of languages. Latin was originally spoken in Rome and it gradually spread throughout the western Mediterranean region through the Roman conquest. Although Latin is no longer a living language, it survives in modified form in the Romance languages. The major subdivisions of this country cluster are France and Belgium; and Spain, Portugal, and Italy.

France

France, the largest West European nation, is two-thirds flat plains or gently rolling hills; the rest is mountainous. A broad plain covers most of northern and western France from the Belgian border in the northeast to Bayonne in the southwest and rises to uplands in Normandy, Britanny, and the east. This large plain is bounded on the south by the steeply rising ridges of the Pyrenees, on the southeast by the mountainous plateau of the Massif Central, and on the east by the rugged Alps, the low ridges of the Jura, and the rounded summits of the densely forested Vosges. The principal rivers are the Rhone in the south, the Loire and the Garonne in the west, and the Seine in the north. The Rhine River forms part of France's eastern border with the Federal Republic of Germany.

The French are socially reserved, and outside Paris the people are more hospitable. Throughout the country they appreciate foreigners who try to speak French. Success in France is to a great extent based on one's educational level, family reputation, and financial situation. And punctuality is a sign of courtesy. Shaking hands is the most common French greeting, but the handshake—unlike the American firm, pumping behavior—is a light grip and a single quick shake. Women usually do not offer their hand to a man until he initiates the contact. When their hand is soiled or wet, Frenchmen may offer their arm or elbow to shake. Close friends often exchange a kiss on either cheek (they touch cheeks and "kiss" the air). The French also shake hands when they depart.

The correct way to sit in France is erect with one's knees together or the legs crossed with one knee over the other. It is impolite to: put your feet on tables or chairs; sit with your legs spread apart; converse with the hands in the pockets; chew gum, yawn, or scratch in public; and sneeze or blow your nose without using a handkerchief or tissue. The American "okay" hand gesture means "zero" in France. In addition, slapping the open palm over a closed fist has a vulgar meaning.

Italy

Italy is a 700-mile-long peninsula shaped like a boot extending into the heart of the Mediterranean. On the west and south of the mainland are the large islands of Sardinia and Sicily, and the smaller islands of Pantelleria and the Eolian group. Italy has seven natural regions: the southern slopes of the Alps, the Po Valley, the Adriatic Plain, the Apennines, the Western Coastal Plain, Sicily, and Sardinia.

The Italians are freedom-loving persons who are known worldwide for their appreciation of beauty, music, and good food. The Italians are very animated during their conversations. They visibly communicate with their entire bodies, verbally and nonverbally. At times there appears to be more talking than listening, as the air is punctuated with noise and gestures. Someone once said that the Italian favorite pastime is talking. U.S. citizens accustomed to staid public interactions are frequently overwhelmed by Italian public interactions; they freely hug, kiss, and shake hands on the streets or in cafes or houses. Older persons should be greeted and introduced first. The handshake is the usual form of greeting for strangers and casual friends. Women frequently greet each other with a kiss on both cheeks. And persons of the same sex often walk arm in arm.

In Italy personal appearance is very important. Dirty and worn clothes are not appropriate public attire. And older women almost always wear dresses. Also, it is not polite to wear curlers or to remove your shoes in public. Men who wear hats are expected to remove them when greeting people and entering edifices. Dark glasses should not be worn inside buildings. When you yawn, it is polite to cover your mouth with a hand.

Portugal

To many visitors Portugal is the threshold to Europe, and Lisbon is the front door to the Continent. Portugal's territory includes the mainland, the Azores, the Madeira Islands, and the protectorate of Macao. Mainland Portugal is divided into three distinct geographical regions. In the northeast corner is a highland region which has many river valleys. In the southwest corner is the lowland country which has rich delta coastal areas. The third region is the central highland. The Azores Islands consist of nine mountainous islands of volcanic origin which lie 800 miles west of Lisbon in the Atlantic Ocean. The Madeira Islands are located 350 miles west of Morocco. And Macao consists of a small peninsula of two small islands off the southern coast of the People's Republic of China near Hong Kong.

The Portuguese people are serious and conservative in their dress and actions. You will seldom see or hear conversations that are animated or loud. Women wear slacks and dresses, but long dresses are usually reserved for evening wear. And men work in suits. In offices and stores you will be greeted politely and formally. A firm handshake is an acceptable greeting, and—as in all countries—a sincere smile is welcome. Portuguese shake hands when they meet and again when the part. To call someone, you should not yell. Instead, you should extend an arm, palm down, and wave the fingers back and forth. First names are used for friends, children and youth; otherwise, Mr. or Miss or some other appropriate title is used before the family name.

Portuguese children are taught to respect their elders, and this socialization extends to adults who respect persons older than themselves. They also respect authority and rank. Military personnel and police officers expect to be treated as their rank dictates they should. Police officers in particular expect to be obeyed. Failure to do so could result in a ticket and possibly a fine.

To show anger (*exaltarse*) in public will result in a loss of respect from those present. Furthermore, the Portuguese do not like to cause embarrassment to others and will do almost everything they can to avoid a conflict. But if their pride is hurt by someone else's action, the Portuguese will let the other person know about it. They are slow to anger but will not let others abuse them. The family is the center of Portuguese life.

Generally, the Portuguese do not stress punctuality in meetings, but they expect visitors to be prompt. Most meetings are well organized and formal; friendly formality prevails in private interviews. But there are certain nuances that must be followed. For instance, it is rude for a younger person to keep an older person waiting. A woman may keep a man waiting, but a gentleman never makes a woman wait for him. Portuguese women are still accorded great respect and protection. They do not go out on dates alone with a man they have just met. The first few dates or meetings are in groups.

LATIN AMERICA

Latin America is mainly comprised of the Spanish- and Portuguese-speaking peoples of the Western Hemisphere. This includes the peoples of Mexico, most of Central and South America, and part of the West Indies. The Latin American and the Latin European clusters differ mainly in their level of industrialization. Latin America is the least industrialized of the two clusters.

Argentina

Argentina shares land borders with Bolivia, Brazil, Chile, Paraguay, and Uruguay. It is bounded by the Atlantic and the Antarctic Oceans. Extending 2,302 miles from north to south and with an Atlantic coastline 1,600 miles long, Argentina is the second-largest country in the Southern Hemisphere, after Brazil, and the eighth largest in the world. Its topography, as varied as that of the United States, ranges from subtropical lowlands in the north to the towering Andean Mountains in the west and the bleak, windswept Patagonian steppe and Tierra del Fuego in the south.

Argentines are quite cosmopolitan and socially progressive. As a whole, they are outgoing and have great respect for individuality. However, they are also very formal during social interactions. Dress is generally conservative. Males remove their hats in buildings and in the presence of women. First names are used only when greeting close acquaintances. It is customary to address people by a title such as "Mr." or "Mrs." and to shake hands while inclining the head. The latter behavior shows special respect. When greeting individuals from a distance, it is impolite to call out—raising a hand and smiling are more appropriate. Women are not likely to talk to strangers without being properly introduced. And one should always greet another person before asking questions.

Argentines speak in a relaxed manner while maintaining eye contact and avoiding excessive gestures. When seated, men may cross their legs (one knee directly over the other one), but women should not. Yawns are frowned upon, and hands should not be placed on the hips during conversation. The conversation distance between persons is much less in Argentina than in the United States. In fact, most Latin Americans stand closer together when conversing than most Americans. During a conversation, a Latin male will often touch the other male's lapel or shoulder. However, affection between a man and a woman is not shown in public. Affection should not be confused with the friendly behavior. Women kiss each other on the cheek when they meet and shake hands with both hands; male friends after a long absence give a full embrace.

Brazil

Occupying the east-central part of South America, Brazil spreads over almost one-half of the continent. It is the fifth-largest country in the world and shares common borders with every South American country except Ecuador and Chile. Brazil's Atlantic coastline is more than 7,200 kilometers (4,500 mi.) long. More than 90 percent of the population live on 10 percent of the land, a 320-kilometer-wide (200 mi.) zone bordering the South Atlantic Ocean south of Fortaleza, in Ceara state, to the Uruguayan border. The country is divided into four topographic regions: (1) The densely forested northern lowlands covering about one-half of the interior and containing the undeveloped Amazon river basin. (2) The semiarid scrubland of the northeast. (3) The rugged hills and mountains interspersed with gently rolling plains of the central west and south. (4) A narrow coastal belt.

Brazilians are warm, friendly people who have a long history of receiving other nationalities as guests. Men and women shake hands upon meeting and departing. But Brazilian handshakes are somewhat less firmer than American handshakes. Women friends usually kiss each other on both cheeks, and men often embrace their male friends and pat them on the back. When departing it is customary for guests to allow the host to open the door for them.

Special attention should be paid to gestures. For example, the traditional American OK sign (thumb and index finger forming a circle) is an obscene gesture, and so too is punching a cupped hand with a fist or holding the arm at a right angle with the fist clenched. In Brazil, waving an outstretched hand with the palm down means "come here" rather than "good-bye." A waiter is called by holding up the index finger or softly saying *"garcon"* (gar-SOHNG), and the check is requested by saying *"Contra, por favor"* (Kohn-tuh POR fah-VOR). Because of the similarity between Portuguese and Spanish, persons who speak Spanish will be understood by most Brazilians.

Mexico

Mexico has six major land regions: (1) the Sierra Madre Mountains, (2) the central plateau, (3) the Chiapas highlands, (4) the Yucatan Peninsula, (5) the coastal plains, and (6) Baja (Lower) California.

The Sierra Madre Mountains cover two-thirds of Mexico, from the southern border up to the northern border. The eastern arm (Sierra Madre Oriental) reaches the Gulf of Mexico, and the western arm (Sierra Madre Occidental) forms the land barrier between the Pacific Coast and the interior.

The Central Plateau, the heart of Mexico, lies between the Sierra Madre Oriental and the Sierra Madre Occidental. Approximately two-thirds of the Mexican population live on the fertile mountain slopes of the plateau. The Chiapas Highlands consist of the mountainous area west of the border of Guatemala and east of the Isthmus of Tehuantepes. Most of the inhabitants of the region raise crops in the fertile Chiapas Valley. The Yucatan Peninsula forms the southeastern tip of Mexico; Honduras and Guatemala border this region. The area consists mainly of tropical jungles and forests. This is the home of the Maya Indians whose ancestors built great cities.

The Coastal Plains are located between the Gulf of Mexico and Sierra Madre oriental on the east, and the Pacific Ocean and Sierra Madre Occidental on the west. This region is mostly desert; with forests and swamps along the Gulf Coast, Baja California is a long, narrow peninsula that forms the western boundary of the Gulf of California. The eastern part has steep mountains and the western part is mainly desert.

Mexico, which is the northernmost country of Latin America, is located immediately south of the United States. In fact, only the Rio Grande River, which forms approximately two-thirds of the boundary between Mexico and the United States, separates these two countries. Because Mexico and the United States are so close in geographic proximity, many people make the erroneous assumption that these two countries are also similar in cultural traditions. In fact, Mexico's social, economic, and language customs are significantly different from the United States. It is thus important for U.S. citizens who do business in Mexico to be familiar with the people and their way of life.

In understanding the people of Mexico, one of the first things you should do is become familiar with their language. When we understand the language of a people, we better understand their social life. More than half of all Mexicans speak Spanish, the official language of Mexico, although a large percentage (approximately 40 percent) are bilingual, speaking both Spanish and English. The second thing you should do is learn what is important in the value systems of the Mexican people and develop a respect for their values.

The Mexican people have a high regard for the inner quality or spirit of the individual. A person's inner spirit represents his or her dignity, and any actions or words against it are considered disrespectful. Also, the family is considered an important part of the individual's frame of reference. U.S. business personnel should learn to take discussions of the family with Mexican business personnel as seriously as they take their business discussions. Mexicans believe that one gets to know a person by knowing about his or her family.

The usual greeting is a handshake or a nod; longtime friends often embrace each other after a long absence. Mexicans stand closer to each other than North Americans when conversing. It is also common for friends to touch the other person's clothing during conversation. "No" can be spoken or indicated by moving the hand left to right (approximately 4–6 inches) with the index finger extended, palm outward. It is considered impolite to toss items to people. They should be handed to them. On the other hand, it is not impolite to beckon people with a "psst-psst" sound. If you beckon with a hand, do so with a palm down, waving motion, taking care not to make it appear that you are waving them away. If someone sneezes, you should say *"salud"* (good health).

The father is the head of the family, but the mother is responsible for running the household. The Mexican family is extended and a household sometimes include other relatives besides the immediate family. Family responsibility supersedes all others. Parental approval of a boyfriend is still important, and single girls who go out alone after dark are considered persons of poor character. Chivalry is very much in vogue. On a bus, for instance, a gentleman is expected to give his seat to a woman. In routine conversation, Mexicans generally use more flowery and charming speech than North Americans. This is due largely to a high regard for the ability of the individual to be witty and charming in interpersonal conversation.

Another difference between Mexican and North American cultures is the concept of truth. Americans perceive truth in terms of reality and fact. Mexicans perceive truth in terms of building good interpersonal relations; that is, Mexicans would rather tell a visitor what they think makes the visitor happy even if they perceive the reality will not. "Untruths" are therefore socially acceptable in many subcultures in Mexico. This is in contrast to North Americans who consider telling an "untruth" to be a reflection of a person's moral character. Although it is understandable that North American business managers expect honesty in business dealings, they should also be familiar with the differences Mexicans hold regarding the concept of truth.

Time is another cultural concept on which Mexicans and U.S. citizens tend to differ. Unlike U.S. citizens who conceptualize time in linear-spatial terms, Mexicans view time in a less linear fashion. Mexicans will do many things in one time frame, while Americans tend to have a set period of time to accomplish one goal. Mexicans use time with less constraints. They believe that what is not achieved today will be achieved *manana.* Given this view, Mexican business executives will place looser time constraints on business deals than their American counterparts. They will also consider interruptions and delays as part of the normal business procedure. Business contacts are usually made during the two- or three-hour lunch break. These are mainly social contacts, however, with business being discussed in the last few minutes.

NEAR EAST COUNTRIES

The Near East has been shaped by Greek, Turkish, Roman, Christian, and Arabic cultures. The countries in this extremely complex grouping include Greece, Yugoslavia, and Turkey. The diversity of language, history, and religion is hardly an adequate reason for the cluster. It is their geography that links these countries into a cluster.

Greece

Most of Greece is located in the southern part of the Balkan Peninsula. Southern Greece covers the Peloponnesus, a peninsula connected with the mainland by the Isthmus of Corinth. Several hundred Greek islands are scattered across the Aegean Sea to Turkey. Greece is bounded on the north by Bulgaria, Turkey, and Yugoslavia; on the west and south by the Ionian and Mediterranean Seas; and on the east by the Aegean Sea and Turkey.

Greeks are used to foreigners, friendly and unfriendly, being in their country. Indeed, Greece has been called the "land where three roads meet—the roads from Europe, Africa, and the Far East." Perhaps it is this constant flow of humanity that causes the Greeks to behave with seemingly undisciplined vitality. Like their Hellenic ancestors, they willingly share thoughts on every conceivable subject. While the pace of living is fast, it is the Greeks, not time, who is the master. They take time to work and play, laugh, and cry. Clock-watching is not characteristic of the Greeks. They live in an unhurried culture. Therefore, if a Greek friend tells you that he will be at your residence by noon, he may arrive early, on time, or later. This is perplexing to individuals who try to determine if people are typically early, on time, or late.

Your Greek friends will often defy such pigeonholing. They greet each other cheerfully. You should be careful not to assume that a shallow, child-like people reside beneath these roles. The Greeks can, when the situation requires, be very serious. Sometimes you will see Greek man fingering a string of beads (*komboloi*). This is a way they get rid of tension and it is strictly a masculine behavior.

When you get to know Greeks, you will find them sincere in their desire to really know you. Many of their questions may be personal. Try to not be offended by their questions. Greeks enjoy close personal relationships, and asking personal questions is their way of establishing close relationships. In essence, it is their way of deciding whether to accept you as "family" or "barbarian." The family is the center of Greek social life. Weekends and holidays are family times. If you are willing to learn some of the language and customs of your hosts, you too can become part of the family. The Greek family is based on *philotimo* (a sense of honor) which makes every Greek extremely protective of his or her family members. An insult to one member is perceived as an insult to all of them.

Ancient Greeks believed that a stranger might be a god in disguise, and it is wise to treat strangers kindly. That tradition of hospitality has been carried over into modern times. Many Greek people shake hands not only when they first meet but everytime they see each other.

Turkey

Turkey lies partly in Europe and partly in Asia. The Bosporus, the Sea of Marmara, and the Dardanelles, known collectively as the Turkish Straits, connect the Black and Mediterranean Seas. The coastal areas receive sufficient rainfall to support intensive cultivation. Various crops, ranging from tea in the northeast to tobacco in the west and cotton in the south, are grown on those relatively narrow coastal plains. The coastal regions, particularly in the south and west, enjoy mild winters.

The handshake is the common form of greeting. Turks clasp hands and kiss both cheeks of a close friend. It is impolite for women to cross their legs if facing someone. It is rude to ask personal questions or bring up controversial topics. Turkey is a highly structured hierarchical society. Therefore, it is more expedient to deal with the individual who has the highest status or most power when trying to get things done. But it is in bad taste to offer tips (*bakhish*) in offices. Trading favors is better than trying to buy them.

It is an insult to direct the sole of one's foot toward a Turk. Visitors should ask permission before smoking. Your host probably will give you permission to smoke even if he or she considers smoking improper. Adult male Turks generally wear suits rather than slacks and sports coats, and adult female Turks generally wear skirts and dresses rather than pantsuits and jeans. Women seldom bare their upper arms. Visitors are expected to refrain from talking about bad news items or asking personal questions or bringing up controversial topics. One should be careful to not refer to Turks as Arabs. Most Turks are Moslim, however.

MIDDLE EAST COUNTRIES

The Arab countries and Israel make up most of the Middle East. An Arab is a person who uses the Arabic language in daily conversation and who identifies with Arab culture. Most Arabs are Moslims. And the Arab countries extend from the Atlantic Ocean to the Persian Gulf. These countries include Aden, Algeria, Bahrain, Egypt, Jordan, Iraq, Iran, Kuwait, Lebanon, Libya, Morocco, Oman, Qatar, Saudi Arabia, Sudan, Syria, Tunisia and Yemen.

Saudi Arabia

Saudi Arabia has four land regions: (1) the Tihama (plain), (2) the western mountains, (3) the interior plateaus, and (4) the eastern coastlands, Jordan, Kuwait, and Iraq, lie to the north. The Persian Gulf, Qatar, and Trucial Coast are on the east. Aden and Oman are on the south and southeast, while Yemen is on the southwest, and the Red Sea and the Gulf of Aqaba are on the west.

The most common form of greeting among men in Saudi Arabia is a not too firm handshake with the right hand and the phrase *"Salaam alekum"* (Peace be upon you). Often, males follow the greeting by extending the left hand to each other's right shoulder and kiss the right and left cheeks. The greeting used depends on the closeness of the relationship and the individuals' status in Saudi Arabian society. It is typical for men not to introduce veiled women accompanying them. It is also common for Saudi Arabian men to walk hand in hand. As with the embraces and kisses, this is a sign of friendship frequently exchanged on meeting and departure. You should be careful not to stare or jump to false conclusions about the sexual preferences of the men.

A word that you will hear often is *"Inshallah"* (God willing). As noted earlier, a Moslim "submits" to God's will. The use of the words is not a means of avoiding responsibility for making decisions, but merely a statement that only those things that God wills will happen. Americans who expect meetings to start on time and get immediate decisions are usually frustrated by Moslims who are not rushed. Eventually things do get done. It is also wise for you to remember that not all Arabs are Moslims, nor are all peoples in the Middle East Arabs.

Separation of males and females is a way of life among Moslims. While Islam's laws have always granted women the right to hold and inherit property, and to obtain a divorce, they are expected to adhere to behavior that reflects feminine modesty and family honor. For example, they must dress modestly. That is, revealing clothing such as short-sleeved blouses and short skirts are to be avoided. Female visitors to Saudi Arabi should also dress conservatively. Most Saudi Arabian men and women still wear traditional Arab dress. The men wear the *ghutra* (head cloth) and *thobe* (white flowing robe). The women wear the veil and *abaya* (black robe that covers them from head to foot, often over long dresses). It is impolite for Saudi Arabians to remove their head coverings.

Women are not permitted to drive vehicles or ride bicycles. And women of all nationalities living in Saudi Arabia are expected to be accompanied by a male anytime they leave home and travel in public places. If you are a guest in an Arab's home, you are not likely to see female members of his family. Furthermore, it is considered impolite to inquire about a man's wife or his female children. Most Saudi Arabian men have only one wife, but a man may have up to four wives as long as he treats them equally. It is proper to make a general query about his family as a whole. Invitations to a Saudi Arabian home are usually given to other men. If a wife is invited, she may be sent to socialize and eat with the other women.

Gifts are not given to the host's wife. If you take a gift for your host, give it to him with your right hand. Gifts normally are given and received with the right hand. Tea or coffee will be served in business meetings and social gatherings. It is impolite for you to refuse a drink, and it is also impolite for you to drink more than three cups. Unless a person is a special friend, the offer of a third cup will signal the end of the meeting. To indicate that you have had enough, put a hand over the cup or tilt it several times and say *"bos"* (enough). Unless your host gives you permission, do not smoke in the presence of Saudi Arabians.

Arabs do not like to be criticized in public. However, they will conduct business in public. Maintain strong eye contact. Arabs believe the eyes are the windows of the soul. Don't gesture with the left hand—it is the Arab's "toilet" hand. Also, do not point at Saudi Arabians or signal with the hand. And avoid showing the soles of your shoes or feet to Saudi Arabians. Nor should you cross your legs. You will not go wrong if you keep both feet on the floor or ground. Unless special permission is received, you should not enter a mosque or even attempt to enter one.

Egypt

Egypt is located in the northeastern corner of Africa and has a land area of about 1 million square kilometers. It is bounded by the Mediterranean Sea, Libya, Sudan, the Red Sea, the Gulf of Aqaba, and Israel. The total area utilized by the people—the Nile Valley and Delta—is less than 40,000 square kilometers, about one-half the size of South Carolina. Egypt is part of the wide band of desert that stretches from the Atlantic coast of Africa into the Middle East. There are four distinct physical divisions: the Nile Valley and Delta, the Western Desert, the Eastern Desert, and the Siani Peninsula. Of twenty-six governorates, four are cities (Cairo, Alexandria, Port Said, and Suez), nine are in Lower Egypt (the Nile Delta region), eight are in Upper Egypt, and five cover the Siani and the desert areas east and west of the Nile.

The Egyptian phrase *"Ma' aleesh,"* which means "don't worry" or "never mind," captures the essence of the Egyptian relaxed approach to life. Like all Moslims, the philosophy of *Inshallah* (if God wills) characterizes both business and leisure activities in Egypt. They exhibit warmth in interpersonal relationships and they like to establish friendship and trust before making business deals. Therefore, Egyptian greetings are quite expressive and lengthy, with the host welcoming visitors several times and inquiring about their family and friends. Reticence to socialize is considered rude behavior. New acquaintances are addressed by their titles or by "Mr.," "Mrs.," or "Miss." French forms of address for women, e.g., "Madam," are also used. However, first names are not used without the appropriate title until friendship is established.

Israel

The State of Israel occupies 7,850 square miles and is located on the eastern end of the Mediterranean Sea where Asia Minor and Africa meet. It is bordered by the Mediterranean Sea on the west, Lebanon on the north, Syria on the northeast, Jordan on the east, and Egypt on the south. There are roughly five land regions in Israel: the highlands of Galilee, the Plain of Esdraelon, the Coastal Plain, the Judean Hills, and the Negev Desert.

About one-half of the Jewish population was born in Israel. They are called *Sabras*. The two main ethnic divisions in Israel are the *Ashkenzim* (Jews of Central and Eastern European origin) and the *Sephardim* (Oriental Jews from the countries of the Near East and the Mediterranean Basin). The latter group now comprises the majority. Of the non-Jewish population, approximately 77 percent are Moslims, 15 percent are Christians, and 8 percent are Druze and others. The Druze are forbidden to reveal the secret teachings of their God, al-Hakim bi-Amr Allah, the sixth caliph of the Fatimid dynasty of Egypt.

Israel is a land of informality. Unlike most countries discussed in this book, titles are relatively unimportant in Israel. For example, army officers and enlisted personnel frequently call each other by their first names or nicknames. Foreigners are also addressed in this informal manner. *Shalom* (sha-LOM) is the usual greeting for either "hello" or "good-bye." This is most often followed with a handshake. However, close friends pat each other on the back or shoulders.

As a whole, the Israelis consider it inappropriate and ill-mannered to speak or use actions that convey pride. They do expect speakers to strongly support their arguments and opinions with facts and evidence. If you use quotations, be exact and paraphrasing should be identified as such. And public speakers are asked "difficult" rather than "polite" questions. This is not done to embarrass the speaker but instead to inform the listeners. In short, Israelis are eager readers and inquisitive listeners.

Israeli parents take an active role in and have a deep responsibility for their children's future. This extends beyond providing children with the best possible education to handling all the business arrangements of their children's weddings. Marriages are significant social events in Israel, and most marriages are performed by a rabbi. After a wedding, singing and dancing often lasts for several hours.

In the large cities, men and women dress casually. Men wear shirts unbuttoned at the neck and untucked. Ties and suits are worn only on special occasions. Women wear shorts and sandals and other casual wear most of the year. For both males and females cotton clothing is most comfortable. Religion also plays a role in dress. On streets you may see Talmudic students wearing long black coats walking side by side with persons in blue jeans. Israel is a nation of dramatic cultural contrasts where old ways co-exist with new ones. This does not minimize the importance of Jewish holidays and customs which range from the ultraorthodox to conservative.

FAR EAST COUNTRIES

The eastern and southeastern parts of Asia are called "the Far East." Eastern Asia is the most developed region of the continent. This area includes China, Hong Kong, Taiwan, and Japan. Southeastern Asia includes Vietnam, Burma, Indonesia, Thailand, Malaysia, the Philippines, and Singapore. Chinese language and customs have greatly influenced all the countries in the Far East.

China

The People's Republic of China, located in eastern Asia, is almost as large as the European Continent. It is the world's third-largest country in total area, after the Soviet Union and Canada. Countries sharing its 14,000-mile border include Korea, the USSR, Mongolia, Afghanistan, Pakistan, India, Nepal, Bhutal, Burma, Laos, and Vietnam. Hong Kong and Macau are on China's southern coastline. Two-thirds of China's area is mountainous or semidesert; only about one-tenth is cultivated. Ninety percent of the people live on one-sixth of the land, primarily in the fertile plains and deltas of the east.

The Chinese are renown for their good manners, hospitality, and humility. However, they do not like to be touched by strangers. A smile is much better received than a pat on the back, and it is impolite to exhibit physical familiarity with older persons or individuals with important positions. Either a nod or a slight bow is an acceptable greeting, but a handshake will suffice too. Chinese names consist of a one-syllable family name followed by a one- or two-syllable given name. The family name is always mentioned first. Thus, Wang Fuming should be addressed as Mr.

Wang, and Li Meili as Madam Li. Married women retain their maiden names. Chinese men and women who participate in social functions with foreigners attend because of their positions and usually do not bring their spouse.

Strict punctuality is observed for business appointments and social occasions. And it is proper to arrive a few minutes before the specified time. It is customary to present business cards. In public and private places the Chinese expect people to conduct themselves with restraint and to refrain from loud, boisterous behavior. Valuable gifts are seldom accepted from strangers, and tipping is forbidden. However, it is appropriate to thank service people for their effort on your behalf. Generally, gifts should be of nominal value and presented to the group host. Individual gifts are not necessary, although little momentos of the occasion are appreciated.

Taiwan

Taiwan, or Formosa, is a mountainous island in the South China Sea. Portuguese traders gave the island the name *Ilha Formosa* (Beautiful Island), and the Chinese call it Taiwan (Terraced Bay). The Formosa Strait separates the islands of Quemay and Matsu. Together, they comprise a space approximately twice the size of New Jersey. Thickly forested mountains cover two-thirds of Taiwan.

In keeping with its belief in "world brotherhood," Taiwan has tried to maintain good international relations by offering its people the dual language mediums of Chinese and English. Today, more than 50 percent of its citizens speak English as a second language. The fact that your host may speak the English language does not eliminate the need for you to know the host country language. I strongly recommend that U.S. business personnel assigned to jobs in Taiwan take a short course in spoken Chinese. Being able to greet your hosts in their native tongue will not only bolster your self-esteem, it will also demonstrate a genuineness of interest on your part.

When meeting someone for the first time, it is appropriate to nod your head. But close friends and acquaintances usually shake hands. A slight bow is a sign of special respect. Adults frequently show affection for children by patting them on the cheek or shoulder but never on the head. Traditional Taiwanese adults believe that the head should not be touched by another person, especially not by strangers. When addressing

Chinese people, the person's title and one-syllable family name are used rather than the first name. Thus, Chen Tsung-fa should be addressed as Mr. Chen. Also in Chinese names, the one-syllable family names comes first and the two-syllable given name second. Only in rare instances are first names used in greetings.

It is considered rude to point with the index finger; the open hand should be used. Nor should you beckon to Chinese with the palms up. If you must beckon, do it with the palms down. When sitting down, place your hands in your lap and don't jiggle your legs. Women may cross their legs, but men seldom cross theirs. It is common for female friends to hold hands when walking in public places, but it is inappropriate for them to put their arms on each other's shoulders.

Even though Taiwan has one of the world's highest population densities, it also has one of the best social orders and some of the most industrious and cooperative people in the world. In fact, the concepts of "teamwork" and "nationalism" permeate the culture and are stressed over "individualism." More importantly, the Taiwanese people believe that the spirit of cooperation should not only be a national concept but also an international reality. This is consistent with their belief in Tatung (World Brotherhood).

The Chinese people may be the only people who pay respect to their senior citizens through a national holiday celebration. Oldster's Day, as it is called, has been an annual celebration in Taiwan since 1966. On this day all senior citizens are presented with gifts from their local government.

The Chinese also have long traditional beliefs in heaven and ancestry worship. They believe that human beings originate from heaven and therefore share a very close relationship with it. When a family worships its ancestors, it also worships its gods who can be traced back to heaven. A pregnant Chinese woman becomes the center of family attention until the baby is born. Three days after, the childbirth is celebrated with the child's ancestors who are notified through special ceremonial rituals. At age one month the child is presented to his or her relatives and friends.

Unlike in the United States where the birthday is a yearly celebration, Taiwanese birthday celebrations are quite different. After the one-month celebration, the next major birthday celebration does not occur until the child reaches adulthood. And the next major celebration is when he or she reaches middle age. Unlike Americans who tend to become depressed upon reaching middle age, this is an upbeat period for the Chinese. If a middle-aged Chinese has a married daughter, the birthday is celebrated more elaborately. According to Taiwanese customs, when a person reaches the age 60, he or she has lived as "small longevity"; the age 70 indicates "middle longevity"; and 80 is a "great longevity."

South Korea

The Republic of Korea (South Korea) occupies the southern portion of a mountainous peninsula, about 600 miles long and 135 miles wide, projecting southeast from China and separating the Sea of Japan from the Yellow Sea (known in Korea as, respectively, the East Sea and West Sea). Japan lies about 120 miles east of Pusan across the Sea of Japan. The most rugged areas are the mountainous east coast and central interior. Good harbors are found only on the western and southern coasts. South Korea's only land boundary is with North Korea, formed by the Military Demarcation Line (MDL) marking the line of separation between the belligerent sides at the close of the Korean War. The Demilitarized Zone (DMZ) extends for 2,000 meters (just over 1 mi.) on either side of the MDL. The North and South Korean Governments both hold that the MDL is not a permanent border but a temporary administrative line.

The family is the foundation of Korean society which is bound together by a strong sense of duty and obligations. Traditional rituals of courtesy, formality, and modesty characterize the Koreans. Compliments are graciously denied, and reluctance to accept high honors is the mark of a socially correct person. Korean men greet their male friends by bowing slightly and shaking hands, either with the right hand or both hands. However, women rarely shake hands. Young children bow and nod their heads unless invited to shake hands, which is a great honor for children. Custom dictates that one should pay complete attention to the person being greeted.

Although Korean men may hold hands in public, it is inappropriate for them to put their arms around another's shoulder or slap each other on the back if they are not very close friends. Koreans are particularly careful about touching in public older people and those of the opposite sex. Also, there is proper posture while standing or sitting. In informal situations visitors may cross their legs only with one knee over the other and with soles and toes pointed downward. It is impolite to cross the legs at all in formal situations. Feet should never be put on furniture, and hands should always remain in the sight of the person one is talking with. It is also impolite to not cover the mouth when yawning or using a toothpick. And both hands should be used for handing things to another person and for receiving objects.

Success depends on social contacts, and gifts frequently are given before asking for a favor. If you wish to avoid an obligation, return gifts to the giver with a comment such as, "I am grateful, but this is too much." Friendships are important as a prelude to long-term business dealings. Open criticism, public disagreement, and rude behavior are to be avoided because Koreans believe that no one has the right to lower the self-esteem of another. It is considered better to accept an injustice to preserve harmony than to assert one's individual rights.

Business etiquette is conditioned largely by the strong Korean work ethic and the basically conservative nature of Korean business. This is reflected in an organizational and managerial approach which emphasizes harmony and structure over innovation and experimentation. This outlook can affect the style, pace, substance, and results of negotiations. Visitors should be punctual for appointments, as an early arrival may disrupt a normally full business schedule. Business cards are customarily exchanged and are regarded as providing insight into the identity, positions, and potential of the presenter.

Japan

The island country of Japan lies off the northeast coast of mainland Asia and faces China, Russia, and Korea. Japan is made up of four large islands and thousands of smaller ones. All of the islands together have a land area slightly smaller than California. The four major islands—Hokkaido, Honshu, Kyushu, and Shikoku—form a curve of about 1,200 miles (1,900 km.) long. The Japanese call their country Nihon Nippon, which means *source of the sun.*

A bow is the traditional greeting, and you should try to bow as low and as long as the other person is bowing. It is incorrect to clasp hands in front of you as you bow. Handshakes also are widespread. When in doubt about proper behavior, act in the same manner as your Japanese host. It is impolite to yawn in formal meetings. Also, avoid making conspicuous gestures and chewing gum in public. Legs, when crossed, should have one knee directly over the other, or they can be crossed at the ankles. Shoes should be removed before stepping into a Japanese-style home. After removing your shoes, place them together pointing toward the outdoors. Slippers may be worn inside Japanese-style homes but should be removed before entering rooms with straw mat floors (*tatami*). Guests should, like the host, deny all compliments graciously. The Japanese feel a deep obligation to return gifts and favors.

AFRICAN COUNTRIES

Africa is the second-largest continent in the world. Only Asia is larger. European countries once governed nearly all Africa. Reflecting the colonization that occurred, many Africans speak English, French, or Portuguese. The chief languages of Africa, however, are native languages and dialects such as the Bantu languages, Khoisan, and Swahili. As in other continents, the ethnic group divisions are intensive.

GHANA

Ghana is bordered by Burkina to the north, Togo to the east, and the Ivory Coast to the west. In the west a forested belt extends north from the coast into the hilly Ashanti region.

Ghanaians are proud of their diverse ethnic populations and also of being the first African nation to gain independence from European colonizers. Traditional religious beliefs and practices still affect Ghanians who are generally sociable, not bound by the Western concept of punctuality, and live at a relaxed pace. However, Ghana's long affiliation with Great Britain is still evident in common English greetings which are considered proper in most circumstances. "Hello" and a firm handshake are daily practices. English is the official language, and Western etiquette is proper when eating with Ghanians, whose food is often spicy.

When first meeting a Ghanian, you should avoid asking questions about the person's "tribe." This word has a negative meaning in Ghana. The word "ethnic group" is acceptable, but questions about a person's ethnic group are reserved for close acquaintances. If you must find out about a person's background, you may get a clue by asking where he or she is from. This is an appropriate query. Although Ghanians do not adhere to the Western concept of "being on time," they expect their Western guests to arrive on schedule. Ghanians will do all that they can to accommodate their guests. But their manner of showing respect varies from most American ways. For example, children are taught to be quiet and respectful around elders, to not look elders in the eyes, and to not aggressively make acquaintances with strangers. Also, an attitude of superiority is offensive.

Kenya

Astride the Equator on the east coast of Africa, Kenya is bounded by Ethiopia, Sudan, Tanzania, Uganda, Lake Victoria, Somalia, and the Indian Ocean. It is a country of striking topographical and climatic variety. The northern three-fifths is arid, much of it semidesert, inhabited only by nomadic pastoralists. Eight-five percent of the population and almost all economic activity are located in the southern two-fifths of the country.

Kenyans are warm, friendly people, most of whom speak Swahili. The common greeting is *Hujambo, hibari?* (Greetings, how are you?), followed by a handshake. When invited into a Kenyan home, it is appropriate to bring small gifts such as cookies and candy. Flowers are usually taken to persons in hospitals, and wine is given at urban weddings. European cuisine is commonplace. In most instances, dinner is eaten before socializing. Visitors must be careful to dress modestly and conservatively. Women should avoid wearing shorts in the cities.

Correspondence and personal calls each play a significant role in the conduct of business in Kenya. Expeditious handling of correspondence is expected and greatly appreciated. Personal visits are warmly welcomed and generally regarded as the most efficient method of establishing new trade contracts. Punctuality is important to Kenyan business people and the business visitor should make every effort to be on time for appointments. As a general rule, appointments should be made in advance of a business call.

Nigeria

Nigeria covers an area of 372,674 square miles. The country takes its name from the Niger River. It extends 475 miles in the south along the Gulf of Guinea. Chad and Cameroon border Nigeria on the east, Dahomey on the west, and Niger on the north. There is a belt of mangrove forests and swamp 10 to 60 miles wide along the coast. Beyond the mangrove belt is a 50- to 60-mile wide tropical forest. Hills lie beyond the tropical forest. The northernmost part of Nigeria merges with the Sahara Desert.

Because of the diversity of customers, cultures, and dialects in Nigeria, the form of greetings vary throughout the country. However, avoid using colloquial greeting and phrases such as "Hi" or "What's happening?" Also, dress varies throughout the country, e.g., in the Moslim north men and women dress very conservative, and non-Moslims in the east and west dress more casual. Individual Nigerians are very proud of their ethnic group and its unique cultural heritage. Because of the negative colonial connotations attached to word "tribe," many Nigerians prefer "ethnic group" to "tribe."

Business visitors should be well dressed. Casual dress in many cases connotes a casual attitude, especially to European-trained Nigerians. Titles should be used, especially the honorific titles of traditional leaders. Company representatives should be flexible in business dealings and be able to make decisions on contractual matters without lengthy referral to their home offices. In Nigeria, business of any consequence is consummated face to face. No worthwhile transactions can be completed either impersonally or quickly.

COMMUNIST COUNTRIES

Under communism the government owns and manages all major productive property in agriculture, industry, and transportation. Communist nations consist of Albania, Bulgaria, Cuba, Czechoslovakia, East Germany, Hungary, North Korea, Peoples Republic of China (discussed earlier), Poland, Romania, the Union of Soviet Socialist Republics, Vietnam, and Yugoslavia.

Union of Soviet Socialist Republics

The USSR is the largest country in the world. Its territory stretches from the Baltic Sea across the northern Eurasian land mass to the Bering Strait, where an island belonging to the Soviet Union lies only 3 miles from one that is part of Alaska. Most of the USSR is above 50 north latitude (Winnipeg, Canada lies on the latitude). The latitude of Moscow is the same as that of southern Alaska.

In the west, from the Pripet Marches near the Polish border to the Ural Mountains, Soviet territory stretches over broad plain broken only by occasional low hills. Crossing this plain to the south are a number of rivers, the most important being the Dnieper, which empties into the Black Sea, and the Volga, which empties into the Caspian Sea. Between the Black and Caspian Seas lie the scenic Caucasian Mountains. The Urals mark the traditional divisions between European and Asiatic Russia. To the east are the vast Siberian lowlands and the deserts of central Asia. Beyond are the barren Siberian highlands and the mountain ranges of the Soviet far east. Farther to the east lie the higher mountain ranges, including the Pamirs, Altai, and Tien Shan.

The people are correctly called "Soviets," not "Russians" who make up about half of the population. Generally, Soviets are thoughtful and friendly people. When first meeting someone and departing, they will shake hands. Greetings and good-byes among friends also include hugging and three kisses on the cheek. Soviets prefer direct and informal interactions and are likely to simply state their name rather than recite a polite phrase after shaking hands. The proper greeting is "Mr.," "Mrs.," "Miss" or title with the last name. It is rude to whistle in public gatherings and, also, to use the following American signs: shaking a raised fist and the "OK" sign with the index finger pressed to the thumb tip. Soviets disapprove of men sitting with ankle on knee or with legs spread wide.

Nor are the Soviets the emotionless people the Western media often portray them to be. In public men may embrace each other, kiss other men on the lips, or cry and not feel guilty or less masculine for such behavior. However, Soviets seldom force a smile. They do not smile if they do not feel like it, which is often misinterpreted as eternally grim behavior. In addition to expressing feelings and displaying emotions, the Soviets usually are frank with each other. And they are generous people. It is a severe insult for a Soviet to be accused of being stingy.

When invited to a Soviet home, it is common practice to bring flowers, a book (avoid dissident literature), or liquor. If you decide to bring a gift made in your country, select something that will not imply the superiority of your country's industry. The most common form of eating is the European style with the fork in the left hand and knife in the right. Hands are kept above the table and not in the lap. Guests should compliment the host on the food and not hurry to leave the table. When dining in a restaurant, the waiter or waitress is called with a slight nod of the head, not by waving an arm or beckoning with a finger. Officially, tipping is not allowed; however, service personnel will keep the change unless you ask for it. Toasts are common during meals eaten in homes and restaurants, and guests are expected to return toasts.

Soviets are very status conscious and resent initial business contacts initiated by low-status foreign personnel. When dealing with the Soviets it is important to remember that they tend to think from the general concept to the particular. Unlike most U.S. citizens, the Soviets deduce implications from axioms rather than the reverse process. That is, Americans tend to be factual, while Soviets tend to be intuitive. However, when conducting business, the roles are often reversed, with Soviets seeking facts and documentation and Americans negotiating with feelings. Soviet negotiators usually are thorough in their preparation, and foreigners are at a tremendous disadvantage if they are not experts in their fields.

REFERENCES

Acosta, F. X. & Sheehan, J. G. (1976). Psychotherapist ethnicity and expertise as determinants of self-disclosure. In M. Miranda (Ed.), *Psychotherapy for the Spanish-Speaking.* Los Angeles: Spanish-Speaking Mental Health Research Center.

Aguilera, D. C. (1967). Relationship between physical contact and verbal interaction between nurses and patients. *Journal of Psychiatric Nursing and Mental Health Services,* 5, 5–21.

Aiello, J. R. & Jones, S. E. (1971). Field study of the proxemic behavior of young school children in three subcultural groups. *Journal of Personality and Social Psychology,* 27, 351–356.

Alamaney, A. J. (1981). Cultural traits of the Arabs: Growing interest for international management. *Management International Review,* 21, 10–28.

Albert, S. & Dabbs, J. M. Jr. (1970). Physical distance and persuasion. *Journal of Personality and Social Psychology,* 15, 265–270.

Allan, J. (Ed.). (1987). Counseling with expressive arts. [Symposium]. *Elementary School Guidance and Counseling,* 21, 251–323.

Allan, W. & Stokes S. (1981). Black family life styles and mental health of black Americans. In R. Endo & F. Munoz (Eds.), *Perspectives on minority group mental health.* Chicago: Charter House.

Anda, D. (1984). Bicultural socialization: Factor affecting the minority experience. *Social Work,* 29, 101–107.

Ansante, M. K., Newmark, E., & Blake, C. A. (Eds.) (1979). *Handbook of intercultural communication.* Beverly Hills, CA: Sage.

Anosike, B. (1982). African and Afro-Americans: The basis for greater understanding and solidarity. *Journal of Negro Education,* 51, 434–448.

Applebaum, H. (Ed.). (1984). *Work in non-market and transitional societies.* Albany: State University of New York Press.

Arcadila, R. (1978). Behavior modification in Latin America. In M. Hersen, R. M. Eishler, & P. M. Miller (Eds.), *Progress in behavior modification.* Vol. 6. New York: Academic Press.

Arlow, J. A. (1989). Psychoanalysis. In R. J. Corsini & D. Wedding (Eds.), *Current psychotherapies.* 4th ed. Springfield, IL: Charles C Thomas.

Arredondo-Dowd, P. M. & Gonsalves, J. (1980). Preparing culturally effective counselors. *Personnel and Guidance Journal,* 58, 657–662.

Atkinson, D. R., Maruyama, M., & Matsui, S. (1978). Effects counselor race and counseling approach on Asian Americans' perceptions of counselor credibility and utility. *Journal of Counseling Psychology,* 25, 76–83.

Atkinson, D. R., Ponterotto, J. D., & Sanchez, A. R. (1984). Attitudes of Vietnamese and Anglo-American students toward counseling. *Journal of College Student Personnel,* 25, 448–452.

Atkinson, D. R. (1985). A meta-review of research on cross-cultural counseling and psychotherapy. *Journal of Multicultural Counseling and Development,* 13, 138–153.

Bagley, C. (1973). Occupational class and symptoms of depression. *Social Science Medicine,* 7, 327–340.

Bahm, A. J. (1964). *The world's living religions.* New York: Dell.

Bandura, A. (1969). *Principles of behavior modification.* New York: Holt, Rinehart & Winston.

Banks, H. C. (1975). The Black person as client and as therapist. *Professional Psychology,* 6, 470–474.

Barcorn, C. N. & Dixon, D. (1984). The effects of touch on depressed and vocationally undecided clients. *Journal of Counseling Psychology,* 31, 489–497.

Barna, L. M. (1970). Stumbling blocks in intercultural communications. In D. S. Hoopes (Ed.), *Readings in intercultural communications.* Vol. 1. Pittsburgh: University of Pittsburgh Intercultural Communication. Network of the Regional Council of International Education.

Barnlund, D. D. (1975). *Public and private self in Japan and the United States.* Tokyo: Simul Press.

Bates, J. E. (1976). Effects of children's nonverbal behavior on adults. *Child Development,* 47, 1079–1088.

Baxter, J. C. (1970). Interpersonal spacing in natural settings. *Sociometry,* 33, 444–456.

Beckhard, R. (1969). *Organization development: Strategies and methods.* Reading, MA: Addison-Wesley.

Becker, H. & Fritzche, D. J. (1987). A comparison of ethical behavior of American, French and German managers. *Columbia Journal of World Business,* 22, 87–95.

Beckett, S. (1965). *Proust.* London: J. Calder.

Berger, P. L. & Luckman, P. (1967). *The social construction of reality.* Garden City, NY: Anchor Books.

Bergman, R. L. (1971). Navajo peyote use—its apparent safety. *American Journal of Psychiatry,* 128, 695–699.

Bernard, M. E. & DiGiuseppe, R. (Eds.). (1988). *Inside rational-emotive therapy.* Orlando, FL: Academic Press.

Berne, E. (1958). *Games people play.* New York: Grove Press.

Berry, J. W. (1979). Research in multicultural societies: Implications of cross-cultural methods. *Journal of Cross-Cultural Psychology,* 10, 415–434.

Beutler, L. E. (1983). *Eclectic psychotherapy: A systematic approach.* Elmsford, NY: Pergamon.

Birdwhistell, R. L. (1970). *Kinesics and content.* Philadelphia: University of Pennsylvania Press.

Blake, R. R. & Mouton, J. S. (1964). *The managerial grid.* Houston, TX: Gulf.

Blalock, H. M. Jr. (1982). *Race and ethnic relations.* Englewood Cliffs, NJ: Prentice-Hall.

Bolen, J. S. (1979). *The Tao of psychology.* New York: Harper & Row.

Brabeck, M. M. & Wolfel, E. R. (1985). Counseling theory: Understanding the trend toward eclecticism from a developmental perspective. *Journal of Counseling and Development*, 63, 343–348.

Brammer, L. M. (1985). Counseling services in the People's Republic of China. *International Journal for the Advancement of Counseling*, 8, 125–136.

Brandon, D. (1976). *Zen in the art of helping*. New York: Dell.

Brenner, C. (1973). *An elementary textbook of psychoanalysis*. New York: International University Press.

Bristline, S. M. (1986). Protocol for foreign guests. *Association Management*, 74, 6–7.

Brockner, J. (1988). *Self-esteem at work: Research theory, and practice*. Lexington, MA: Lexington Books.

Buber, M. (1957). *Pointing the way*. New York: Harper & Row.

Buber, M. (1965). *The knowledge of man*. New York: Harper & Row.

Buck, R. (1984). *The communication of emotion*. New York: Guilford.

Buck R. & Teng, W. (1987). *Spontaneous emotional communication and social biofeedback: A cross-cultural study of emotional expression and communication in Chinese and Taiwanese students*. Symposium on Social and Biological Influences on Expressivity. American Psychological Association Convention, New York. August 30.

Bugental, D. E., Love, R. L., & Gianetto, R. M. (1971). Perfidious feminine faces. *Journal of Personality and Social Psychology*, 27, 314–318.

Casas, J. M., Ponterotto, J. G., & Gutierrez, J. M. (1986). An ethical indictment of counseling research and training: The cross-cultural perspective. *Journal of Counseling and Development*, 64, 347–349.

Chang, B. (1981). Asian-American patient care. In G. Henderson & M. Primeaux (Eds.), *Transcultural health care*. Menlo Park, CA: Addison-Wesley.

Chang, S. K. C. (1985). American and Chinese managers in U.S. companies in Taiwan: A comparison. *California Management Review*, 27, 144–156.

Cherniss, C. (1968). *Professional burnout in human services organizations*. New York: Praeger.

Chin, R. (1982). Conceptual paradigm for a racial-ethnic community: The case of the Chinese American Community. In S. Sye & T. Moore (Eds.), *The pluralistic society: A community mental health perspective*. Los Angeles: Spanish Speaking Mental Health Research Center.

Claver, R. G. (1976). Problemees de guerissage en cote d'Ivoire. *Annales Medico-Psychologiques*, 134, 23–30.

Clements, F. E. (1932). *Primitive concepts of disease*. University of California Publications in American Archaeology and Ethnology, 32, 2.

Collomb, H. (1972). *Psychiatries sans psychiatres*. Cairo: Etudes Medicales.

Constantelos, D. (1967). *The Greek Orthodox Church*. New York: Seabury Press.

Contino, R. & Lorusso, R. M. (1982). The Theory Z turnaround of a public agency. *Public Administration Review*, 42, 66–71.

Copeland, E. J. (1982). Minority populations and traditional counseling programs: Some alternatives. *Counselor Education and Supervision*, 21, 187–193.

Corey, G. (1977). *Theory and practice of consulting and psychotherapy*. Monterey, CA: Brooks/Cole.

Corsini, R. J. & Wedding, D. (Eds.). (1989). *Current Psychotherapies.* 4th ed. Itasca, IL: F. E. Peacock.

Curt, C. J. N. (1980). *Hispanic-Anglo conflicts in nonverbal communication.* Second Annual Conference of the Institute of Nonverbal Research at Teachers College, Columbia University, March 21.

Davids, T. W. & Davids, C. A. F. (Trans.). (1939). *The sacred books of the Buddhists.* Vol. 3. Oxford: Clarendon Press.

Davis, M. & Skupier, J. (1982). *Body movement and nonverbal communication: An annotated bibliography, 1971–1980.* Bloomington: Indiana University Press.

Dawson, J. M. L. (1975). *Psychological effect of bio-social change in West Africa.* New Haven, CT: Hraflex.

deKeyser, V., Qvale, T., & Wilpert, B. (Eds.). (1988). *The meaning of work and technological options.* New York: John Wiley & Sons.

del Portillo, C. T. (1987). Poverty, self-concept, and health: Experience of Latinas. *Women and Health,* 12, 229–247.

Deloria, V. Jr. (1969). *Custer died for your sins: An Indian manifesto.* New York: Seabury Press.

DeVos, G. (1985). Dimensions of the self in Japanese culture. In A. J. Marsella, G. DeVos, & F. L. K. Hsu (Eds.), *Culture and self: Asian and Western perspectives.* New York: Tavistock.

DeWitt, J. (1971). *The Christian Science way of life.* Boston: Christian Science Publishing Company.

Dillard, J. L. (1972). *Black English: Its history and usage in the United States.* New York: Random House.

Disara, J. (1988). African children's attitude toward learning. *Journal of Multicultural Counseling and Development,* 16, 16–23.

Dohrenwend, B. P. & Dohrenwend, B. S. (1969). *Social status and psychological disorder: A casual inquiry.* New York: John Wiley & Sons.

Dohrenwend, B. P. & Dohrenwend, B. S. (1974). Social and cultural influences on psychopathology. *Annual Review of Psychology,* 25, 417–452.

Doi, L. T. (1964). Psychoanalytic therapy and "Western Man": A Japanese view, *International Journal of Social Psychiatry.* Special Edition, No. 1.

Dolliver, R. (1981). Some limitations in Perls' Gestalt therapy. *Psychotherapy, Research and Practice,* 8, 38–45.

Draguns, J. G. (1973). Comparisons of psychopathology across cultures: Issues, findings, directions. *Journal of Cross-Cultural Psychology,* 4, 9–47.

Draguns, J. G. (1980). Psychological disorders of clinical severity. In H. C. Triandis & J. G. Draguns (Eds.), *Handbook of cross-cultural psychology.* Vol. 6. Boston: Allyn & Bacon.

Draguns, J. G. (1981). Cross-cultural counseling and psychotherapy: History, issues, current state. In A. J. Marsella & P. B. Pedersen (Eds.), *Cross-cultural counseling and psychotherapy.* New York: Pergamon Press.

Dryden, W. (1984). *Rational-emotive therapy: Fundamentals and innovations.* Beckenham, England: Croom-Helm.

Dunham, H. W. (1976). Society, culture and mental disorder. *Archives of General Psychiatry*, 33, 247–256.

Dusay, J. M. & Dusay, K. M. (1989). Transactional analysis. In R. J. Corsini & D. Wedding (Eds.), *Current psychotherapies*. 4th ed. Itasca, IL: F. E. Peacock.

Edgerton, R. B., Karno, M., & Fernandez, I. (1970). Curanderismo in the metropolis. *American Journal of Psychotherapy*, 24, 130–135.

Egan, G. (1985). *The skilled helper: Model, skills, and methods of effective helping*. 3rd ed. Monterey, CA: Brooks/Cole.

Egeland, J. (1967). *Beliefs and behavior related to illness*. Doctoral dissertation, Yale University.

Ekman, P. & Friesen, W. V. (1974). Detecting deception from the body or face. *Journal of Personality and Social Psychology*, 30, 288–298.

Ekman, P. & Friesen, W. V. (1986). A new pan-cultural expression of emotion. *Motivation and Emotion*, 20, 159–168.

Ekman, P., Friesen, W. V., O'Sullivan, M., Diucoyanni-Tarlatzis, I., Krause, R., Pitcairn, T., Schere, K., Chan, A., Heider, K., Le Compte, W. A., Ricci-Bitte, P., & Tomita, M. (1987). Universals and cultural differences in judgments of facial expressions of emotion. *Journal of Personality and Social Psychology*, 43, 712–717.

Eliot, C. E. (1925). *Hinduism and Buddhism: An historical sketch*. London: Longmans, Green.

Elliott, R., Barker, C. B., Caskey, N., & Pistrang, N. (1982). Differential helpfulness of counselor verbal response modes. *Journal of Counseling Psychology*, 29, 354–361.

Elliott, R. (1985). Helpful and nonhelpful events in brief counseling interviews: An empirical taxonomy. *Journal of Counseling Psychology*, 32, 307–322.

Ellis, A. (1962). *Reason and emotion in psychotherapy*. New York: Lyle Stuart.

Ellis, A. (1989). Rational-emotive therapy. In R. J. Corsini & D. Wedding (Eds.), *Current psychotherapies*. 4th ed. Itasca, IL: F. E. Peacock.

Engel, G. (1971). Sudden and rapid death during psychological stress: Folklore or folk wisdom? *Annals of Internal Medicine*, 74, 771–782.

England, G. W. & Lee, R. (1974). The relationship between managerial values and managerial success in the United States, Japan, India, and Australia. *Journal of Applied Psychology*, 4, 411, 419.

Eron, L. D. & Peterson, R. A. (1982). Abnormal behavior: Some approaches. *Annual Review of Psychology*, 33, 231–264.

Erskine, R. G. (1982). Transactional analysis and family therapy. In A. M. Horne & M. M. Olhsen (Eds.), *Family counseling and therapy*. Itasca, IL: F. E. Peacock.

Esen, A. (1972). A view of guidance from Africa. *Personnel and Guidance Journal*, 50, 792–799.

Esser, A. H., Chamberlain, A. S., Chapple, E. D., & Kine, N. S. (1965). Territoriality of patients on a research ward. In J. Wortis (Ed.), *Recent advances in biological psychiatry*. Vol. 7. New York: Plenum Press.

Feagin, J. R. (Ed.). (1984). *Racial and ethnic relations*. Englewood Cliffs, NJ: Prentice-Hall.

Feder, B. & Ronall, R. (Eds.). (1980). *Beyond the hot seat*. New York: Brunner/Mazel.

Fernandez, M. S. (1988). Issues in counseling Southeast-Asian students. *Journal of Multi cultural Counseling and Development*, 16, 157–166.

Fiedler, F. A. (1950). A comparison of the therapeutic effectiveness of empathy, nonpossessive warmth, and genuineness. In A. S. Gurman & A. M. Razin (Eds.), *Effective psychotherapy: A handbook of research.* New York: Pergamon Press.

Fiedler, F. A. (1951). Factor analysis of psychoanalytic, nondirective, and Adlerian therapeutic relationships. *Journal of Psychology,* 15, 35–38.

Fiedler, F. A. (1967). *A theory of leadership effectiveness.* New York: McGraw-Hill.

Fieg, J. (1979). Concept of oneself. In E. L. Smith & L. F. Luce (Eds.), *Toward internationalism: Readings in cross-cultural communication.* Rowley, MD: Newbury House.

Firestone, S. (1970). *The dialects of sex.* New York: Bantam Books.

Fisch, S. (1968). Botanicas and spiritualism in a metropolis. *Milbank Memorial Fund,* 41, 378.

Fisher, J. D., Rytting, M., & Heslin, R. (1976). Hands touching hands: Affective and evaluative effects of interpersonal touch. *Sociometry,* 39, 416–421.

Fondetti, D. (1976). *Care in working class ethnic neighborhoods: Implications for policy and programming.* New York: Institute on Pluralism and Group Identity.

Foster, G. M. (1953). Relationship between Spanish and Spanish-American folk medicine. *Journal of American Folklore,* 66, 201–217.

Foster, G. M. & Anderson, B. G. (1978). *Medical anthropology.* New York: John Wiley & Sons.

Foster, P. (1982). How attitudes are sometimes formed. In S. Fresh (Ed.), *Learning about peoples and cultures.* Evanston, IL: McDougal, Littell.

Franks, C. M., Wilson, G. T., Kendall, P., & Brownell, K. (1982). *Annual review of behavior therapy: Theory and practice.* Vol. 1. New York: Guilford Press.

Fraser, J. (1980). *The Chinese portrait of a people.* New York: Summit Books.

Freeberg, N. E. (1969). Assessment of disadvantaged adolescents: A different approach to research and evaluation measures. *Research Bulletin.* Princeton, NJ: Educational Testing Service, May.

Freud, S. (1920). *A general introduction to psychoanalysis.* Garden City, NY: Garden City Publishing Co.

Freudenberger, H. J. (1980). *Burnout: The high cost of achievement.* New York: Doubleday.

Fromm, E. (1967). *Man for himself: An inquiry into the psychology of ethics.* New York: Fawcett.

Fromm, E. (1968). *The sane society.* New York: Fawcett.

Gbekobou, K. N. (1984). Counseling African children in the United States. *Elementary School Guidance and Counseling Journal,* 18, 225–230.

Gelfand, D. E. & Kutzik, A. J. (Eds.). (1979). *Ethnicity and aging.* New York: Springer.

Gelson, C. J. & Carter, J. A. (1985). The relationship in counseling and psychotherapy: Components, consequences, and theoretical antecedents. *The Consulting Psychologist,* 13, 155–243.

Gibbs, J. T. (1985). Can we continue to be color-blind and class-bound? *The Consulting Psychologist,* 13, 426–435.

Giles, H. & Edwards, J. R. (Eds.). (1983). Language and attitude in multicultural settings. [Symposium] *Journal of Multilingual and Multicultural Development.* 4.

Giordano, J. (1973). *Ethnicity and mental health.* New York: Institute on Pluralism and Group Identity.

Giordano, J. & Giordano, G. P. (1977). *The ethno-cultural factor in mental health: A literature review and bibliography.* New York: Institute on Pluralism and Group Identity.

Gladstein, G. (1983). Understanding empathy: Integrating counseling, development, and social psychology perspectives. *Journal of Counseling Psychology, 30,* 467–482.

Glasser, W. (1965). *Reality therapy.* New York: Harper & Row.

Glasser, W. (1981). *Stations of the mind.* New York: Harper & Row.

Glen, M. & Kunnes, R. (1973). *Repression or revolution? Therapy in the United States Today.* New York: Harper & Row.

Goffman, E. (1959). *The presentation of self in everyday life.* Garden City, NJ: Doubleday.

Goldberg, M. M. (1941). A quantification of the marginal man theory. *American Sociological Review, 6,* 52–58.

Goldstein, K. (1959). Health as value. In A. H. Maslow (Ed.), *New Knowledge in values.* Chicago: Henry Regnery.

Gonzales, M., Urbano, S. C., & Mesa, R. (Eds.). (1984). *Economy and society in the transformation of the world.* New York: United Nations University.

Gonzales, N. S. (1966). Human behavior in cross-cultural perspective: A Guatemalan example. *Human Organizations, 25,* 122–125.

Gospel, H. F. (1988). The management of labour: Great Britain, the U.S., and Japan. *Business History, 30,* 104–115.

Gottesfeld, M. L. (1981). Countertransference and ethnic similarity. In G. Henderson & M. Primeaux (Eds.), *Transcultural health care.* Menlo Park, CA: Addison-Wesley.

Graham, J. L. (1985). The influence of culture on the process of business negotiations: An Exploratory study. *Journal of International Business Studies, 16,* 81–96.

Grantham, R. J. (1973). Effects of counselor sex, race, and language style on Black students in initial interviews. *Journal of Counseling Psychology, 20,* 553–559.

Greeley, A. M. (1969). *Why can't they be like us?* New York: Institute of Human Relations Press.

Green, J. (1982). *Cultural awareness in the human services.* Englewood Cliffs, NJ: Prentice-Hall.

Groves, J. E. (1974). Taking care of the hateful patient. *New England Journal of Medicine, 29,* 301–306.

Gudykunst, W. B. (1985). The influence of cultural similarity and type of relationship on uncertainty reduction processes. *Communication Monographs, 52,* 203–217.

Gudykunst, W. B. & Ting-Toomey, S. (1988). Culture and affective communication. *The American Behavioral Scientist, 31,* 384–400.

Gulick, J. (1976). The ethos of insecurity of Middle Eastern culture. In G. DeVos (Ed.), *Responses to changed society, culture, and personality.* New York: Van Nostrand.

Guthrie, G. M. & Tanco, P. P. (1980). Alienation and anomie. In H. C. Triandis & J. G. Draguns (Eds.), *Handbook of cross-cultural psychology.* Vol. 6. Boston: Allyn & Bacon.

Hall, E. T. (1959). *The silent language*. New York: Doubleday.

Hall, E. T. (1976). *Beyond Culture*. New York: Doubleday.

Hall, J. A. (1980). Voice tone and persuasion. *Journal of Personality and Social Psychology*, 27, 924-234.

Halleck, S. L. (1971). *The politics of therapy*. New York: Harper & Row.

Hamilton, E. (1942). *Mythology*. Boston: Little, Brown.

Hamilton, G. G. & Biggart, N. W. (1988). Market, culture, and authority: A compara— tive analysis of management and organization in the Far East. *American Journal of Sociology*, 94, 352-394

Hanna, J. L. (1984). Black, white nonverbal differences, dance and dissonance: Implications for desegregation. In A. Wolfgang (Ed.), *Nonverbal behavior, perspec- tives, applications, and intercultural insights*. Toronto: C. J. Hogrefe.

Harding, M. E. (1965). *The "I" and the "Not-I"*. Princeton: Princeton University Press.

Hardy-Fanta, C. & MacMahon-Herra, E. (1981). Adopting family therapy to the Hispanic family. *Social Casework*, 63, 138–148.

Harris, O. & Balgopal, P. (1980). Intervening with the Black family. In C. Janzen & O. Harris (Eds.), *Family treatment in social work*. Itasca, NY: F. E. Peacock.

Harris, T. A. (1969). *I'm OK— You're OK*. New York: Harper & Row.

Harrison, S. I. & Carek, D. J. (1966). *A guide to psychotherapy*. Boston: Little, Brown.

Hartman, H. (1958). *Ego psychology and the problem of adaptation*. New York: Interna- tional Universities Press.

Harvey, E. (1933). *The mind of China*. New Haven: Yale University Press.

Harvey, Y. K. & Wintrob, R. M. (1981). The self-awareness factor in intercultural psychiatry: Some personal reflections. In P. B. Pedersen, J. G. Draguns, W. J. Lonner, & J. E. Trimble (Eds.), *Counseling across cultures*. Honolulu: University of Hawaii Press.

Hayes, W. A. (1980). Radical Black behaviorism. In E. L. Jones (Ed.), *Black Psychology*. New York: Harper & Row.

Hecht, M. & Ribeau, S. (1984). Ethnic communication. A comparative analysis of satisfying communication. *International Journal of Intercultural Relations*, 8, 135–152.

Heikal, M. (1980). Communication across cultural barriers. *Editors and Publishers*, 113, 120+.

Henderson, G. (Ed.). (1979). *Understanding and counseling ethnic minorities*. Springfield, IL: Charles C Thomas.

Henderson, G. & Primeaux, M. (Eds.). (1981). *Transcultural health care*. Menlo Park, CA: Addison-Wesley.

Hendrick, C., Stikes, C. S., & Murray, D. J. (1972). Race versus belief similarity as determinants of attraction in a live interaction situation. *Journal of Experimental Research in Personality*, 6, 162–168.

Hendrick, S. S. (1988). Counselor self-disclosure. *Journal of Counseling and Development*, 66, 419–424.

Henkin, W. A. (1985). Toward counseling the Japanese in America: A cross-cultural primer. *Journal of Counseling and Development*. 63, 500–503.

Henley, N. M. (1977). *Body politics*. Englewood Cliffs, NJ: Prentice-Hall.

Hermansson, G. L., Webster, A. C., & McFarland, K. (1988). Counselor deliberate postural lean and communication of facilitative conditions. *Journal of Counseling Psychology*, 35, 144–158.

Herr, E. L. (1987). Cultural diversity for an international perspective. *Journal of Multicultural Counseling and Development*, 15, 99–109.

Herzberg, F. (1959). *The motivation to work*. New York: John Wiley & Sons.

Herzberg, F. (1982). *The managerial choice: To be efficient and to be human*. Salt Lake City, UT: Olympus.

Herzberg, F. (1984). Managing egos: East vs. West. *Industry Week*, 223, 56–61, 100–104.

Heslin, R. & Patterson, M. L. (1982). *Nonverbal behavior and social psychology*. New York: Plenum Press.

Heyer, R. (1987). Empirical research on ego state theory. *Transactional Analysis Journal*, 17, 286–294.

Higginbotham, H. N. (1979). *Delivery of mental health services in three developing Asian nations: Feasibility and cultural sensitivity of "modern Psychiatry."* Doctoral dissertation, University of Hawaii.

Hill, C., Thames, T., & Rardin, D. (1979). Comparison of Rogers, Perls, and Ellis in the Hill Counselor Verbal Response Category System. *Journal of Counseling Psychology*, 26, 198–203.

Ho, D. (1979). Psychological implications of collectivism: With special references to the Chinese case and Maoist dialects. In L. Eckensberger, W. Lonner, & Y. Poortinga (Eds.), *Cross-cultural contributions to psychology*. Amsterdam: Swets and Zeitlinger.

Ho, D. Y. E. (1985). Cultural values and professional issues in clinical psychology: Implication for the Hong Kong experience. *American Psychologist*, 40, 1212–1218.

Ho, M. K. (1987). *Family therapy with ethnic minorities*. Beverly Hills, CA: Sage.

Hofstede, G. H. (1980). Motivation, leadership, and organization. *Organization Dynamics*, 9, 42–63.

Hofstede, G. H. (1984). *Culture's consequences: International differences in work-related values*. Beverly Hills, CA: Sage.

Hollingshead, A. B. & Redlich, R. C. (1958). *Social class and mental health*. New York: John Wiley & Sons.

Horton, P. B. (1965). *Sociology and the health sciences*. New York: McGraw-Hill.

Howe, R. W. (1988). *The Koreans: Passion and Grace*. San Diego, CA: Harcourt Brace Jovanovich.

Hsu, F. L. K. (1953). *Americans and Chinese*. New York: Doubleday.

Hsu, F. L. K. (1985). The self in cross-culture perspectives. In A. J. Marsella, G. DeVos, & F. L. K. Hsu (Eds.), *Culture and self: Asian and Western perspectives*. New York: Tavistock.

Ibrahim, F. A. (1985). Effective cross-cultural counseling and psychotherapy: A framework. *The Counseling Psychologist*, 64, 134–145.

Idowu, A. (1985). Myths and superstitions in traditional African healing. *American Mental Health Counselors Association Journal*, 7, 78–86.

Ishii, S. (1973). Characteristics of Japanese nonverbal communicative behavior. *Journal of Communication Association of the Pacific*, 11, 43–60.

Ivey, A. E. (1981). Counseling and psychotherapy: Toward a new perspective. In A. J. Marsella & P. B. Pedersen (Eds.), *Cross-cultural counseling and psychotherapy*. New York: Pergamon Press.

Ivey, A. E., Ivey, M. B., & Simek-Downing, L. (1987). *Counseling and psychotherapy: Integrating skills, theory, and practice*. Englewood Cliffs, NJ: Prentice-Hall.

Jellnick, E. M. (1962). Cultural differences in the meaning of alcoholism. In D. J. Pittman & C. R. Snyder (Eds.), *Society, culture and drinking patterns*. New York: John Wiley & Sons.

Jersild, A. T. (1952). *In search of self*. New York: Columbia University Teachers College.

Johnson, F. (1975). Some problems of reification in existential psychiatry. In R. G. Geyer & D. R. Schweitzer (Eds.), *Theories of alienation*. Leiden: Martinus Nijhoff.

Johnson, F. A. (1981). Ethnicity and interactional rules in counseling and psychotherapy: Some basic considerations. In A. J. Marsella & P. B. Pedersen (Eds.), *Cross-cultural counseling and psychotherapy*. New York: Pergamon Press.

Jones, E. E. (1974). Social class and psychotherapy: A critical review of research. *Psychiatry*, 37, 307–320.

Jones, E. E. (1985). Psychotherapy and counseling with Black clients. In P. Pedersen (Ed.), *Handbook of cross-cultural counseling and therapy*. Westport, CT: Greenwood Press.

Jones, M. (1988). Managerial thinking: An African perspective. *Journal of Management Studies*, 25, 481–505.

Jones, S. E. (1971). A comparative proxemics analysis of dyadic interaction in selected subcultures of New York City. *Journal of Social Psychology*, 84, 35–44.

Jung, C. G. (1957). *The undiscovered self*. New York: Mentor.

Jung, C. G. (1961). *Psychological reflections: An anthology of writings of C. G. Jung*. New York: Harper & Row.

Jung, C. G. (1968). Civilization in transition. In G. Adler (Ed.), *Collected Works of Carl Jung*. Vol. 10. Princeton, NJ: Princeton University Press.

Kagan, N. (1964). Three dimensions of counselor encapsulation. *Journal of Counseling Psychology*, 11, 361–365.

Kanungo, R. N. & Wright, R. W. (1983). A cross-cultural comparative study of managerial attitudes. *Journal of International Business Studies*, 14, 115–129.

Kaplan, B. H. (1965). The structure of sentiment in a lower-class group in Appalachia. *Journal of Social Issues*, 21, 126–141.

Kaplan, L. (1959). *Foundations of human behavior*. New York: Harper & Row.

Katz, J. H. (1985). The sociopolitical nature of counseling. *The Counseling Psychologist*, 13, 615–624.

Katz, M. M. & Sanborn, K. O. (1976). Multiethnic studies of psychopathology and normality in Hawaii. In J. Westermeyer (Ed.), *Anthropology and mental health*. The Hague: Mouton.

Kay, M. (1978). Clinical anthropology. In E. E. Bauwens (Ed.), *The anthropology of health*. St. Louis: C. V. Mosby.

Kazdin, A. E. (1978). *History of behavior modification*. Baltimore: University Park Press.

Keith-Lucas, A. (1972). *Giving and taking help.* Chapel Hill: University of North Carolina Press.

Kelly, E. W., Jr. & True, J. H. (1980). Eye contact and communication of facilitative conditions. *Perceptual and Motor Skills,* 51, 815–820.

Kiesler, C. A. & Kiesler, S. B. (1970). *Conformity.* Reading, MA: Addison-Wesley.

Kim, B. L. C., Okamura, A. I., Ozawa, N. & Forrest, V. (1981). *Women in shadows: A handbook for service providers working with Asian wives of U.S. military personnel.* La Jolla, CA: National Committee Concerned with Asian Wives.

Kim, Y. S. E. (1987). *Korean families and family therapy: Projection of a therapeutic paradigm for Korean urban middle-class families.* New York: Lang.

Kim, Y. Y. (1984). Searching for creative integration. In W. B. Gudykunst & Y. Y. Kim (Eds.), *International communication annual,* Vol. 7. Beverly Hills, CA: Sage.

Kim, Y. Y. (Ed.). (1986). *Interethnic communication: Current research.* Beverly Hills, CA: Sage.

King, D. (1983). *Egyptian psychology: Subjective impressions and survey results.* Paper presented at the American Psychological Association Convention, Anaheim, CA.

King, L. M. (1978). Social and cultural influences on psychopathology. *Annual Review of Psychology,* 29, 405–433.

Kitano, D. L. (1985). Applying Taoist thought to counseling and psychotherapy. *American Mental Health Counselors Association Journal,* 7, 52–63.

Kitano, H. H. L. (1981). Counseling and psychotherapy with Japanese Americans. In A. J. Marsella & P. B. Pedersen (Eds.), *Cross-cultural counseling and psychotherapy.* New York: Pergamon Press.

Kleinman, A. (1977). Depression, somatization and the "new cross-cultural psychiatry." *Social Science and Medicine,* 11, 3–9.

Kleinman, A. (1979). *Patients and healers in the context of culture.* Berkeley: University of California Press.

Kohut, H. (1959). Introspection, empathy and psychoanalysis. *Journal of the American Psychoanalysis Association,* 7, 459–483.

Kohut, H. (1959). *The restoration of self.* New York: International Universities Press.

Kondo, A. (1953). Morita therapy: A Japanese therapy for neurosis. *American Journal of Psychoanalysis,* 13, 31–37.

Kopp, S. B. (1972). *If you meet the Buddha on the road, kill him!* New York: Bantam.

Lambert, M. J. (1981). Evaluating outcome variables in cross-cultural counseling and psychotherapy. In A. J. Marsella & P. B. Pedersen (Eds.), *Cross-cultural counseling and psychotherapy.* New York: Pergamon Press.

Lambo, T. A. (1978). Psychotherapy in Africa. *Human Nature,* 1, 32–39.

Landy, D. (1974). Role adaptation: Traditional curers under the impact of Western medicine. *American Ethnologist,* 1, 103–127.

Lao-tse. (1944). *The way of life according to Lao-tsu: An American version.* Trans. by W. Bynner. New York: John Day.

Lazarus, A. A. (1981). *The practice of multimodal therapy.* New York: McGraw-Hill.

Lefkowitz, D. & Baker, J. (1971). Black youth: A counseling experience. *School Counselor,* 18, 290–293.

Lefley, H. P. & Bestman, E. W. (1984). Community mental health and minorities: A multi-ethnic approach. In S. Sue & T. Moore (Eds.), *The pluralistic society: A community mental health perspective*. New York: Human Sciences Press.

Leong, F. T. L. (1986). Counseling and psychotherapy with Asian-Americans: A long review. *Journal of Counseling Psychology, 33*, 196–206.

LeVine, E. S. & Campbell, D. T. (1972). *Ethnocentrism: Theories of conflict, ethnic attitudes, and group behavior*. New York: John Wiley.

LeVine, E. & Franco, J. N. (1981). A reassessment of self-disclosure patterns among Anglo-Americans and Hispanics. *Journal of Counseling Psychology, 28*, 522–524.

Lewin, K. (1935). *A dynamic theory of personality*. New York: McGraw-Hill.

Lewis, W. C. (1972). *Why people change: The psychology of influence*. New York: Holt, Rinehart & Winston.

Likert, R. (1967). *The human organization: Its management and values*. New York: McGraw-Hill.

Lofquist, L. H. & Dawis, R. V. (1969). *Adjustment to work*. New York: Appleton-Century-Crofts.

Lonner, W. J. & Sundberg, N. D. (1985). Assessment in cross-cultural counseling and therapy. In P. Pedersen (Ed.), *Handbook of cross-cultural counseling and therapy*. Westport, CT: Greenwood Press.

Lott, J. T. (1976). Migration of a mentality: The Filipino community. *Social Casework, 57*, 165–172.

MacArthur, R. (1975). Differential ability patterns: Invit, Nsenga and Canadian Whites. In J. W. Berry & W. J. Lonner (Eds.), *Applied cross-cultural psychology*. Amsterdam: Swets & Zeitlinger.

Magnusson, D. & Stattin, H. A. (1978). A cross-cultural comparison of anxiety responses in an interactional frame of reference. *International Journal of Psychology, 13*, 317–332.

Malinowski, B. (1922). *Argonauts of the Western Pacific*. London: George Routledge & Sons.

Mann, J. (1965). *Changing human behavior*. New York: Charles Scribner's Sons.

Marcos, L. R., Urcoyo, L., & Kesselman, M. (1973). The language barrier in evaluating Spanish-American patients. *Archives of General Psychiatry, 29*, 655–659.

Marmor, J. (1971). Dynamic psychotherapy and behavior therapy. *Archives of General Psychiatry, 31*, 121–128.

Marsella, A. J., DeVos, G., & Hsu, F. L. K. (Eds.). (1985). *Culture and self: Asian and Western perspectives*. New York: Tavistock.

Marshall, D. (1979). Implications for intercultural counseling. *Multiculturism, 3*, 9–13.

Maslach, C. (1976). Burned-Out. *Human Behavior, 519*, 16–22.

Maslow, A. H. (1954). *Motivation and personality*. New York: Harper & Row.

Maslow, A. H. (1971). *The farther reaches of human nature*. New York: New Directions.

Matsumoto, D. & Kudoh, T. (1987). Cultural similarities and differences in the semantic dimensions of body postures. *Journal of Nonverbal Behavior, 11*, 166–179.

Maupin, E. W. (1962). Zen Buddhism: A psychological review. *Journal of Consulting Psychology, 24*, 262–378.

May, R. (1953). *Man's search for himself.* New York: W. W. Norton.

Mayo, C. & Henley, N. M. (Eds.). (1981). *Gender and nonverbal behavior.* New York: Springer-Verlag.

McAdoo, H. (1977). Family therapy in the Black community. *American Journal of Orthopsychiatry,* 45, 75–79.

McCaffrey, A. & Hafner, C. R. (1985). When two cultures collide: Doing business overseas. *Training and Development Journal,* 39, 26–31.

McClelland, D. C. (1961). *The achieving society.* New York: D. Van Nostrand.

McFadden, J. (1981). Stylistic dimensions of counseling Blacks. In R. H. Dana (Ed.), *Human Services for cultural minorities.* Baltimore, MD: University Park Press.

McGinley, H., LeFevre, R., & McGinley, P. (1975). The influence of a communicator's body position on opinion change in others. *Journal of Personality and Social Psychology,* 31, 686–690.

McGoldrick, M., Pearce, J. K., & Giordano, J. (Eds.). (1982). *Ethnicity and family therapy.* New York: Guilford Press.

McGregor, D. (1957). The human side of enterprise. *Anniversary Convocation of the School of Management.* Cambridge, MA: MIT.

McNickle, D. (1968). The sociocultural setting of Indian life. *Journal of Psychiatry,* 125, 115–120.

Mead, M. (1970). *Cultural commitment.* Garden City, NY: Doubleday.

Meadow, A. & Vetter, H. J. (1959). Freudian theory and the Judaic value system. *International Journal of Social Psychiatry,* 5, 197–207.

Meara, N., Shannon, J., & Pepinsky, H. (1979). Comparison of the stylistic complexity of the language of counselor and client across three theoretical orientations. *Journal of Counseling Psychology,* 26, 181–189.

Mehrabian, A. (1972). *Nonverbal communication.* Chicago: Aldine.

Melzoff, J. & Kornreich, M. (1970). *Research in psychotherapy.* New York: Atherton Press.

Menninger, K. (1930). *The human mind.* New York: Alfred A. Knopf.

Menninger, K. (1942). *Love against hate.* New York: Harcourt, Brace

Messer, S. B. (1986). Behavioral and psychoanalytic perspectives at therapeutic choice points. *American Psychologist,* 41, 1261–1272.

Metraux, A. (1959). *Voodoo in Haiti.* New York: Oxford University Press.

Miller, J. G. (1955). Toward a general theory for the behavioral sciences. *American Psychologist,* 10, 513–531.

Miller, R. C. & Berman, J. S. (1983). The efficacy of cognitive behavior therapies: A quantitative review of the research evidence. *Psychological Bulletin,* 94, 39–53.

Millikan, R. L. (1965). Prejudice and counseling effectiveness. *Personnel and Guidance Journal,* 43, 710–712.

Mindel, C. (1980). Extended familism among urban Mexican Americans, Anglos, and Blacks. *Hispanic Journal of Behavioral Sciences,* 2, 21–34.

Mitchell, K. M., Bozarth, J. D., & Krauft, C. C. (1977). A reappraisal of the therapeutic effectiveness of empathy, nonpossessive warmth, and genuineness. In A. S.

Gurman & A. M. Razin (Eds.), *Effective psychotherapy: A handbook of research.* New York: Pergamon Press.

Mohan, R. (1984). The effect of population growth, the pattern of demand, and technology on the process of urbanization. *Journal of Urban Economics,* 15, 125–156.

Montagu, A. (1974). *Man's most dangerous myth: The fallacy of race.* 5th ed. London: Oxford University Press.

Moore, W. E. & Tumin, M. M. (1949). Some social functions of ignorance. *American Sociological Review,* 14, 787–795.

Moracco, J. C. (1983). Some correlates of the Arab character. *Psychology,* 20, 47–70.

Moracco, J. C. (1985). Counseling in the Middle East: Some considerations for mental health practitioners. *American Mental Health Counselors Association Journal,* 7, 64–71.

Morley, P. & Wallis (Eds.). (1978). *Culture and caring: Anthropological perspectives on traditional medical beliefs.* Pittsburgh: University of Pittsburgh Press.

Morrow, R. S. (1975). Introduction: Symposium in ethnic differences in therapeutic relationships. *Professional Psychology,* 6, 470–474.

Morten, G. H. (1984). Racial self-labeling and preference for counselor race. *Journal of Non-White Concerns in Personnel and Guidance,* 12, 105–109.

MOW International Research Team. (Eds.). (1987). *The meaning of work.* London: Academic Press.

Mumford, E. & Skipper, J. K., Jr. (1967). *Sociology in hospital care.* New York: Harper & Row.

Murase, T. (1976). Naikan therapy. In W. P. Lebra (Ed.), *Culture-bound syndromes, ethnopsychiatry and alternative therapies.* Honolulu: University Press of Hawaii.

Murdock, G. P. & Provost, C. (1973). Measurement of cultural complexity. *Ethnology,* 12, 379–392.

Murillo-Rhode, I. (1979). Cultural sensitivity in the care of the Hispanic patient. *Washington State Journal of Nursing.* Special Suppl., 25–32.

Murphy, G. & Murphy, L. (1968). *Asian psychology.* New York: Basic Books.

Nash, M. (1984). *Unfinished agenda: The dynamics of modernization in developing nations.* Boulder, CO: Westview Press.

Neff, W. S. (1985). *Work and human behavior.* 3rd ed. New York: Aldine.

Neimeyer, G. T. & Fong, M. C. (1983). Self-disclosure flexibility and counselor effectiveness. *Journal of Counseling Psychology,* 30, 258–261.

Nevis, E. C. (1983). Using an American perspective in understanding another culture: Toward a hierarchy of needs for the People's Republic of China. *Journal of Applied Behavioral Science,* 19, 249–264.

Nicoll, M. (1964). *Psychological commentaries.* London: Vincent Stuart & John M. Watkins.

Norwine, J. & Gonzalez, A. (Eds.). (1988). *The Third World: States of mind and being.* Boston: Unwin Hyman.

Obermann, C. E. (1965). *A history of vocational rehabilitation in America.* Minneapolis: T. S. Denison.

Okonogi, K. (1978). The Ajase complex of Japanese. *Japan Echo,* 5, 88–105.

Olatawura, M. O. (1975). Psychotherapy for the Nigerian patient. *Psychotherapy and Psychosomatics*, 25, 259–266.

O'Leary, K. D. & Wilson, G. T. (1987). *Behavior therapy: Application and outcome*. 2nd ed. Englewood Cliffs, NJ: Prentice-Hall.

O'Malley, K. M. & Richardson, S. (1985). Sex bias in counseling: Have things changed? *Journal of Counseling and Development*, 63, 294–295+.

Ouchi, W. (1982). *Theory Z: How American business can meet the Japanese challenge*. Reading, MA: Addison-Wesley.

Ouchi, W. & Johnson, J. B. (1978). Types of organizational control and their relationship to well being. *Administrative Quarterly*, 23, 393–317.

Papajohn, J. & Spiegel, J. (1975). *Transactions in families*. San Francisco: Jossey-Bass.

Papper, S. (1970). The undesirable patient. *Journal of Chronic Diseases*, 22, 771–779.

Paradis, F. E. (1981). Themes in the training of culturally effective psychotherapists. *Counselor Education and Supervision*, 21, 136–151.

Paranjpe, A. C., Ho, D. Y. E., & Rieber, R. W. (Eds.). (1988). *Asian contributions to psychology*. New York: Praeger.

Parham, T. A. & Helms, J. E. (1981). Influence of black students' racial identity attitudes on preference for counselor ethnicity and willingness to use counseling. *Journal of Counseling Psychology*, 30, 258–161.

Park, R. E. (1928). Human migration and the marginal man. *American Journal of Sociology*, 33, 881–893.

Parker, W. M. (1987). Flexibility: A primer for multicultural counseling. *Counselor Education and Supervision*, 26, 176–180.

Pasteur, A. B. & Toldson, I. L. (1982). *Roots of soul: The psychology of Black expressiveness*. Garden City, NY: Doubleday.

Patterson, C. H. (1984). Empathy, warmth, and genuineness in psychotherapy: A review of reviews. *Psychotherapy*, 21, 431–438.

Patterson, C. H. (1985). *The therapeutic relationship: Foundations for an eclectic psychotherapy*. Monterey, CA: Brooks/Cole.

Pattison, J. E. (1973). Effects of touch on self-exploration and the therapeutic relationship. *Journal of Consulting and Clinical Psychology*, 40, 170–175.

Pearce, W. B. & Conklin, F. (1971). Nonverbal vocalic communication and perceptions of a speaker. *Speech Monographs*, 30, 235–241.

Pedersen, P. B., Lonner, W., & Draguns, J. (Eds.). (1976). *Counseling across cultures*. Honolulu: University Press of Hawaii.

Pedersen, P. B. (1979). *Alternative futures for cross-cultural counseling and psychotherapy*. Paper presented at DISC Conference on Cross-cultural Counseling and Psychotherapy Foundations Evaluations and Training. Honolulu, June 12–18.

Pedersen, P. B. (1981). The cultural inclusiveness of counseling. In P. B. Pedersen, J. G. Draguns, W. J., Lonner, & J. E. Trimble (Eds.), *Counseling across cultures*. Honolulu: University of Hawaii Press.

Pedersen, P. B. (Ed.). (1985). *Handbook of cross-cultural counseling and therapy*. Westport, CT: Greenwood Press.

Pedersen, P. B. & Lefley, H. P. (Eds.). (1986). *Cross-cultural training for mental health professionals*. Springfield, Il: Charles C Thomas.

Perlman, H. H. (1957). *Social casework: A problem-solving process.* Chicago: University of Chicago Press.

Perls, F. S. (1969). *Ego, hunger and aggression: The beginning of Gestalt therapy.* New York: Random House.

Pike, K. L. (1954). *Language in relation to a unified theory of the structure of human behavior.* (Part I). Glendale, CA: Summer Institute of Linguistics.

Pollack, E. & Menacker, J. (1971). *Spanish-speaking students and guidance.* Boston: Houghton Mifflin.

Pomales, J., Clairborn, C. D., & LaFromboise, T. D. (1986). Effects of Black students' racial identity on perceptions of white counselors varying in cultural sensitivity. *Journal of Counseling Psychology, 33,* 57–64.

Ponterotto, J. G., Anderson, W. H., & Grieger, I. Z. (1986). Black students' attitudes toward counseling as a function of racial identity. *Journal of Multicultural Counseling and Development, 14,* 50–59.

Ponterotto, J. G. (1987). Counseling Mexican Americans: A Multimodal approach. *Journal of Counseling and Development, 65,* 310–313.

Ponterotto, J. G. (1988). Counseling Mexican Americans: A multidimensional approach. *Journal of Counseling and Development, 65,* 310–313.

Ponterotto, J. G., Alexander, C. M., & Hinkston, J. A. (1988). Afro-American preferences for counselor characteristics: A replication and extension. *Journal of Counseling Psychology, 35,* 175–182.

Poortinga, M. H. (Ed.). (1977). *Basic problems in cross-cultural psychology.* Amsterdam: Swets & Zeitlinger.

Press, P. U. (1971). The urban curandero. *American Anthropologist, 77,* 741–756.

Prince, R. H. (1976). Psychotherapy as the manipulation of endogenous healing mechanisms: A transcultural survey. *Transcultural Psychiatric Research, 13,* 115–138.

Prince, R. H. (1980). Variations in psychotherapeutic experience. In H. C. Trandis & J. G. Draguns (Eds.), *Handbook of cross-cultural psychology.* Boston: Allyn & Bacon.

Rabkin, J. G. (1980). Ethnic density and psychiatric hospitalization: Hazards of minority status. *American Journal of Psychology, 137,* 1469–1470.

Raskin, J. & Rogers, C. R. (1989). Person-centered therapy. In R. J. Corsini & D. Wedding (Eds.), *Current Psychotherapies.* 4th ed. Itasca, IL: F. E. Peacock.

Reichenbach, H. (1947). *Elements of symbolic logic.* New York: Macmillan.

¼Reusch, J. & Prestwood, A. R. (1950). Interaction processes and personal codification. *Journal of Psychiatry, 18,* 391–430.

Reynolds, D. & Kiefer, C. (1977). Cultural adaptability as an attribute of therapies: The case of Morita psychotherapy. *Culture, Medicine, and Psychiatry, 1,* 395–412.

Rhee, Y. W. (1984). *Korea's competitive edge: Managing the entry into world markets.* Baltimore, MD: Johns Hopkins University Press.

Rich, A. L. (1974). *Interracial communication.* New York: Harper & Row.

Ridley, C. R. (1984). Clinical treatment for the nondisclosing Black client: A therapeutic paradox. *American Psychologist, 39,* 1234–1244.

Ridley, C. R. (1985). Imperative for ethnic and cultural relevance in psychology training programs. *Professional Psychology: Research and Practice*, 165, 611–622.

Riesman, D. (1950). *The lonely crowd.* New Haven: Yale University Press.

Rogers, C. R. (1958). The characteristics of a helping relationship. *Personnel and Guidance Journal*, 48, 721–729.

Rogers, C. R. (1961). The process equation of psychotherapy. *American Journal of Psychotherapy*, 15, 27–45.

Rogers, C. R. (1950). *Client-centered therapy.* Boston: Houghton Mifflin.

Rogers, C. R. (1986). Client-centered therapy. In I. L. Kutash & A. Wolf (Eds.), *Psychotherapist's casebook: Therapy and techniques in practice.* San Francisco: Jossey-Bass.

Root, M., Ho, C., & Sue, S. (1986). Issues in the training of counselors for Asian Americans. In H. P. Lefley & P. B. Pedersen (Eds.), *Cross-cultural training for mental health professionals.* Springfield, IL: Charles C Thomas.

Rotenberg, M. (1974). The Protestant ethic versus Western people-changing sciences. In J. L. M. Dawson & W. Lonner (Eds.), Readings in *cross-cultural psychology.* Hong Kong: University of Hong Kong Press.

Row, A. (1956). *The psychology of occupations.* New York: John Wiley & Sons.

Ruiz, D. S. (1982). Epidemiology of schizophrenia: Some diagnostic and sociocultural considerations. *Phylon*, 43, 315–326.

Ruiz, P. (1982). The Hispanic patient: Sociocultural perspectives. In R. M. Becerra, M. Karno, & J. I. Escobas (Eds.), *Mental health and Hispanic Americans.* New York: Grune & Stratton.

Rushing, W. A. (1980). Race as a contingency in mental hospitalization. *Sociology and Social Research*, 64, 168–182.

Sachs, C. (1937). *World history of dance.* New York: W. W. Norton.

Saeki, C. & Borow, H. (1958). Counseling and Psychotherapy: East and West. In P. Pedersen (Ed.), *Handbook of cross-cultural counseling and therapy.* Westport, CT: Greenwood Press.

Sanchez, A. R. & Atkinson, D. R. (1983). Mexican American cultural commitment, preference for counselor ethnicity and willingness to use counseling. *Journal of Counseling Psychology*, 30, 215–220.

Sandoval, M. C. & De La Roza, M. (1986). A cultural perspective for serving the Hispanic client. In H. P. Lefley & P. B. Pedersen (Eds.), *Cross-cultural training for mental health practitioners.* Springfield, IL: Charles C Thomas.

Sanua, V. D. (1966). Sociocultural aspects of psychotherapy treatment: A review of the literature. In L. E. Abt & B. F. Riess (Eds.), *Programs in clinical psychology.* New York: Grune & Stratton.

Sartre, J. (1965). Quoted in W. A. Kaufman (Ed.), *Existentialism.* New York: Meridian Books.

Schefler, A. E. (1972). *Body language and social order: Communication as behavioral control.* Englewood Cliffs, NJ: Prentice-Hall.

Scherer, K. R., London, H., & Wolf, J. J. (1973). The voice of confidence: Paralinguistic cues and audience evaluation. *Journal of Research in Personality*, 7, 31–44.

Schroeder, D. G. & Ibrahim, F. A. (1982). *Cross-cultural couple counseling.* Paper presented at the annual meeting of the American Association for Marriage and Family Therapy, Dallas, Texas.

Schulz, R. & Barefoot, J. (1974). Nonverbal responses and affiliative conflict theory. *British Journal of Social and Clinical Psychology,* 13, 237–243.

Schwartz, L. R. (1969). The hierarchy of resort in curative practices: The Admiralty Islands, Melansia. *Journal of Health and Social Practices,* 10, 205–209.

Scott, C. C. (1974). Health and healing practices among five ethnic groups in Miami, Florida. *Public Health Reports,* 89, 524–532.

Seeman, J. (1984). The fully functioning person: Theory and research. In R. F. Levant & J. M. Shilen (Eds.), *Client-centered therapy: New directions in theory, research and practice.* New York: Praeger.

Sekaran, U. (1981). Are U.S. organizational concepts and measures transferable to another culture?: An empirical investigation. *Academy of Management Journal,* 24, 409–417.

Seligman, L. (1985). The mental health field in Egypt. *American Mental Health Counselors Association Journal,* 7, 87–94.

Sengoku, T. (1985). *Willing workers: The worth ethic in Japan, England, and the United States.* Trans. by K. Koichi & Y. Ezaki. Westport, CT: Quorum Books.

Sertorio, G., Nuciari, G., Martinengo, C., & Lazzarini, G. (1976). Cultural practices and social consciousness: Emerging patterns in the family framework with reference to the Italian society. In M. Biskup, V. Filias, & I. Vitanyi (Eds.), *The family and its culture: An investigation in seven East and West European countries.* Budapest: European Coordination Centre for Research and Documentation in Social Sciences.

Seymour, D. L. (1972). Black English. *Intellectual Digest,* 2, 72–80.

Sheehan, P. W. & White, K. D. (Eds.). (1976). *Behavior modification in Australia.* Victoria: Australian Psychological Society.

Simmons, O. G. (1955). Popular and modern medicine in Mestizo communities of coastal Peru and Chile. *Journal of American Folklore,* 68, 57–71.

Skinner, B. F. (1953). *Science and human behavior.* New York: Macmillan.

Sladen, B. J. (1982). Effects of race and socioeconomic status on the perception of process variables in counseling. *Journal of Counseling Psychology,* 29, 260–366.

Smedley, S. R. & Zimmerer, T. W. (1986). Doing business in Third World countries. *Business,* 36, 52–56.

Smith, E. M. J. (1985). Ethnic minorities: Life stress, social support, and mental health issues. *The Counseling Psychologist,* 13, 537–579.

Smith, J. (1971). *The book of Mormon.* Salt Lake City, Desert Book.

Smith, W. D. (1978). Black perspectives on counseling. In G. R. Walz and L. Benjamin (Eds.), *Transcultural counseling: Needs, programs and techniques.* New York: Human Sciences Press.

Smith, W. D., Burlew, A. K., Mosley, M. H., & Whitney, W. M. (1978). *Minority issues in mental health.* Reading, MA: Addison-Wesley.

Snow, L. F. (1974). Folk medical beliefs and their implications for care of patients: A review based on studies among Black Americans. *Annals of Internal Medicine*, 81, 82–96.

Snowden, S. (1985). P's and Q's of international protocol. *Marketing Communications*, 10, 127.

Stadler, H. A. (Ed.). (1985). Attitudes toward counseling and mental health in non-Western societies. [Symposium] *American Mental Health Counselors Association Journal*, 7, 52–96.

Staples, R. & Miranda, A. (1980). Racial and cultural variations among American families: A decennial review of the literature on minority families. *Journal of Marriage and Family*, 42, 887–903.

Steinberg, M. D., Pardes, H., Bjork, D., & Sporty, L. (1977). Demographic and clinical characteristics of Black psychiatric patients in a private general hospital. *Hospital and Community Psychiatry*, 28, 128–132.

Stephens, D. B. (1981). Cultural variations in leadership style: A methodological experiment comparing managers in the U.S. and Peruvian textile industries. *Management International Review*, 3, 79–82.

Stephens, J. (1946). *The crock of gold*. New York: Macmillan.

Stikes, C. S. (1972). Culturally specific counseling: The Black client. *Journal of Nonwhite Concerns*, 1, 15–23.

Storr, A. (1961). *The integrity of personality*. New York: Atheneum.

Strasser, S. (1988). *Working it out: Sanity and success in the workplace*. Englewood Cliffs, NJ: Prentice-Hall.

Strauss, J. S. (1979). Social and cultural influences on psychopathology. *Annual Review of Psychology*, 30, 397–416.

Strong, S. R. (1980). Christian counseling: A synthesis of psychological and Christian concepts. *Personnel and Guidance Journal*, 58, 589–597.

Strupp, H. H. (1977). A reformulation of the therapist's contribution. In A. S. Gurman & A. M. Razin (Eds.), *Effective Psychotherapy: A handbook of research*. New York: Pergamon Press.

Sudarkasa, N. (1980). African and Afro-American family structure: A comparison. *Black Scholar*, 11, 37–60.

Sue, D. W. & Sue, S. (1972). Counseling Chinese-Americans. *Personnel and Guidance Journal*, 50, 637–644.

Sue, D. W. & McKinney, H. (1975). Asian-Americans in the community mental health care system. *American Journal of Orthopsychiatry*, 45, 111–118.

Sue, D. W. & Sue, S. (1977). Barriers to cross-cultural counseling. *Journal of Counseling Psychology*, 24, 637–644.

Sue, D. W. & Sue, S. (1985). Asian-Americans and Pacific Islanders. In P. Pedersen (Ed.), *Handbook of cross-cultural counseling and therapy*. Westport, CT: Greenwood Press.

Sue, D. W., McKinney, H., Allen, D., & Hall, J. (1974). Delivery of community mental health services to Black and White clients. *Journal of Consulting and Clinical Psychology*, 42, 794–801.

Sue, D. W. (1981). Evaluating process variables in cross-cultural counseling and psychotherapy. In A. J. Marsella and P. B. Pedersen (Eds.), *Cross-cultural counseling and psychotherapy.* New York: Pergamon Press.

Sue, D. W., Bernier, J. B., Duran, A., Feinberg, L., Pedersen, P. B., Smith, E. Jr. & Vasquez-Nuttal, E. (1982). Position paper: Cross-cultural counseling competencies. *Counseling Psychologist,* 10, 45–52.

Sue, S. & Morishma, J. (1982). *The mental health of Asian Americans.* San Francisco: Jossey-Bass.

Sue, S. (1983). Ethnic minority issues in psychology. *American Psychologist,* 38, 583–592.

Suiter, R. L. & Goodyear, R. K. (1985). Male and female counselor and client perceptions of four levels of counselor touch. *Journal of Counseling Psychology,* 32, 645–648.

Sundal-Hansen, L. S. (1985). Sex-role issues in counseling women and men. In P. Pedersen (Ed.), *Handbook of cross-cultural counseling and therapy.* Westport, CT: Greenwood Press.

Sundberg, N. D. (1981). Cross-cultural counseling and psychotherapy: A research overview. In A. J. Marsella & P. B. Pedersen (Eds.), *Cross-cultural counseling and psychotherapy.* New York: Pergamon Press.

Suinn, R. M. (1985). Research and practice in cross-cultural counseling. *The Counseling Psychologist,* 13, 673–684.

Taft, R. (1966). *From stranger to citizen.* London: Tavistock.

Taussig, I. M. (1987). Comparative responses of Mexican Americans and Anglo Americans to early goal setting in a public mental health clinic. *Journal of Counseling Psychology,* 34, 214–217.

Thomas, A. & Sillen, S. (1972). *Racism and psychotherapy.* New York: Brunner/Mazel.

Thomas, C. W. (1985). Counseling in a cultural context. *The Counseling Psychologist,* 13, 657–663.

Torrey, E. F. (1972). *The mind game: Witch doctors and psychiatrists.* New York: Emerson Hall.

Tournier, P. (1957). *The meaning of persons.* New York: Harper & Row.

Townsend, J. M. (1979). Stereotypes of mental illness: A comparison with ethnic stereotypes. *Cultural Medicine and Psychiatry,* 3, 205–229.

Trotter, J. R. (1979). The other hemisphere. *Science News,* 109, 218.

Trout, D. L. & Rosenfield, H. M. (1980). The effect of postural lean and body congruence on the judgment of psychotherapeutic rapport. *Journal of Nonverbal Behavior,* 4, 176–190.

Tseng, W. S. & Hsu, J. (1980). Subclinical disorders. In H. C. Triandis & J. G. Draguns (Eds.), *Handbook of cross-cultural psychology.* Vol. 6. Boston: Allyn & Bacon.

Tseng, W. S. & McDermott, J. F. (1981). *Culture, mind and therapy: An introduction to cultural psychiatry.* New York: Brunner/Mazel.

Tsu, C. (1974). *Inner chapters.* Trans. by G. Feng & J. English. New York: Alfred A. Knopf.

Turner, J. C. & Giles, H. (Eds.). (1981). *Intergroup behavior.* Chicago: University of Chicago Press.

Turner, V. (1969). *The ritual process.* Chicago: Aldine.

Vayhinger, J. M. (1973). *Protestantism: Conservative evangelism in North America.* St. Louis: Concordia.

Vexliard, A. (1968). Temperamet et modalities d'adaptation. *Bulletin de Psychodogie,* 21, 1–15.

Vroom, V. H. (1964). *Work and motivation.* New York: John Wiley & Sons.

Wachtel, P. L. (1977). *Psychoanalysis and behavior therapy: Toward an integration.* New York: Basic Books.

Watts, A. (1961). *Psychotherapy: East and West.* New York: Pantheon Books.

Watts, A. (1975). *Tao — the water way.* New York: Pantheon Books.

Watzlawick, P., Beavin, A. B., & Jackson, M. D. (1967). *Pragmatics of human communication.* New York: W. W. Norton.

Weaver, J. I. & Garrett, S. D. (1978). Sexism and racism in the American health care industry: A comparative analysis. *International Journal of Health Services,* 8, 695–698.

Weaver, T. (1970). Use of hypothetical situations in a study of Spanish-American illness referral systems. *Human Organization,* 29, 141.

Weber, M. (1930). *The Protestant ethic and the spirit of capitalism.* New York: Scribner.

Weekes-Vagliani, W. (1976). *Family life and structure in southern Cameroon.* Paris: Development Centre of the Organization for Economic Co-Operation and Development.

Wehrly, B. & Deen, N. (1983). International guidance and counseling. *Personal Guidance Journal,* 61, 451–514.

Wehrly, B. (1988). Cultural diversity from an international perspective. Part 2. *Journal of Multicultural Counseling and Development,* 16, 3–15.

Wei-ming, T. (1985). Selfhood and otherness in Confucian thought. In A. J. Marsella, G. DeVos, & F. L. K. Hsu (Eds.), *Culture and self: Asian and Western perspectives.* New York: Tavistock.

Weisz, J. R., Weisz, B., Walter, B. R., Suwanlert, S., Cheiyasit, W., & Anderson, W. W. (1988). Thai and American perspectives on over and undercontrolled child behavior problems: Exploring the threshold model among parents, teachers, and psychologists. *Journal of Consulting and Clinical Psychology,* 56, 601–609.

Welty, P. T. (1970). *The Asians: Their heritage and their destiny.* Philadelphia: J. B. Lippincott.

Werner, R. S. (1983). Utilizing the Hispanic family as a strategy in adjustment counseling. *Journal of Non-White Concerns in Personnel and Guidance,* 11, 122–127.

Westwood, M. J. (1983). Cross-cultural counseling: Some special problems and recommendations for the Canadian counselors. *Canadian Counsellor/Counseiller Canadian,* 17, 62–66.

Williams, B. M. (1974). Trust and self-disclosure among black college students. *Journal of Counseling Psychology,* 21, 522–525.

Williams, R. L. (1970). Black pride, academic relevance, and individual achievement. *Counseling Psychologist,* 2, 18–22.

Willison, B. G. & Masson, R. L. (1988). The role of touch in therapy: An adjunct to communication. *Journal of Counseling and Development,* 64, 497–500.

Wilson, G. T. (1989). Behavior therapy. In R. J. Corsini & D. Wedding (Eds.), *Current psychotherapies*. 4th ed. Itasca, IL: F. E. Peacock.

Wolfgang, A. (1975). Basic issues and plausible answers in counseling new Canadians. In A. Wolfgang (Ed.), *Education of immigrant students: Issues and answers*. Toronto: Ontario Institute for Studies in Education.

Wolfgang, A. (1985). The function and importance of nonverbal behavior in intercultural counseling. In P. Pedersen (Ed.), *Handbook of cross-cultural counseling and therapy*. Westport, CT: Greenwood Press.

Wolpe, J. (1958). *Psychotherapy by reciprocal inhibition*. Stanford: Stanford University Press.

Wrenn, C. G. (1962). The culturally encapsulated counselor. *Harvard Educational Review*, 32, 444–449.

Yu, E. & Philips, E. H. (Eds.). (1983). *Traditional thoughts and practices in Korea*. Los Angeles: Center for Korean-American and Korean Studies.

Yum, J. O. (1988). The impact of Confucianism on interpersonal relationships and communication patterns in East Asia. *Communication Monographs*, 55, 374–378.

Yun, H. (1976). The Korean personality and treatment considerations. *Social Casework*, 57, 173–178.

Zahra, S. (1982). Organizational behavior in Islamic firms: Critique, clarification, and elaboration. *Management International Review*, 3, 79–82.

AUTHOR INDEX

SUBJECT INDEX